THE PENGUIN POETS

D43

FRENCH VERSE

2: SIXTEENTH TO EIGHTEENTH CENTURIES

THE PENGUIN BOOK OF

FRENCH VERSE

2

SIXTEENTH TO EIGHTEENTH
CENTURIES

*

INTRODUCED AND EDITED BY

GEOFFREY BRERETON

*

WITH PLAIN PROSE TRANSLATIONS
OF EACH POEM

PENGUIN BOOKS

Penguin Books Ltd, Harmondsworth, Middlesex

U.S.A.: Penguin Books Inc, 3300 Clipper Mill Road, Baltimore 11, Md

AUSTRALIA: Penguin Books Pty Ltd, 762 Whitehorse Road,
Mitcham, Victoria

—

First published 1958

—

Made and printed in Great Britain
by Richard Clay & Company, Ltd,
Bungay, Suffolk

GENERAL EDITOR'S FOREWORD

The purpose of these Penguin books of verse in the chief European languages is to make a fair selection of the world's finest poetry available to readers who could not, but for the translations at the foot of each page, approach it without dictionaries and a slow plodding from line to line. They offer even to those with fair linguistic knowledge the readiest introduction to each country's lyrical inheritance, and a sound base from which to make further explorations. The anthologist too gains a considerable advantage from this method, since he can choose much more freely among medieval, dialect, and difficult modern poems when he knows that all the reader's problems can be solved by a glance at the bottom of the page.

But these anthologies are not intended only for those with a command of languages. They should appeal also to the adventurous who, for sheer love of poetry, will attack a poem in a tongue almost unknown to them, guided only by their previous reading and some Latin or French. In this way, if they are willing to start with a careful word for word comparison, they will soon dispense with the English, and read a poem by Petrarch, Campanella, or Montale, by Garcilaso, Góngora, or Lorca, straight through. Even German poetry can be approached in this unorthodox way. Something will, of course, always be lost, but not so much as will be gained.

The selections in each book have been made by the anthologist alone. But all alike reflect contemporary trends in taste, and include only poetry that can be read for pleasure. No specimens have been included merely for their historical interest, or to represent some particular school or phase of literary history.

J. M. COHEN

THE PENGUIN
FOREIGN VERSE ANTHOLOGIES

The following foreign verse anthologies have already been published in this series:

The Penguin Book of Spanish Verse, edited by J. M. Cohen

The Penguin Book of French Verse: (3) *The Nineteenth Century*, edited by Anthony Hartley

The Penguin Book of German Verse, edited by L. W. Forster

The Penguin Book of Italian Verse, edited by George Kay

TABLE OF CONTENTS

*

MELLIN DE SAINT-GELAIS (1491–1558) was a court poet of Marot's school whose work sometimes shows Italian Renaissance influences. He wrote some of the first French sonnets.

CLÉMENT MAROT (1496–1544), the dominant poet of the early sixteenth century. He wrote largely in the medieval tradition, but with new playfulness and humour. His songs, *ballades*, and *rondeaux* established a familiar vein to which later poets constantly returned.

MAURICE SCÈVE (1501?–c. 1563), the greatest of the Lyons group of poets. Condensed, learned, and passionate, he is the most nearly 'metaphysical' of French poets. The influences of late medieval rhetoric, of Petrarch, and of Neo-Platonism meet in his principal work, *Délie, objet de plus haute vertu* (1544), a collection of 450 *dizains* which was his amorous and spiritual diary.

PERNETTE DU GUILLET (*c.* 1520–1545), the literary
disciple of Scève and the human inspiration of his *Délie*. Her
Rimes (1545) were published posthumously.

PONTUS DE TYARD (1521–1605), a youthful disciple of
Scève who was later included in Ronsard's group. His *Erreurs
amoureuses* (1549 *etc.*) is a typical product of French Neo-
Platonism.

JOACHIM DU BELLAY (1522–1560) was Ronsard's companion in the early days of the Pléiade, whose manifesto he
wrote in *La Défense et Illustration de la langue francaise*. His
early verse, partly of Platonic inspiration, is in *L'Olive* and the
Treize Sonnets de l'honnête amour. He then spent five years in
Rome as steward to his relative, Cardinal Jean Du Bellay, dying shortly after his return to France. In Rome he wrote *Les
Antiquités de Rome* and *Les Regrets*, in which his mastery of
the sonnet reaches its peak.

TABLE OF CONTENTS

LOUISE LABÉ (*c.* 1524–1566) belonged to the Lyons group of poets. She wrote a score of sonnets and three elegies, all on the theme of unsatisfied physical passion (*Œuvres,* 1555).

PIERRE DE RONSARD (1524–1585) was the leader of the Pléiade group and undoubtedly the greatest poet of the French Renaissance. He helped to renew French poetry by

A 2   ix

assimilating Greek, Latin, and Italian models, but most of his work reads as entirely native. His immense virtuosity appears most effectively in his love-poems, from the early *Amours* to the *Sonnets pour Hélène* of his late middle age, but his range also includes philosophical verse, political verse, pastoral, light poems, queer poems, and the sombre sonnets of his last years.

RÉMY BELLEAU (1528–1577) was a member of the Pléiade group who excelled in whimsical descriptions – of insects, fruit, and other natural objects in the *Petites Inventions* (1556) and of precious gems, with their physical and occult proper-

ROBERT GARNIER (*c.* 1544–1590) was the only considerable dramatist of the sixteenth century. His best tragedy, *Les Juives*, is partly lyrical and the choruses can be detached. He also wrote a number of occasional poems.

GUILLAUME DE SALLUSTE DU BARTAS (1544–1590) was a Gascon Protestant who set out in *La Semaine* (1578) to describe the whole process and product of the Creation. His second *Semaine* (unfinished) continued the story of mankind from Eden. These long cosmic poems, packed with quaint and often fantastic information, are one of the noble curiosities of literature. They survive through Du Bartas's extraordinary powers of invention, verbal and otherwise.

PHILIPPE DESPORTES (1546–1606), a favourite court poet whom his contemporaries saw as the successor to Ronsard. In his love poems he drew freely on the Italians, from Petrarch to Ariosto, to produce verse of great sentimental sophistication, foreshadowing *préciosité*.

GABRIELLE DE COIGNARD (?–1594). The wife of a judge at Toulouse. Her children published her *Œuvres chrétiennes* posthumously.

JEAN DE LA CEPPÈDE (*c.* 1550–1622). A Provençal legal
official and a devout Catholic, whose work was recently re-
discovered after three centuries of neglect. The two parts of
his *Théorèmes spirituels* (1613–21) contain some 500 sonnets,
remarkable for their vigorously corrupt imagery; also paraphrases of psalms.

AGRIPPA D'AUBIGNÉ (1551–1630) was a soldier, politician,
and writer who remained a militant Protestant throughout his
life. He was Madame de Maintenon's grandfather. In his chief
work, *Les Tragiques*, he wrote the epic of the Protestant
cause. His early love poems, *Le Printemps*, show that the violence and morbidity of his epic verse extended to his private
emotions.

JACQUES DAVY, CARDINAL DU PERRON (1555–
1618), a theologian who influenced Malherbe in the direction
of formality. The *Cantique* is one of his more uninhibited
pieces.

FRANÇOIS DE MALHERBE (1555–1628) is regarded as one
of the law-givers of classicism. Regularity, sonority, and the

avoidance of particularized language are his hallmarks – as in his paraphrases of the Psalms. His earlier poems show the same love of rhetoric displayed with far greater flamboyance.

JEAN DE SPONDE (1557–1595). A Protestant theologian and scholar, converted to Catholicism near the end of his life. He is a comparatively recent discovery. A style at once impassioned and ornamental distinguishes both his religious verse (*Essai de quelques poèmes chrétiens*, 1588) and his earlier love poems, which he repudiated.

JEAN-BAPTISTE CHASSIGNET (*c.* 1570–*c.* 1635) is another recent discovery, like Sponde and La Ceppède. The 434 sonnets of his *Mépris de la vie et consolation contre la mort* (1594) are meditations on the single theme of mortality, worked out through a rich variety of comparisons and metaphors.

TABLE OF CONTENTS

THÉOPHILE DE VIAU (1590–1626) was the first of the 'libertine' poets, free-and-easy in manner and choice of subject. He invests his country scenes with a certain courtly artificiality.

ANTOINE-GIRARD DE SAINT-AMANT (1594–1661) was a courtier and soldier and a friend of Théophile de Viau. He has qualities of a Cavalier poet, added to a feeling for nature, a strain of melancholy, a pinch of *préciosité* and an overriding vein of exuberant humour. With such varied gifts, he could not be troubled to specialize.

CLAUDE DE MALLEVILLE (1597–1647), a minor *précieux* poet. Contemporaries preferred the sonnet given here to Voiture's version with the same title. Both were after an Italian original.

VINCENT VOITURE (1598–1648), an outstanding writer of society verse, but not confined to the *précieuse* mentality. He is one of the wittiest of French poets. He revived the *rondeau* and the *ballade*, dead since Marot.

CHARLES VION DE DALIBRAY (1600?–1653?), a disciple of Saint-Amant who wrote both 'burlesque' and serious
  poetry.

TRISTAN L'HERMITE (c. 1601–1655) wrote a number of
  plays and an autobiographical novel, *Le Page disgracié*. His
  verse, influenced by *préciosité*, shows an unusual blend of
  affectation and personal feeling. The passage given here is
  from his long poem, *Les Plaintes d'Acante* (1633).

GEORGES DE SCUDÉRY (1601–1667) was a literary ad-
  venturer who wrote plays, verse, and criticism and collabor-
  ated in the novels of his more famous sister, Madeleine.

PIERRE LE MOYNE (1602–1672), a Jesuit theologian, author
  of an epic poem, *Saint Louis*, from which the lines on the pyramids are taken. He also wrote a series of descriptive sonnets
  on biblical and other heroines, *La Galerie des femmes fortes*
  (1647), in which morbidity and *préciosité* are strangely combined.

DU BOIS HUS (?). Nothing is known of him except that his
  poem *La Nuit des nuits et le Jour des jours, ou la Naissance des
  deux Dauphins du Ciel et de la Terre* appeared in 1640. The ex-
  tract given appears reminiscent of Milton's *On the Morning of
  Christ's Nativity* (1629).

TABLE OF CONTENTS

NICOLAS BOILEAU (1636–1711), a satirist and critic with a
   shrewdly realistic outlook who represents the rational strain in
   Classicism. His chief works were *L'Art poétique*, the *Satires*
   and the *Épîtres*.

JEAN-BAPTISTE ROUSSEAU (1671–1741), the foremost
   eighteenth-century exponent of the grand manner in verse,
   ultimately developed from Malherbe. He spent most of his life
   in exile as the result of a literary feud.

VOLTAIRE (1694–1778) was the most brilliant of eighteenth-
   century rationalist writers and outstanding in several fields of
   literature. He used verse skilfully as a vehicle for ideas, satire,
   and the occasional expression of light melancholy.

JEAN-FRANÇOIS DE SAINT-LAMBERT (1716–1803),
   the author of *Les Saisons* (1769), inspired by James Thomson's
   Seasons. Using the noble diction of his time, he described
   nature with perception and feeling.

ANTOINE-LÉONARD THOMAS (1732–1785), a man-of-
   letters and general essayist, remembered only for the poem
   given here.

JACQUES DELILLE (1738–1813), a descriptive and didactic
   poet of great fecundity. This passage is from *Les Jardins*
   (1782).

ÉVARISTE DE PARNY (1753–1814) was born in Réunion of a minor aristocratic family. His love poems, light but tinged with sadness, appeared as the *Poésies érotiques* (1778). Some of them point forward to Romanticism.

ANDRÉ CHÉNIER (1762–1794), born in Constantinople of a French father and a mother with a Greek background. He began a diplomatic career, wrote journalistic and other occasional prose, and was guillotined in the Revolution. His verse was hardly known in his lifetime and remained unpublished until 1819. It consists mainly of poems of Greek and Latin inspiration, fragments of ambitious descriptive poetry like *L'Amérique*, and the *Odes* and *Iambes*, which are largely concerned with political events. Whatever the subject, Chénier's passionate enthusiasms made him the most openly personal of the eighteenth-century poets and commended him to the Romantics.

ANONYMOUS BALLADS AND SONGS. France has a rich popular poetry, mostly in the form of songs, which has rarely touched the poetry of literature and has qualities which that lacks. Dates of origin are usually uncertain, since the traditional song is often the most subject to change. But many of the most attractive examples belong to the period of this anthology, at least in their best form. *La Blanche Biche*, *La Courte Paille*, and *En passant par la Lorraine* all go back to the sixteenth century. *Renaud le tueur de femmes* is a seventeenth-century version of a much older theme. The same seems true of *Les douze mois de l'année*, which has local variations. The King in *Le Mariage anglais* was very possibly Charles I. *Les Menteries*, of which there are several versions, seems to have been a popular seventeenth-century joke-fantasy. The remaining pieces are all dated round 1700, or a little later.

INTRODUCTION

I

THE French poetry of nearly three hundred years is represented in this volume, which runs from poets still influenced by medieval tradition to the precursors of Romanticism. Between those two limits, the great poetic movement of the Renaissance grew up and declined, to be succeeded by types of verse which were neglected until quite recently and whose rediscovery has entailed a new assessment of the resources of French poetry. The face of this, as it is now seen, differs appreciably from the older presentation. Although, on a long view, it may not need to be re-drawn completely, the changes of emphasis are considerable and for the modern reader the results seem pure gain. The chief beneficiaries of the research of the past twenty years are the poets writing between about 1580 and 1650. They have an interest scarcely suspected by critics who regarded most of that period as a long and somewhat uninspired prelude to classicism. Classicism itself, however—with the outstanding exceptions of La Fontaine and the great dramatists—still appears as inimical to poetry as before. Its final triumph as an academic doctrine marked a decline of the lyrical faculty which became fully apparent in the eighteenth century. The Age of Reason, so rich in prose-writers, confronts the verse-anthologist with a relatively barren field, only partially redeemed by Chénier towards its end.

Since the literature of France forms an inseparable part of Western culture as a whole, one might expect her poetry to have gone through the same phases as the poetry of neighbouring countries. On broadly general lines, it is possible to say that it did. But a reader who approaches this anthology with an ordered picture of the development of the English poetry of the same period in his mind is just as likely to be struck by differences as by resemblances. The two outlines have roughly the same shape, but at no point do they truly coincide. It would, in fact, be surprising if they did. Quite apart from such fundamentals as language and national character, the temporary circumstances which influence poets to write as they do can hardly combine in the same proportions in two literatures simultaneously. They include the social moment, the religious and philosophical climate, the impact of foreign literatures, and a number of other factors. In the period of this volume, the Renaissance reached the two countries with somewhat different emphasis, the Counter-Reformation set up different reactions (especially since it failed in England while succeeding in France), and the standing and tone of the various courts, universities, and urban societies had diverse effects on the poets who lived and worked in them.

Yet in spite of this, the English reader of this volume will sometimes find himself on more familiar ground than he would in the nineteenth and twentieth centuries. Ronsard, Du Bellay, and Desportes are likely to remind him of the Elizabethan sonneteers, some of whom imitated the French poets directly. He will quite often be reminded of Milton, although there was no Milton in France. Again, one cannot point with confidence to any French 'metaphysical' poets, but one recognizes features of metaphysical poetry across the Channel. So long as one does not try to match two patterns and is prepared for things to occur at different times and in different orders, it is remarkable how frequently they prove to be the same things. A common background of literary culture – the Bible, or Greek, Latin, and Italian poetry – explains many of them. Yet sometimes the resemblance is harder to define: it may be a mere tone of voice, a similar way of looking at physical objects, an unconscious mannerism which has only become noticeable through the passage of time. To recognize these without always scrutinizing them very closely is one of the minor yet real pleasures to be had from the French poetry of this period. But even without it, the principal pleasure remains. Most of the original qualities of good poetry should be able to reach the reader directly over any interval of space and time. If they completely failed to do that, the poem would hardly be worth reprinting.

The historical outline which follows may help to place those qualities in better perspective.

II

In the sixteenth century French poetry was dominated by the Pléiade, the group of poets whose work marked the coming of the full Renaissance. Their achievement was so considerable that it has tended to obscure their immediate predecessors, some of whom deserve a better fate. It is true that at the beginning of the century French poetry was at a low ebb. The old medieval forms and themes were still in use, but the spirit had died out of them. The wind was beginning to blow from Italy, but so far its force had hardly been felt. In those circumstances Clément Marot wrote his verse. He had something of the new humanist learning; he wrote some of the earliest French sonnets—as did his disciple and contemporary, Mellin de Saint-Gelais—but he still belonged essentially to the medieval tradition, the tradition of Villon. His main achievement was to have developed this at a time when other poets were either continuing it mechanically or preparing to reject it. He combined the blunt humour and naïveté of an earlier age with a lightness of touch which was novel and still natively French. Particularly by his skill in the traditional *rondeau* and *ballade*, he succeeded in handing on some of the medieval vein, even if only in a playful form. Much later poets, from Voiture and La Fontaine to Voltaire, looked on him as a model for familiarly satirical verse. Even today his short song-poems can awaken a more immediate response than the more sophisticated work of the Pléiade.

Like his contemporary Rabelais, Marot was entirely untouched by Neo-Platonism, the new idealism which was spreading from Italy and which represented the most serious attempt of the Renaissance mind to bridge the medieval distinction between the physical and the spiritual. For the Neo-Platonists, intent on finding some kind of wholeness in man and in the universe, the activities of the senses were reflections of those of the soul—lower in degree but not essentially different in nature. Such a philosophy transformed love, which for Marot had been little more than an agreeable pastime, into something approaching a religious cult, in which earthly beauty was revered as an image of divine beauty. Neo-Platonism in France is often inseparable from the influence of Petrarch and other Italian poets who imitated him. For these, the poet's mistress becomes assimilated—in pagan terms—to a goddess, or, in Christian terms, takes on some of the prestige enjoyed by the Virgin in medieval literature. Combined or separately, Neo-Platonism and Petrarchism colour a great deal of sixteenth-century poetry, though they often take on distorted forms. They were first given memorable expression by a group of poets who flourished at Lyons, a city whose geographical position made it particularly open to Italian influences. Maurice Scève, the leader of the group, followed the Petrarchan pattern in his best work, *Délie*, in which he traces his love for an idealized mistress in terms which make a complete human experience of it. The work is at once sensual and abstract, but its chief originality lies in the intellectual element which controls its beautifully regulated symbolism. In form, it is a long succession of short separate poems known as *dizains*, and has analogies with the sonnet sequence. The brevity of the *dizain* is intimately connected with Scève's condensed thought and carefully chosen language. Its discipline and compression occasionally suggest Mallarmé, but Scève is a much clearer – if also a more limited – poet.

Two poetesses also belonged to the Lyons group. The more varied was Pernette du Guillet, a young woman who was Scève's literary disciple and in part, at least, the model for his *Délie*. She replies to his verse in hers which, unlike his, is fluid and caressing, full of a half-playful love casuistry which is still largely medieval. Some of her songs are not so far from Marot's manner. Her delightfully intelligent verse has none of the intensity of Louise Labé's better-known elegies and sonnets, which harp very movingly on the single theme of frustrated passion. In contrast to this, the Platonic abstractions of Pontus de Tyard – a follower of Scève who later entered Ronsard's orbit – may seem mathematical and bloodless. But such a poem as *Disgrâce* shows how the cosmogony of the Platonists could be used to suggest an always valid picture of a universe which seems to have turned black and hostile in sympathy with some personal depression. The theme is basically that of Marot's light little song:

> *D'amours me va tout au rebours*,
> In love it goes all the wrong way for me,

but de Tyard has built it up by intellectual elaboration into a total disorganization of life.

All this verse belongs to the dawn of the Renaissance. The decisive innovations were made by Ronsard's group in the middle of the century. The Pléiade poets began by consciously turning their backs on medieval tradition and seeking their models in Greek and Latin literature. They continued also to absorb Italian influences and enthusiastically adopted the sonnet, so that it became very easily the dominant short verse-form of the age and the vehicle of much of its poetry. They gave France what was virtually a new metre – the *alexandrin* – and in other ways, also, greatly increased the scope and suppleness of French verse. Of their two major poets, Du Bellay can be seen at his best in the sonnet. He used it for his early verse, which is largely Platonic in inspiration, as well as for the *Antiquités* and the *Regrets* of his maturity. These last books were the fruit of his exile in Rome, where he spent five unhappy years in the suite of his uncle, Cardinal Jean du Bellay. They show the wide variation of tone of which he was capable. In the same narrow form he can lament the fall of ancient Rome with all the appropriate pomp, can achieve a fastidious elegance in such a sonnet as *Cependant que Magny suit son grand Avanson*, or recall a chatty session with his barber or the drinking capacities of the Swiss. Another manner appears in the *Jeux rustiques*, whose main originality consists in their metrical lightness, since they were adaptations of Latin pieces by the Italian poet Andrea Navagero. Such borrowings, sometimes hardly distinguishable from free translations, were too common in the sixteenth and seventeenth centuries to need constantly pointing out. They were not considered as plagiarisms and can be judged now, as they were then, on their poetic merits in their new language.

Du Bellay died comparatively young, and in any case his more volatile talent was never likely to challenge Ronsard's title to supremacy. Ronsard was a court poet with a scholarly formation and a wide culture. Within the inescapable limits of his age he comes nearer to being a universal poet than any other in France, with the possible exception of Hugo. He is a virtuoso in several domains. His love-sonnets – often courtly but never Platonic – are as varied in their way as Du Bellay's, but the diversity is as much an effect of art as of changing mood. The passionate rhythms of certain sonnets are quite unlike the formal precision of others. The grave pathos of the sonnets on the death of Marie, or of *Quand vous serez bien vieille, au soir, à la chandelle*, has little in common with the swirl and sway of the lines describing the dance in *Le soir qu'Amour vous fit dans la salle descendre*. The rhetorical opening of the *Sonnet pour Sinope* differs again from the generally colloquial tone of many of the *Sonnets pour Hélène*, a work of his mature years and undoubtedly his masterpiece. The virtue of this poetry is more in its execution than in any particular intensity of feeling, beyond the direct human appeal. When Ronsard writes on less personal themes, he does so in poems which are usually too long to be anthologized, though an occasional passage can be extracted. As an unofficial poet laureate he commanded a firm and noble style fully adequate to the political occasion. He brooded on destiny, as in the *Élégie à Philippe Desportes*, with a pomp of language which Malherbe would hardly surpass. He speculated on the natural and the supernatural with a picturesque curiosity which may now seem quaint, but which was in step with the current knowledge of his time. He could write delightful pastoral and did not disdain the humour of the *folâtrie* and the drinking-song.

While Ronsard and Du Bellay between them represent the highest achievements of the Pléiade, its range is extended in various directions by several lesser poets. The 'scientific' impulse to catalogue knowledge of the natural world and to give it some kind of philosophical explanation underlies Rémy Belleau's charming descriptive verse, light and playful though it is in the main. (This is the same tendency which appeared in Du Bartas's much vaster work, undertaken in a completely serious spirit.) Among the numerous sonneteers who followed Du Bellay, Pontus de Tyard, and Ronsard in writing their sequences of *Amours*, Jodelle strikes a distinctive note which is sometimes reminiscent of Scève. In form, he cultivated a curious 'ternary' technique, used to good effect in the first of his sonnets given in this book. Other poets were to use it after him, including Sponde in the sonnet beginning:

> *Tout s'enfle contre moi, tout m'assaut, tout me tente.*
> Everything swells up against me, everything assails me,
> everything tempts me.

More radical experiments with metre were made by Jean-Antoine de Baïf, as well as by poets who were not of the Pléiade, such as Passerat and Rapin. Though their attempts to write in Greek and Latin metres came to nothing, some of their pieces are much better than curiosities. They deserve remembering as some of the earliest poets who questioned the purely syllabic basis of French verse and who did not invariably consider rhyme to be sacrosanct.

III

Most French critics refuse to see the Pléiade movement as an early phase of classicism. They prefer to reserve that term for the seventeenth century. Nevertheless, it is plain that Ronsard and his group were 'classical' in intention, even if their performance was incomplete. They believed in a fixed hierarchy of literary standards, at the summit of which they placed the Greeks and Latins. They set out to create new forms and styles which would be permanently suitable for French poetry, not merely for the individual poet and the moment. Here, they had a large measure of success. They established the rule for their own century, while few of the prosodic innovations of the seventeenth century are not to be found already in Ronsard, if only in embryo. The Pléiade were also classical in another sense of the word in supposing an ordered universe which could be known and described by the poet, and within that conception of a settled order some of them achieved a noteworthy serenity of outlook and style. One may point to some of Du Bellay's more turbulent poems or to an occasional fantastic piece by Ronsard, but these were not typical of their work as a whole. Their mature work at least is distinguished by its simplicity and sobriety and by that balance between imagination and reason which is a dominant feature of classicism in any age.

If one sees the Pléiade as a classicist movement which for various reasons failed to establish itself conclusively, the succeeding developments follow the theoretically normal order. (The norm is based on the development of Italian art and, to a certain degree, on that of the ancient Greek and Latin literatures.) According to theory, a classical period is followed by a decadent phase, in which its forms are aped and elaborated by writers who have lost touch with its spirit. In France, the poetry of Desportes, who, in his mannered way, attempted to continue the Pléiade tradition, answers to such a description. The next important phase is the Baroque, which in the plastic arts means a rejection of the classical harmony and purity of line in favour of fluid and swirling forms; these are often accompanied by an excessive love of decoration for its own sake. The underlying state of mind is taken to be one of anguish and uncertainty. The balanced order of classicism has broken down and in its place is a whirlpool which the human eye cannot reduce to any rational design. It can only perceive constant movement and a series of disquieting impressions.

To call poetry Baroque on the analogy of painting and architecture is to risk some confusion. The term is not really well enough defined, and different critics have applied it to different kinds of poetry. However, it can be pressed into service as the best guide at present available to some newly-discovered territory. The Baroque doubt may be said to have affected all the great religious poets of the late sixteenth century with the single exception of Du Bartas. In setting out to describe the divine ordering of the universe, Du Bartas seems to have felt no inner misgivings at all. Where he appears Baroque is in his exuberant use of language and in his ostensibly fantastic vision of the natural world. Plants can move and animals have roots; the stars dance and the earth is constituted anthropomorphically. Such things, however, belonged for the most part to contemporary theories of the physical universe and cannot be credited to the poet's individual imagination. Yet there still remains something basically anti-rational and anti-classical in his attitude towards them. The greater the excess, the more enthusiastically he elaborates upon it.

In d'Aubigné the Baroque strain goes deeper. The strength and strangeness of his language derive principally from the Bible, and he lacks the loquacious exuberance of Du Bartas. But the underlying anguish is intense. It was already apparent in the morbid violence of his early love-poems. When he came to write his epic poem, *Les Tragiques*, he had canalized it by an effort of will and, by making the Protestant cause his own, had identified his psychological conflict with the struggle between the two religious parties. The scenes of suffering and destruction which recur throughout this long poem remain as evidence of his obsessions. His contemporary, Sponde, and a younger poet, Chassignet, are also at war with themselves. They are afflicted by a spiritual disquiet which makes them profoundly aware of the impermanence of human life and of worldly values. This had been one of Ronsard's favourite themes, expressed in terms of the flower which fades – a universally accepted metaphor which he presents with a calm and almost static melancholy. But Sponde treats the matter as one of spiritual survival and fights out the issue before the reader with a display of highly mannered antitheses which give his verse an extraordinary flavour of decadence without detracting from its urgency. Chassignet, who published his sonnets at the age of about twenty-four and then ceased to write original verse, conveys the effect of mutability by an almost inexhaustible range of similes, from the constantly changing waters of a river to the evanescent smell of fruit. Here again the contrast with Ronsard is apparent and even more pointed. Such a sonnet as *A beaucoup de danger est sujette la fleur* opens with the exact idea of the doomed rose, but Chassignet immediately expands and varies this in compliance with his own shifting vision. There is none of the unity which gives a sense of slow inevitability and finally of acceptance to Ronsard's classically lovely *Comme on voit sur la branche, au mois de mai, la rose*. Instead, there is a fluidity of metre and of thought, ending with one of those 'surprises' characteristic of the literary Baroque.

In La Ceppède, another remarkable sonneteer, the variety of the imagery and of the allusions has a different purpose. His sonnets, called 'theorems' by their author, were intended to suggest the various mystic implications of the Passion and Resurrection of Christ and to encourage meditation by the use of a symbolism which is sometimes deliberately abstruse. La Ceppède weaves together the biblical and the classical, draws similes from astrology, alchemy, hunting, and other sources, and succeeds in erecting one of the strangest monuments to piety which France or any other Catholic country has produced.

All these poets have a basic violence or restlessness which belongs to the dark period of the Wars of Religion, although neither La Ceppède nor d'Aubigné was published until the next century. From then on, the Baroque entered a lighter phase, which for some critics, who see it as essentially a seventeenth-century mode of art, is its only true form.

IV

In the Baroque poetry of the seventeenth century the interest is transferred to external qualities. The poet may still harbour a sense of instability, but he quickly projects it on to the outward scene, leaving the impression that he is not moved by deep feeling. The most that he reveals is the quiet melancholy of the 'fantastical' mind. One of the reasons for this widespread melancholia was evidently the removal of religion as a poetic catalyst. The victory of the Counter-Reformation – which in France looked more like a return to civic sanity than the triumphant conclusion of a crusade – had put an end to a conflict with which the poet could openly identify his emotions. He was now limited to the ordinary sentiments of piety, which found abundant expression in numerous volumes of conventional verse. The most vital element left for religious poetry was praise – praise of the Deity, of his goodness and his works. This is the theme of almost every religious poem which rises above the average, from some of Malherbe's paraphrases of the Psalms to Martial de Brives's rich and ecstatic *Paraphrase du Cantique des Trois Enfants*. A poet can appropriately express his delight in nature or a mood of personal exultation in such verse, but it offers him no means of expressing the mood of frustration or of discontent. Denied this outlet, sharpness of feeling became diffused in a more vague and passive melancholy, which often reached the surface in eccentric forms.

An English poet of the early seventeenth century throws out a definition which fits much of the French poetry of the time:

> From witty men and mad
> All poetry conception had.
>
> … Only these two poetic heat admits:
> A witty man, or one that's out of's wits.

This notion of 'wit' was common to all the West European literatures. Combined in various degrees with the 'fantastic' element, it complicates and enriches the conception of the Baroque. It appears in a relatively pure state in French *précieux* verse, where it takes the form of an ingenious ringing of the changes on a limited number of sentiments and metaphors. This cultivated strain owed much to the literary *salons* and was connected with a social movement towards greater refinement in language and manners. It also reflected the influence of a new generation of Italian poets headed by Marino, in whose work the same qualities of ingenuity were developed to the full. A sonnet such as *La Belle Matineuse*, of which versions of an Italian original by two different French poets are printed in this book, is typical of this kind of poetry. Vincent Voiture, the author of the second version, was the most accomplished of the various writers of *salon* verse and his reputation has suffered since because of it. He deserves rehabilitating as one of the best of French light poets, by no means limited to the *précieux* conventions. He parodies these as often as he obeys them and he is quite capable of ignoring them altogether and writing with a humour as open as that of Marot, whom he consciously imitated.

A type of wit which is often deliberately anti-*précieux* and always anti-idealistic flourished at the same time. It appears in numerous epigrammatists, in 'burlesque' poets like Scarron, in minor humorists like Vion de Dalibray and in such poems as Saint-Amant's *L'Enamouré*. Some of the same poets who affect this bluff Philistine manner can write on other occasions in the most delicate *précieux* vein.

Préciosité cannot be confined to society verse. It mingles with the Baroque to introduce the conceit and the ornamental classical allusion both into religious poetry and into what is now thought of as nature-poetry. The descriptive verse of seventeenth-century poets admits a degree of artificiality quite at variance with post-Wordsworthian ideas of the way 'nature' should be approached. Yet to conclude that these poets were looking only with an urban eye, or were technically ill-equipped for their subjects, would be to ignore the true qualities of their work.

There is much direct observation of the countryside in poems such as Saint-Amant's *La Solitude*, or Théophile de Viau's *Lettre à son frère* (both are too long to be given here in their entirety). The first is coloured with melancholy, the second with nostalgia, and conventional classical allusions appear in both, yet the predominant vision in each is realistic. Elsewhere, the same poets write with greater artificiality. The reason is certainly not incompetence, but because they are seeking a different effect. In Théophile's poem *Le Matin* the mythological and the natural alternate to present a kaleidoscopic succession of small, clearly-defined pictures appropriately capped by the conceit in the final verse:

Il est jour, levons-nous, Philis:
Allons à notre jardinage
Voir s'il est, comme ton visage,
Semé de roses et de lis.

It is day, let us get up, Phyllis: let us go to our garden and see
if, like your face, it is sprinkled with roses and lilies.

The conceits in such a poem as Saint-Amant's *L'Hiver des
Alpes* help to convey the impression of whiteness and glitter
more strongly than merely naturalistic description would do:

Ces atomes de feu qui sur la neige brillent,
Ces étincelles d'or, d'azur et de cristal
Dont l'hiver, au soleil, d'un lustre oriental
Pare ses cheveux blancs que les vents éparpillent.

These fiery atoms glittering on the snow, these sparks of gold,
of azure and of crystal, with which Winter, in sunshine, with
oriental splendour, adorns its white hair tossed by the winds.

Other poets in their various landscapes and skyscapes – Tristan l'Hermite, La Mesnardière, Du Bois Hus – show us a world
of changing lights and colours, of little mechanical figures
moving to the sound of running water, of flowers, birds and
fishes constantly transformed by the imagination into something
else: in short a world of movement and metamorphosis in which
nothing retains the same shape for very long. Conventionalized,
these transformations can become tedious – Phyllis outshines
the sun and appears herself to be the daystar – but in fresher con-
texts they represent a particular way of looking at phenomena
which goes deeper than mere literary fashion. They tend to show
that the sense of mutability, which for the earlier religious poets
had gone to the foundations of the individual and of the universe, still ran through the more polished poetry of the seventeenth century. To suggest it on this more superficial level was a
delicate art, very open to abuse by exaggeration and to the
ridicule of common sense. Once lost, it disappeared almost entirely from French poetry, to reappear only in quite recent times.

V

After 1650 the whole trend of French literature was towards a definitive classicism and against the kind of poetry just described. The positive virtues of classicism are those associated with the clean, clear line and with a sense of proportion in fitting the means to the end. Such a conception of art precludes 'madness' and requires 'wit' to be kept under close control – an almost crippling condition for the poetic imagination as this is usually conceived. It happens that the greatest of the classical poets, Racine, was a dramatist. His best verse is all in his plays and so is outside the scope of this anthology. His non-dramatic verse, which is predominantly religious, cannot be taken to represent him worthily. Similar considerations exclude Corneille, who belonged, however, to an earlier generation and whose verse is less purely classical. There remains La Fontaine – justly remembered as the best of all writers of verse fables, but also a poet of much wider accomplishment whose early work, such as *Adonis* and *Le Songe de Vaux*, illustrates the classical qualities at their most attractive. There is also Boileau, the theorist of late seventeenth-century classicism and the satirist of the *précieux* and the Baroque (though even Boileau's work shows traces of a mild 'fantasy', just as Racine's still shows traces of 'wit'). Although not one of the great creative writers, Boileau represented the doctrine of the golden mean and set an example of sound sense and sound craftsmanship in the making of verse. In this last field he and his contemporaries are generally supposed to have continued and completed the reform begun by Malherbe earlier in the century. This is one of those half-truths which can now be seen to require some adjustment.

Malherbe had laid down certain principles of verse-technique which were aimed at achieving greater regularity and dignity. He had also set up models for 'official' poetry in some of his odes. But his influence had been neither conclusive nor continuous. The verse of his immediate disciples, Maynard and Racan, appears elegantly empty today and, although these poets were esteemed in their own time, their prestige was considerably lower than that of Théophile de Viau, who stood for ease and naturalness of style. As a reformer of language and prosody,

Malherbe represented at first little more than an interlude between the two phases of the Baroque, and even this would be
untrue of the earlier part of his career. He himself was unequi-
vocally a Baroque poet when he began writing. He indulged
without restraint in the hyperbolic flourish and the far-fetched
simile. A poem such as his *Ode à la Reine mère du Roi*, written in
1600, shows this flamboyant manner only partially tamed: it
may well appeal more strongly to the modern reader than the
more cramped, though still rhetorical, manner of his later verse.
It was, in fact, the *panache* of his poetry, combined with its firm
metrical basis, which seems to have impressed later poets; they
included the youthful Racine, who admired and quoted the ode
just mentioned in his correspondence. But this was only one kind
of poetry, and for some thirty years after Malherbe's death it was
not the chief kind. When the true classical movement emerged,
it contained much more than had ever been in Malherbe. In spite
of Boileau's rather tendentious praise, it is only very partially
true to say of Malherbe that 'everything recognised his laws'.
His influence had not predominated up to the sixteen-sixties,
nor, although strongly felt, was it to do so afterwards. One of
his most lasting legacies to French poetry was the ten-line stanza
which he handled with such assurance. It will be found in a number of the longer poems in this book and it continued in favour
long after the eighteenth century.

VI

The eighteenth century inherited an exhausted tradition from
Racine, La Fontaine, and Boileau. When those three had ceased
to write there remained little more than the empty shell of classicism for their successors. Grandiloquent verse, derived ultimately
from Malherbe, but modified by Boileau and others, had wide
currency and occasional successes. For his contemporaries,
Jean-Baptiste Rousseau (once called 'the great Rousseau' to dis-
tinguish him from Jean-Jacques, who now alone can claim the
epithet) was the finest exponent of this rhetorical art. 'Wit' was
still alive, but it was divorced from the fantasy which had once

made it a poetic force. It could be pointed and amusing, but it was the wit of the clubman and no longer of the eccentric. Voltaire's epigram on the Abbé de Saint-Pierre is typical club humour. The gentler wit of the Vicomte de Parny, a minor poet who was one of Lamartine's models, should no doubt be excepted. Parny combines it with a pervading tone of nostalgia which, if it went rather deeper, might be called Romantic.

'Madness' has disappeared, but in its place an entirely new kind of personal feeling begins to manifest itself dimly. In the descriptive and didactic poetry of the time, flat and excessively long though much of it is, there is sometimes an attempt to discern a spirit in the scene described and even to associate it with the mood of the poet. Such emotions are only faintly present in Saint-Lambert and Delille, who on the whole are concerned only with visual aspects. But there is something of the true Romantic ecstasy in Thomas's remarkable *Ode sur le Temps*, and much more in such a poem as Chénier's *Invocation*.

Chénier, who perished in the Revolution while he was still young, was easily the greatest poet of the century. With his emotional enthusiasms, his impassioned rhetoric, he is as much an eighteenth-century figure as Edmund Burke. His satirical manner reaches its height in the savage oratory of the *Ode à Charlotte Corday*. It appears as well in the *Iambes*, which he composed during the last months of his life in prison. Rather than give one of the more smoothly polished of these well-known poems, I have preferred a short, unfinished fragment which catches more realistically the peculiar absurdity and horror of a situation still actual in too many countries today. As for Chénier's earlier poems on classical themes, they may appear excessively sentimental in places, yet they have a suppleness and flow hardly matched elsewhere in French poetry, and certainly not in their own century. Chénier fittingly closes an epoch. He stands at the limit of the classical tradition: a step or two further and it would relax and cease to be classical altogether.

Since the Renaissance at least, French poetry has tended to flourish on a more literary plane than that of other countries.

Its qualities of sophistication are largely due to the fact that it has been closed to popular influences. But France has a rich though separate body of popular ballads and songs of various kinds. I have included at the end of this volume a handful which belong to the period. Most of them will be familiar, though sometimes in later forms. They may help to remind the reader that the French poetic sense can be found in other places than books.

VII

The ideal anthology would no doubt consist only of complete poems, but within any practical limits of space that would mean omitting the best work of too many poets. I have therefore compromised with principle in a number of cases by including extracts from longer poems, but have aimed at choosing passages which are reasonably complete in themselves and do not smack of the specimen. I must ask the reader's indulgence where I have failed, and point in compensation to the greater variety of work which cutting has made it possible to include. Cuts are indicated by three dots, usually at the beginning of the line which immediately follows an omitted passage. Spelling has been modernized throughout, except where requirements of rhyme or metre (and, exceptionally, other considerations) demand the retention of an old form. The punctuation of early editions has also been modified where it was misleadingly archaic. When the title of a poem is in square brackets, it has been supplied editorially.

As in the other volumes in this series, the prose translations are intended as practical guides to the sense of the verse and, in a lesser degree, to its idiom. The general principle of the series has also been followed in the arrangement of the poets, which is chronological according to dates of birth.

I have profited by the help and advice of the general editor, Mr J. M. Cohen, and I owe a special debt to Professor R. C. Knight and the French Department in the University College of Swansea for their help in solving several knotty points of interpretation. Like every anthologist, I have also benefited by the published work of others. The present volume, containing as it does a good deal of verse which may be unfamiliar, demands a short bibliography – both to acknowledge a vigorous movement in modern scholarship and criticism, and as a reassurance that it does not represent an over-personal choice.

G. B.

ANTHOLOGIES AND COLLECTIONS

A. Dumas: *Anthologie des poètes français du 17ᵉ siècle* (Paris, 1934).
C.-F. Ramuz: *Anthologie de la poésie française, 16ᵉ et 17ᵉ siècles* (Paris, 1943).
D. Aury: *Anthologie de la poésie religieuse française* (Paris, 1943).
T. Maulnier: *Poésie du 17ᵉ siècle* (Paris, 1945).
P. Éluard: *Première Anthologie vivante de la poésie du passé* (Paris, 1951).
A.-M. Schmidt: *Poètes du 16ᵉ siècle* (Paris, 1953).
A. J. Steele: *Three Centuries of French Verse* (Edinburgh, 1956).
G. Doncieux: *Le Romancero populaire de la France* (Paris, 1904).
H. Davenson: *Le Livre des Chansons* (Neuchâtel, 1946).
Claude Roy: *Trésor de la poésie populaire* (Paris, 1954).

RECENT EDITIONS OF VERSE NOT READILY ACCESSIBLE ELSEWHERE

Du Bartas, selections in M. Braspart: *Du B., poète chrétien* (Neuchâtel, 1947).
La Ceppède, selections in F. Ruchon: *Essai sur la vie et l'œuvre de J. de La C.* (Geneva, 1953).
Chassignet, *Le Mépris de la vie ...,* selection ed. A. Muller (Geneva, 1953).
D'Aubigné, *Le Printemps* I and II, ed. B. Gagnebin and F. Desonay (Geneva, 1948-52).
Sponde, *Poésies*, ed. F. Ruchon and A. M. Boase (Geneva, 1949).
La Fontaine, *Œuvres diverses*, ed. P. Clarac (Paris, 1942).

CRITICISM AND EXEGESIS

I. Buffum: *Studies in the Baroque from Montaigne to Rotrou* (Yale, 1957).
R. Lebègue: *La Poésie française de 1560 à 1630* (Paris, 1951).
O. de Mourgues: *Metaphysical, Baroque and Précieux Poetry* (Oxford, 1953).
M. Raymond: *Génies de France* (Neuchâtel, 1942) and *Baroque et Renaissance poétique* (Paris, 1956).
J. Rousset: *La Littérature de l'âge baroque en France* (Paris, 1953).
V.-L. Saulnier: *Maurice Scève* (Paris, 1948).
R. Winegarten: *French Lyric Poetry in the Age of Malherbe* (Manchester, 1954).

MELLIN DE SAINT-GELAIS

Sonnet

IL n'est point tant de barques à Venise,
D'huîtres à Bourg, de lièvres en Champagne,
D'ours en Savoie et de veaux en Bretagne,
De cygnes blancs le long de la Tamise;

Ni tant d'amours se traitant en l'église,
Ni différends aux peuples d'Allemagne,
Ni tant de gloire à un seigneur d'Espagne,
Ni tant se trouve à la cour de feintise;

Ni tant y a de monstres en Afrique,
D'opinions en une république,
Ni de pardons à Rome aux jours de fête;

Ni d'avarice aux hommes de pratique,
Ni d'arguments en une Sorbonnique,
Que m'amie a de lunes en la tête.

Sonnet

THERE are not so many boats in Venice, oysters at Bourg, hares
in Champagne, bears in Savoy, and calves in Brittany, white swans
along the Thames;

Nor so many love-affairs negotiated in church, nor disputes
among the peoples of Germany, nor haughtiness in a Spanish
grandee, nor is so much deceit found at court;

Nor are there so many monsters in Africa, opinions in a repub-
lic, nor pardons at Rome on feast days;

Nor avarice among lawyers, nor arguments at a meeting of the
Sorbonne, as my darling has whims in her head.

Malédictions contre un envieux

JE prie à Dieu qu'il vous doint pauvreté,
Hiver sans feu, vieillesse sans maison,
Grenier sans blé en l'arrière-saison,
Cave sans vin tout le long de l'été.

Je prie à Dieu qu'à bon droit et raison
N'ayez chez vous rien qui ne vous déplaise,
Tant que pour être un peu mieux à votre aise
Vous pourchassiez d'être mis en prison.

. . . Je prie à Dieu, le roi de paradis,
Que mendiant votre pain alliez querre
Seul, inconnu, et en étrange terre,
Non entendu par signes ni par dits.

Je prie à Dieu que vous puissiez attendre
Qu'on ouvre l'huis, une nuit toute entière,
Tout en pourpoint dessous une gouttière,
Et que la belle à vous ne veuille entendre. . . .

Curses upon a Spiteful Person

I PRAY God to give you poverty, winters with no fire, old age with
no house, a barn empty of corn in the autumn, a cellar without wine
all the summer through.

I pray God that with good cause and justly you may have nothing in your house which does not displease you, so that, to have a
little more comfort, you seek to be put in prison.

I pray God, the King of Heaven, that, begging your bread, you
may go searching alone, unknown, in a strange land, not understood by signs or words.

I pray God that you may wait for the door to be opened a whole
night long, clad only in your doublet beneath a rain-gutter, and that
the lady should refuse to listen to you.

2

CLÉMENT MAROT

De sa grande amie

Rondeau

Dᴇᴅᴀɴs Paris, ville jolie,
Un jour passant mélancolie,
Je pris alliance nouvelle
A la plus gaie demoiselle
Qui soit d'ici en Italie.

D'honnêteté elle est saisie,
Et crois – selon ma fantaisie –
Qu'il n'en est guère de plus belle
    Dedans Paris.

Je ne la vous nommerai mie,
Sinon que c'est ma grand'amie,
Car l'alliance se fit telle
Par un doux baiser que j'eus d'elle,
Sans penser aucune infamie
    Dedans Paris.

On His Darling

Rondeau

Iɴ Paris, that pretty town, throwing off melancholy one day, I began a new friendship with the gayest young lady that there is from here to Italy.

    She's as virtuous as she could be and I think – according to my ideas – that there is hardly a prettier girl in Paris.

    I shall certainly not tell you her name, except (to say) that she's my darling, for our friendship was sealed by a sweet kiss I had from her, with no thought of any harm, in Paris.

De trois couleurs

Rondeau

GRIS, Tanné, Noir porte la fleur des fleurs
Pour sa livrée, avec regrets et pleurs;
Pleurs et regrets en son cœur elle enferme,
Mais les couleurs dont ses vêtements ferme,
Sans dire mot exposent ses douleurs.

Car le Noir dit la fermeté des cœurs;
Gris le travail; et Tanné les langueurs:
Par ainsi c'est *langueur en travail ferme*,
    Gris, Tanné, Noir.

J'ai ce fort mal par elle et ses valeurs,
Et en souffrant ne crains aucuns malheurs,
Car sa bonté de mieux avoir m'afferme:
Ce nonobstant, en attendant le terme,
Me faut porter ces trois tristes couleurs:
    Gris, Tanné, Noir.

On Three Colours

Rondeau

GREY, tan, black the flower of flowers wears for her livery, with
sorrow and tears; tears and sorrow in her heart she hides, but the
colours with which she decks her clothes show out her grief without a word said.

   For black spells constancy of heart; grey, distress; and tan,
sighs: so it is *sighing in constant distress*, grey, tan, black.

   I have this affliction through her and her emblems, and in suffering I fear no misfortune, for her kindness assures me of better
things: this notwithstanding, until the time is up I have to wear
these three sad colours: grey, tan, black.

Du baiser de s'amie

Rondeau

EN la baisant m'a dit: Ami, sans blâme
Ce seul baiser, qui deux bouches embâme,
Les arrhes sont du bien tant espéré.
Ce mot elle a doucement proféré,
Pensant du tout apaiser ma grand'flamme.

Mais le mien cœur adonc plus elle enflamme,
Car son haleine, odorant plus que bâme,
Soufflait le feu qu'Amour m'a préparé
En la baisant.

Bref, mon esprit sans connaissance d'âme
Vivait alors sur la bouche à ma Dame,
Dont se mourait le corps enamouré:
Et si la lèvre eût guère demouré
Contre la mienne, elle m'eût sucé l'âme
En la baisant.

On His Darling's Kiss

Rondeau

WHEN I kissed her, she said: 'Darling, in all good faith, this single kiss which makes two mouths fragrant is on account for the bliss so much desired.' She uttered these words softly, meaning entirely to calm my hot flame.

But by this she inflamed my heart all the more, for her breath, more fragrant than balsam, fanned the fire which Love prepared for me when I kissed her.

Yes, though not a soul knew it, my spirit lived at that moment on the mouth of my lady, whose amorous body seemed to die. And if her lips had stayed much longer against mine, she would have sucked out my soul, when I kissed her.

De l'amour du siècle antique

Rondeau

Au bon vieux temps un train d'amour régnait
Qui sans grand art et dons se démenait,
Si qu'un bouquet donné d'amour profonde
C'était donné toute la terre ronde,
Car seulement au cœur on se prenait.

Et si par cas à jouir on venait,
Savez-vous bien comme on s'entretenait?
Vingt ans, trente ans, cela durait un monde
    Au bon vieux temps.

Or est perdu ce qu'Amour ordonnait;
Rien que pleurs feints, rien que changes on oit.
Qui voudra donc qu'à aimer je me fonde,
Il faut premier que l'amour on refonde,
Et qu'on la mène ainsi qu'on la menait
    Au bon vieux temps.

Love in the Old Days

Rondeau

In the good old days a way of love prevailed which was carried on
without great subtlety and gifts, so that a bunch of flowers given
with true love was like giving the whole round earth, for people
were concerned only with the heart.

And if it happened that people became lovers, do you know how
long they stayed together? Twenty years, thirty, it lasted an age in
the good old days.

Now what Love ordained has gone. Feigned tears, fickleness, is
all we hear of. So if anyone expects me to build on love, love (itself) must first be recast, and carried on as it used to be in the good
old days.

6

Ballade du Jour de Noël

OR est Noël venu son petit trac,
Sus donc aux champs, bergères de respec;
Prenons chacun panetière et bissac,
Flûte, flageol, cornemuse et rebec,
Ores n'est pas temps de clore le bec,
Chantons, sautons, et dansons ric à ric.
Puis allons voir l'Enfant au pauvre nic,
Tant exalté d'Élie, aussi d'Énoc,
Et adoré de maint grand roi et duc;
S'on nous dit nac, il faudra dire noc.
Chantons Noël, tant au soir qu'au déjuc.

Colin Georget et toi, Margot du Clac,
Écoute un peu et ne dors plus illec:
N'a pas longtemps, sommeillant près d'un lac,
Me fut avis qu'en ce grand chemin sec
Un jeune enfant se combattait avec
Un grand serpent et dangereux aspic;
Mais l'enfanteau, en moins de dire pic,

Ballade of Christmas Day

Now Christmas has come on its way; so out into the fields, shep-
herdesses, out of respect for it. Let's each take scrip and wallet,
flute, flageolet, pipes, and rebeck, this is no time to keep our mugs
shut, let us sing, leap, and foot it neatly. Then let us go to see the
Child in his poor nest, so exalted by Elias, also by Enoch, and
adored by many a great king and duke. If anyone says *gotcher* to
us, we must say *wotcher*. Let's sing Noel, both at evening and at
rising.

Colin Georgie and you, Margot Clatter-Clack, just listen to me
and stop sleeping there. Not long ago, dozing near a lake, it seemed
to me that on that wide dry road a young child was fighting with a
great serpent and dangerous asp. But the kiddy, before you could

7

D'une grand'croix lui donna si grand choc
Qu'il l'abattit et lui cassa le suc;
Garde n'avait de dire en ce défroc:
Chantons Noël tant au soir qu'au déjuc.

Quand je l'ouis frapper, et tic et tac,
Et lui donner si merveilleux échec,
L'ange me dit d'un joyeux estomac:
«Chante Noël, en français ou en grec,
Et de chagrin ne donne plus un zec,
Car le serpent a été pris au bric.»
Lors m'éveillai, et comme fantastic
Tous mes troupeaux je laissai près un roc.
Si m'en allai plus fier qu'un archiduc
En Bethléem. Robin, Gauthier et Roch,
Chantons Noël tant au soir qu'au déjuc.

Envoi

Prince dévot, souverain catholic,
Sa maison n'est de pierre ou de bric,
Car tous les vents y soufflent à grand floc;

say Jack Robinson, gave him such a bang with a great cross that he
knocked him flat and broke his backbone. He had no heart to say
in that sorry state: Let's sing Noel both at evening and at rising.
  When I heard him hitting, with bing and bang, and giving him
such a wonderful drubbing, the angel said to me with joyful heart:
'Sing Noel, in French or in Greek, and don't give a fig for sorrow,
for the serpent has been caught in the trap.' Then I woke up, and
all in a daze I left my sheep near a rock, and I went off prouder
than an archduke to Bethlehem. Robin, Gautier, and Roch, let's
sing Noel both at evening and at rising.

Envoi

Pious Prince, Catholic sovereign, his house is not of stone or of
brick, for all the winds blow loudly through it; and whether it is

8

Et qu'ainsi soit, demandez à Saint Luc.
Sus donc avant, pendons souci au croc,
Chantons Noël tant au soir qu'au déjuc.

Ballade de Frère Lubin

POUR courir en poste à la ville
Vingt fois, cent fois, ne sais combien,
Pour faire quelque chose vile,
Frère Lubin le fera bien.
Mais d'avoir honnête entretien,
Ou mener vie salutaire,
C'est à faire à un bon chrétien,
Frère Lubin ne le peut faire.

Pour mettre, comme un homme habile,
Le bien d'autrui avec le sien
Et vous laisser sans croix ni pile,
Frère Lubin le fera bien:
On a beau dire: Je le tiens,
Et le presser de satisfaire,
Jamais il ne vous rendra rien;
Frère Lubin ne le peut faire.

so, just ask St Luke. Up then, get going, let's hang care on the
hook, let's sing Noel both at evening and at rising.

Ballade of Brother Lubin *

To hurry post-haste to the town, twenty times, a hundred times,
I don't know how often, to do some dirty thing, Brother Lubin will
do it gladly. But to have honest dealings with you, or lead a whole-
some life, that's a matter for a good Christian, Brother Lubin cannot do it.

To place, like a smart fellow, other people's property with his,
and leave you without a dime, Brother Lubin will do it gladly. It is
no good saying: 'I have got him', and pressing him to settle, he
will never give you back a thing: Brother Lubin cannot do it.

* 'Brother Lubin' was a stock name given to mendicant friars.

Pour débaucher par un doux style
Quelque fille de bon maintien,
Point ne faut de vieille subtile,
Frère Lubin le fera bien.
Il prêche en théologien,
Mais pour boire de belle eau claire,
Faites-la boire à votre chien,
Frère Lubin ne le peut faire.

Envoi

Pour faire plus tôt mal que bien,
Frère Lubin le fera bien:
Mais si c'est quelque bonne affaire,
Frère Lubin ne le peut faire.

Chanson

TANT que vivrai en âge fleurissant,
Je servirai Amour le dieu puissant,
En faits, en dits, en chansons et accords.
Par plusieurs jours m'a tenu languissant,
Mais après deuil m'a fait réjouissant,
Car j'ai l'amour de la belle au gent corps.

To seduce with smooth words some attractive-looking girl, no crafty old woman is needed: Brother Lubin will do it gladly. He preaches like a true theologian, but as for drinking clean clear water – give it to your dog to drink: Brother Lubin cannot do it.

Envoi

To do harm rather than good, Brother Lubin will do it gladly: but if it is some good matter, Brother Lubin cannot do it.

Song

As long as I live in youth and health, I will serve Love the powerful god, with deeds, with words, with songs, with tunes. For many days he kept me sorrowing, but after grief he has made me gay, for I have the love of the girl with the graceful body.

Son alliance,
C'est ma fiance;
Son cœur est mien,
Le mien est sien.
Fi de tristesse!
Vive liesse,
Puisqu'en amours j'ai tant de bien!
Quand je la veux servir et honorer,
Quand par écrits veux son nom décorer,
Quand je la vois et visite souvent,
Les envieux n'en font que murmurer.
Mais notre amour n'en saurait moins durer:
Autant ou plus en emporte le vent.
Maugré envie
Toute ma vie
Je l'aimerai
Et chanterai:
C'est la première,
C'est la dernière
Que j'ai servie, et servirai.

Her pledge of friendship is my guarantee; her heart is mine and mine is hers. Away with sadness, up with joy, since I have so much luck in love!

When I try to serve and honour her, when I try to praise her name in my writings, when I see and visit her often, spiteful tongues do nothing but wag. But our love will last no less long for that. As much or more (than the spiteful tongues) have gone with the wind.

Despite envy, I shall love her all my life and shall sing: She's the first, she's the last, that I have served and shall serve.

Chanson

D'AMOURS me va tout au rebours,
Jà ne faut que de cela mente.
J'ai refus en lieu de secours:
M'amie rit, et je lamente.
C'est la cause pourquoi je chante:
D'amours me va tout au rebours,
Tout au rebours me va d'amours!

MAURICE SCÈVE

Délie

Objet de Plus Haute Vertu

Dizains

LIBRE vivais en l'avril de mon âge,
De cure exempt, sous cette adolescence
Où l'œil, encor non expert de dommage,
Se vit surpris de la douce présence
Qui par sa haute et divine excellence
M'étonna l'âme et le sens tellement

Song

IN love it goes all wrong for me; I really must not lie about that.
I get refusal instead of encouragement; my darling laughs and I
lament. That's the reason why I sing: In love it goes all wrong for
me, all wrong for me it goes in love!

I LIVED free in the April of my life, untouched by care, in that
youthful time when my eye, not yet accustomed to danger, saw
itself surprised by that sweet presence which, by its high and divine
excellence, so stunned my soul and my sense that the archer of her

Que de ses yeux l'archer, tout bellement,
Ma liberté lui a tout asservie:
Et dès ce jour continuellement
En sa beauté gît ma mort, et ma vie.

COMME Hécaté tu me feras errer,
Et vif et mort, cent ans parmi les ombres;
Comme Diane au ciel me reserrer,
D'où descendis en ces mortels encombres;
Comme régnante aux infernales ombres,
Amoindriras ou accroîtras mes peines.
    Mais comme Lune infuse dans mes veines,
Celle tu fus, es, et seras DÉLIE,
Qu'Amour a jointe à mes pensées vaines
Si fort que Mort jamais ne l'en délie.

LE voir, l'ouïr, le parler, le toucher
Finaient le but de mon contentement,
Tant que le bien, qu'amants ont sur tout cher,
N'eut onques lieu en notre accointement.

eyes, without more ado, wholly enslaved my freedom to her. And since that day continually, in her beauty lies my death and my life.

LIKE Hecate you will make me wander alive and dead a hundred years among the shades; like Diana, will shut me up in heaven, whence you came down among these mortal pitfalls; as queen of the infernal shades, will lessen or increase my torments.
    But as Moon infused in my veins, this you were, are, and will be Delia – whom love has joined to my fruitless thoughts so closely that death can never separate her from them.

SEEING, hearing, speaking, touching, marked the limit of my satisfaction, so that that supreme happiness, which lovers hold dear above all else, never had place in our intercourse.

Que m'a valu d'aimer honnêtement
En sainte amour chastement éperdu?
Puisque m'en est le mal pour bien rendu,
Et qu'on me peut pour vice reprocher
Qu'en bien aimant j'ai promptement perdu
La voir, l'ouïr, lui parler, la toucher.

EN devisant un soir me dit ma Dame:
Prends cette pomme en sa tendresse dure,
Qui éteindra ton amoureuse flamme,
Vu que tel fruit est de froide nature:
Adonc aura congrue nourriture
L'ardeur qui tant d'humeur te fait pleuvoir.
    Mais toi, lui dis-je, ainsi que je puis voir,
Tu es si froide, et tellement en somme
Que, si tu veux de mon mal cure avoir,
Tu éteindras mon feu mieux que la pomme.

What has it profited me to love virtuously, chastely beguiled in a sacred love? Since evil is given me in exchange for good, and it can be imputed to me as a fault that by loving rightly I have suddenly lost (the right) to see her, to hear her, to speak to her, to touch her.

WHILE we were chatting one evening, my lady said to me: 'Take this apple so firmly tender, and it will quench your amorous flame, since this fruit is cold by nature. So the ardour which makes you rain so much moisture will have appropriate food.'
    'But you,' I said to her, 'as I can well see, you are so cold, and in short such that, if you are willing to treat my disease, you will quench my fire better than the apple.'

A L'EMBRUNIR des heures ténébreuses
Que Somnus lent pacifie la terre,
Enseveli sous courtines ombreuses,
Songe à moi vient qui mon esprit desserre,
Et tout auprès de celle-là le serre
Qu'il révérait pour son royal maintien.
    Mais par son doux et privé entretien
L'attrait tant sien que puis sans crainte aucune
Il m'est avis, certes, que je la tiens,
Mais ainsi comme Endymion la Lune.

DÉLIA ceinte, haut sa cotte attournée,
La trousse au col, et arc et flèche aux mains,
Exercitant chastement la journée,
Chasse et prend cerfs, biches, et chevreuils maints.
    Mais toi, Délie, en actes plus humains
Mieux composée, et sans violents dards,
Tu vènes ceux par tes chastes regards
Qui tellement de ta chasse s'ennuient,
Qu'eux tous étant de toi saintement ards,
Te vont suivant, où les bêtes la fuient.

IN the gloaming of the darkening hours, when slow Somnus brings peace to the earth, to me, sunk deep under shady curtains, comes a dream which sets my spirit free and presses it close beside her whom it revered for her royal bearing.

But by her sweet and private society, she draws it so close to her, making it hers, that then with no doubt at all it seems to me, yes, that I hold her – but as Endymion held the Moon.

DELIA (Diana) belted, her tunic girded up, the quiver round her neck, the bow and arrow in her hands, chastely occupying the day, hunts and catches stags, does, and many a roe-deer.

But you, my Delia, more pacific in less cruel acts and without brutal arrows, you hunt with your chaste looks those who are so harried by your pursuit that, all being burnt by your sacred fire, they follow after you, while the beasts flee from her.

SEUL avec moi, elle avec sa partie,
Moi en ma peine, elle en sa molle couche:
Couvert d'ennui je me vautre en l'ortie,
Et elle nue entre ses bras se couche.
    Ah, lui indigne, il la tient, il la touche:
Elle le souffre et, comme moins robuste,
Viole Amour par ce lien injuste
Que droit humain, et non divin, a fait.
    O sainte loi à tous, fors à moi, juste,
Tu me punis pour elle avoir méfait!

SANS lésion le Serpent Royal vit
Dedans le chaud de la flamme luisante:
Et en l'ardeur qui à toi me ravit
Tu te nourris sans offense cuisante;
Et, bien que soit sa qualité nuisante,
Tu t'y complais, comme en ta nourriture.

I ALONE by myself, she with her husband, I in my pain, she in her soft bed: covered with torments, I wallow in nettles, and she lies naked in his arms.

    Ah, unworthy he, he holds her, he touches her: she suffers him and, though the weaker, violates love by that unjust bond, which human equity, not divine, has made.

    O holy law, just to all except to me, you punish me for her misdoing.

THE Royal Serpent* lives unscathed in the heat of the shining flame; and in the fire which bars me from you, you feed with no scorching hurt; and, though its properties are harmful, you delight in it, as though it were your native food.

· * 'Royal' because the salamander was the emblem of Francis I, with the motto: *Nutrisco et extinguo* (I feed on fire and extinguish it).

O fusses-tu par ta froide nature
La Salamandre en mon feu résidente!
Tu y aurais délectable pâture
Et éteindrais ma passion ardente.

Tu cours superbe, ô Rhône, florissant
En sablon d'or et argentines eaux.
Maint fleuve gros te rend plus ravissant,
Ceint de cités et bordé de châteaux,
Te pratiquant par sûrs et grands bateaux
Pour seul te rendre en notre Europe illustre.
  Mais la vertu de ma Dame t'illustre
Plus qu'autre bien qui te fasse estimer.
Enfle-toi donc au parfait de son lustre,
Car fleuve heureux plus que toi n'entre en mer.

Phébus dorait les cornes du Taurcau,
Continuant son naturel office;
L'air tempéré et en son serein beau
Me conviait au salubre exercice.

O would that by your cold nature you were the salamander
dwelling in my fire; there you would find delectable nourishment
and would quench my ardent passion.

You proudly flow, O Rhône, prospering in golden sands and silvery waters. Many a swollen river makes you more delightful,
girded with cities and fringed with castles, navigating you with
stout and great ships, to send you on alone through our noble
Europe.
  But the virtue of my lady ennobles you more than any other
quality for which you are prized. Swell yourself, then, to the height
of her perfection, for no more fortunate river joins the sea.

Phoebus was gilding the horns of Taurus, continuing his natural
function; the air, mild and lovely in its serenity, invited me to
healthful exercise.

Par quoi pensif, selon mon naïf vice,
M'ébattais seul, quand celle me vint contre
Qui devant moi si soudain se démontre
Que, par un bref et doux salut de l'œil,
Je me défis à si belle rencontre
Comme rosée au lever du soleil.

NOUVELLE amour, nouvelle affection,
Nouvelles fleurs parmi l'herbe nouvelle:
Et, jà passée, encor se renouvelle
Ma primevère en sa verte action.
  Ce néanmoins, la rénovation
De mon vieux mal et ulcère ancienne
Me détient tout en cette saison sienne,
Où le meurtrier m'a meurtri, et noirci
Le cœur si fort que plaie égyptienne,
Et tout tourment me rend plus endurci.

LA blanche aurore à peine finissait
D'orner son chef d'or luisant et de roses,

Wherefore pensively, as is my natural bent, I was sporting alone,
when she came towards me and appeared before me so suddenly
that, at the brief, sweet greeting of her eye, I melted at such a delightful encounter like dew before the rising sun.

NEW love, new feeling, new flowers in the new grass: and, though
now past, my spring renews itself yet again in its green effects.
  This notwithstanding, the recurrence of my old pain and former
wound shackles me wholly in this its season, when the slayer slew
me and darkened my heart with the virulence of a plague of Egypt,
and every torment hardens me still more.

THE white dawn had scarcely finished bedecking her head with
gleaming gold and roses, when my spirit, which was wholly perish-

Quand mon esprit, qui du tout périssait
Au fond confus de tant diverses choses,
Revint à moi sous les custodes closes
- Pour plus me rendre envers Mort invincible.
    Mais toi qui as – toi seule – le possible
De donner heur à ma fatalité,
Tu me seras la Myrrhe incorruptible
Contre les vers de ma mortalité.

Toute fumée en forme d'une nue
Départ du feu avec grave maintien:
Mais tant plus haut s'élève et se dénue,
Et plus soudain se résout tout en rien.
    Or que serait à pénétrer au bien
Qui au parfait d'elle jamais ne faut?
Quand seulement pensant plus qu'il ne faut,
Et contemplant sa face à mon dommage,
L'œil et le sens peu à peu me défaut,
Et me perds tout en sa divine image.

ing in the confused depths of so many various things, came back
to me under the drawn curtains, to make me more invincible
against death.

But you who have – you only the power to bring happiness to
my destiny, you will be for me the incorruptible myrrh against the
worms of my mortality.

All smoke in cloudlike shape leaves the fire with stately bearing:
but the higher it rises and despoils itself, the quicker it is resolved
into nothing.

What, then, would it be like to reach into the bliss which in the
perfection of her is never wanting? When only by thinking more
than is fitting, and contemplating her face to my peril, my eye and
sense gradually fail me, and I am wholly lost in her divine image.

Quand je te vis, miroir de ma pensée,
D'auprès de moi en un rien départie,
Soudain craignant de t'avoir offensé,
Devins plus froid que neige de Scythie.
    Si ainsi est, soit ma joie avortie
Avec ma flamme auparavant si forte;
Et plus ma foi ne soit en quelque sorte
Sur l'émeri de fermeté fourbie,
Voyant plutôt, que l'espérance morte,
Fleurir en moi les déserts de Libye.

PERNETTE DU GUILLET

La nuit était pour moi si très-obscure
Que terre et ciel elle m'obscurcissait,
Tant qu'à midi de discerner figure
N'avais pouvoir – qui fort me marrissait:
    Mais quand je vis que l'aube apparaissait
En couleurs mille, et diverse et sereine,
Je me trouvai de liesse si pleine –
Voyant déjà la clarté à la ronde –

When I saw you, mirror of my mind, gone in an instant from beside me, suddenly fearing to have offended you, I grew colder than Scythian snows.

If I did offend you, let my joy abort with my flame so strong before; and let my faith no more at all be polished on the emery of constancy – seeing rather, since hope is dead, the deserts of Libya flowering within me.

The night was so very dark for me that it hid earth and heaven from me, so that even at noon I had no power to discern a face, which grieved me sorely.

But when I saw the dawn appearing, diverse and clear with its thousand colours, I felt myself so full of joy – already seeing the

Que commençai louer à voix hautaine
Celui qui fait pour moi ce jour au monde.

QUAND vous voyez que l'étincelle
Du chaste amour sous mon aisselle
Vient tous les jours à s'allumer,
Ne me devez-vous bien aimer?
    Quand vous me voyez toujours celle
Qui pour vous souffre et son mal cèle,
Me laissant par lui consumer,
Ne me devez-vous bien aimer?
    Quand vous voyez que pour moins belle
Je ne prends contre vous querelle,
Mais pour mien vous veux réclamer,
Ne me devez-vous bien aimer?
    Quand pour quelque autre amour nouvelle
Jamais ne vous serai cruelle,
Sans aucune plainte former,
Ne me devrez-vous bien aimer?

light around me — that I began to lift up my voice in praise of him who brings this daylight for me to the world.

WHEN you see that the spark of chaste love under my armpit (in my heart) is kindled every day anew, are you not bound to love me well?

When you see that I am always she who suffers for you and hides her suffering, letting myself be consumed by it, are you not bound to love me well?

When you see that I seek no quarrel with you over a less fair one, but wish to claim you back as mine, are you not bound to love me well?

Since for any new love of yours I shall never be cruel to you, and will utter no complaint, will you not be bound to love me well?

Quand vous verrez que sans cautèle
Toujours vous serai été telle
Que le temps pourra affermer,
Ne me devrez-vous bien aimer?

Non que je veuille ôter la liberté
A qui est né pour être sur moi maître:
Non que je veuille abuser de fierté,
Qui à lui humble et à tous devrais être:
Non que je veuille à dextre et à senestre
Le gouverner, et faire à mon plaisir:
Mais je voudrais, pour nos deux cœurs repaître,
Que son vouloir fût joint à mon désir.

Qui dira ma robe fourrée
De la belle pluie dorée
Qui Daphnès enclose ébranla:
Je ne sais rien moins que cela.

When you see that without guile I shall always have been towards you such as time will be able to prove, will you not be bound to love me well?

Not that I would wish to take away the freedom of him who was born to be master over me: not that I would wish to be proud to excess, I who should be humble towards him and all others: not that I would wish to drive him to right and left at my own pleasure: but I would wish, to content both our hearts, that his will should unite with my desire.

If they say that my dress is lined with the beautiful golden rain which stirred imprisoned Danaë, I know nothing at all of that.

Qui dira qu'à plusieurs je tends
Pour en avoir mon passetemps,
Prenant mon plaisir çà et là:
Je ne sais rien moins que cela.

Qui dira que t'ai révélé
Le feu longtemps en moi celé
Pour en toi voir si force il a:
Je ne sais rien moins que cela.

Qui dira que, d'ardeur commune
Qui les jeunes gens importune,
De toi je veux ... et puis holà!
Je ne sais rien moins que cela.

Mais qui dira que la vertu,
Dont tu es richement vêtu,
En ton amour m'étincela:
Je ne sais rien mieux que cela.

Mais qui dira que d'amour sainte
Chastement au cœur suis atteinte,
Qui mon honneur onc ne foula:
Je ne sais rien mieux que cela.

If they say that I incline to several to have my amusement with them, taking my pleasure here and there, I know nothing at all of that.

If they say that I have revealed to you the fire long hidden within me to see what power it has on you, I know nothing at all of that.

If they say that (fired) with the common ardour by which young people are importuned I want from you ... and then, hey there! I know nothing at all of that.

But if they say that the virtue with which you are richly clad kindled a love for you in me, there's nothing I know better than that.

If they say that I am chastely stricken in my heart with a virtuous love which has never stained my honour, there's nothing I know better than that.

En Dauphiné Cérès faisait encor moisson,
Étant à Millery Bacchus en sa boisson:
Par quoi je puis juger, voyant les vins si verts,
Que Vénus sera froide encor ces deux hivers.

A qui plus est un amant obligé:
Ou à Amour, ou vraiment à sa Dame?
Car son service est par eux rédigé
Au rang de ceux qui aiment los et fame.
    A lui il doit le cœur, à elle l'âme,
Qui est autant comme à tous deux la vie.
L'un à l'honneur, l'autre à bien le convie.
Et toutefois voici un très grand point,
Lequel me rend ma pensée assouvie:
C'est que sans Dame, Amour ne serait point.

Si le servir mérite récompense,
Et récompense est la fin du désir,
Toujours voudrais servir plus qu'on ne pense,
Pour non venir au bout de mon plaisir.

In Dauphiné Ceres was still gathering in the corn-harvest while at Millery Bacchus was already in his cups (the vine-harvest was complete): whereby I can guess, seeing the wines so raw, that Venus will be cold these two winters to come.

To whom is a lover most beholden? Is it to Love, or in truth to his Lady? For Love's service is by them (those who ask such questions) reduced to the level of those who love praise and fame.
    To Love he owes his heart, to her his soul, which is the same as owing both of them his life. One invites him to honour, the other to joy. And yet here is a very important point, which sets my doubts at rest: it is that without Lady there would not be Love.

If service merits reward, and reward is the end of desire, I would choose always to serve longer than is expected, in order not to come to the end of my pleasure.

PONTUS DE TYARD

Disgrâce

La haute Idée à mon univers mère,
Si hautement de nul jamais comprise,
M'est à présent ténébreuse Chimère.

Le Tout, d'où fut toute ma forme prise,
Plus de mon tout, de mon tout exemplaire,
M'est simplement une vaine feintise.

Ce qui soulait mon imparfait parfaire
Par son parfait, sa force a retirée,
Pour mon parfait en imparfait refaire.

Le Ciel, qui fut mon haut Ciel Empyrée,
Fixe moteur de ma force première,
Pour m'affaiblir rend sa force empirée.

La grand' clarté, à luire coutumière
En mon obscur, me semble être éclipsée,
Pour me priver du jour de sa lumière.

Desolation

The high Idea which is the mother of my universe, in its height
never understood by any, is now a dark illusion to me.

The Whole, from which my whole form was taken – more than
my whole, the pattern of my whole – is simply a vain pretence
to me.

That which used to perfect my imperfection by its perfection has
withdrawn its power, to throw back my perfection into imperfection.

Heaven, which was my high Empyrean, the fixed mover of my
primal force, decreases its force to weaken me.

The great brightness which was accustomed to shine in my darkness appears eclipsed to me, in order to deprive me of the light of
its day.

La Sphère en rond, de circuit lassée
Pour ma faveur, malgré sa symétrie
En nouveau cours contre moi s'est poussée.

La harmonie, en doux concens nourrie
Des sept accords, contre l'ordre sphérique
Horriblement entour mon ouïr crie.

Le clair Soleil par la ligne écliptique
De son devoir mes yeux plus n'illumine,
Mais (puis que pis ne peut) se fait oblique.

La déïté, qui de moi détermine,
De ne prévoir que mon malheur m'asseure,
Et au passer du temps mon bien termine.

L'âme, qui fit longtemps en moi demeure,
Iniquement d'autre corps s'associe,
Et, s'éloignant de moi, veut que je meure,
Pour s'exercer en palingénésie.

The round sphere, weary of turning in my favour, denies its symmetry and launches out on a new course against me.

The harmony, fed by sweet concordant strains of the seven tunes, against the order of the spheres screeches hideously around my ears.

The bright sun no longer lights my eyes by the ecliptic line of its true function, but – since it can do no worse – becomes oblique.

The divine power which disposes of me confirms me only in the promise of misfortune, and with the passing of time ends my happiness.

The soul, which long dwelt within me, joins iniquitously with another body and, deserting me, desires me to die in order to practise palingenesis.*

* Palingenesis: the revival of an apparently dead body by the introduction of another soul.

Vicieux peuple, ô vil peuple ignorant,
Enflé du fiel du mensonger médire,
Ois les durs mots, les plaints que je soupire
Pour l'honneur saint que tu vas dévorant.

Le ciel sans cesse en sa rondeur courant
Rien que douleur en mon âme m'inspire,
Pleuvant sur moi les flèches de son ire,
Tant que toujours je languisse en mourant.

Tant je me trouve à moi-même ennuyeux,
Que tout clair jour soit obscur à mes yeux
Si j'ai pensé, malin, ce que tu penses.

Mais si les cœurs de ma Dame et de moi
Ne sont tachés, tombe ce mal sur toi,
Meurtrier cruel de nos deux innocences.

Père du doux repos, Sommeil père du songe,
Maintenant que la nuit d'une grande ombre obscure
Fait à cet air serein humide couverture,
Viens, Sommeil désiré, et dans mes yeux te plonge.

Depraved people, O vile ignorant people, puffed up with the venom of lying slander, listen to my desolate words, my complaining sighs for the sacred honour which you are devouring.

Heaven ceaselessly rolling round inspires nothing but grief in my heart, raining upon me the arrows of its anger, so that I languish continually at the point of death.

I find myself so irksome to myself, that may every bright day be darkened in my eyes, if I have thought, evil slanderer, what you think.

But if the hearts of my lady and myself are unspotted, may that curse fall upon you, cruel assassin of our two innocencies.

Father of sweet rest, Sleep, father of dreams, now that the night with its great dark shadow makes a moist covering for this clear air, come, longed-for Sleep, and plunge into my eyes.

Ton absence, Sommeil, languissamment allonge
Et me fait plus sentir la peine que j'endure.
Viens, Sommeil, l'assoupir et la rendre moins dure,
Viens abuser mon mal de quelque doux mensonge.

Jà le muet silence un escadron conduit
De fantômes ballants dessous l'aveugle nuit;
Tu me dédaignes seul qui te suis tant dévot!

Viens, Sommeil désiré, m'environner la tête,
Car d'un vœu non menteur un bouquet je t'apprête
De ta chère morelle et de ton cher pavot.

JOACHIM DU BELLAY

L'Olive

Déjà la nuit en son parc amassait
Un grand troupeau d'étoiles vagabondes,
Et pour entrer aux cavernes profondes,
Fuyant le jour, ses noirs chevaux chassait.

Your absence, Sleep, tediously lengthens the pain which I endure and makes me feel it more keenly. Come, Sleep, to lull it and make it less sharp, come and beguile my suffering with some sweet illusion.

Already mute silence leads out a band of fluttering phantoms under the blind night; you disdain me alone who am your votary!

Come, longed-for Sleep, and surround my head, for with a sincere prayer I have got ready for you a bunch of your beloved nightshade and your beloved poppies.

Night was already gathering into its fold a great flock of wandering stars, and to enter the deep caves, fleeing from day, was driving its black horses.

Déjà le ciel aux Indes rougissait,
Et l'aube encor de ses tresses tant blondes
Faisant grêler mille perlettes rondes,
De ses trésors les prés enrichissait:

Quand d'occident, comme une étoile vive,
Je vis sortir dessus ta verte rive,
O fleuve mien! une nymphe en riant.

Alors, voyant cette nouvelle aurore,
Le jour honteux d'un double teint colore
Et l'Angevin et l'Indique orient.

Si notre vie est moins qu'une journée
En l'éternel, si l'an qui fait le tour
Chasse nos jours sans espoir de retour,
Si périssable est toute chose née,

Que songes-tu, mon âme emprisonnée?
Pourquoi te plaît l'obscur de notre jour,
Si pour voler en un plus clair séjour,
Tu as au dos l'aile bien empennée?

The sky was already reddening in the Indies and the dawn, still raining down a thousand round pearlets from its fair tresses, was enriching the meadows with its treasures:

When from the west, like a living star, I saw coming out upon your green bank, O river of mine, a smiling nymph.

Then, seeing this new dawn, the day, ashamed, colours with a double flush both the Angevin and the Indian east.

If our life is less than a day in eternity, if the returning year carries off our days without hope of recall, if each thing born is perishable,

Why do you linger here, my imprisoned soul? Why does the darkness of our day please you, if, to fly to a brighter home, you have a well-fledged wing on your back?

Là est le bien que tout esprit désire,
Là, le repos où tout le monde aspire,
Là est l'amour, là le plaisir encore.

Là, ô mon âme, au plus haut ciel guidée,
Tu y pourras reconnaître l'Idée
De la beauté qu'en ce monde j'adore.

Sonnets de l'honnête amour

Non autrement que la prêtresse folle,
En grommelant d'une effroyable horreur,
Secoue en vain l'indomptable fureur
Du Cynthien, qui brusquement l'affole:

Mon estomac, gros de ce dieu qui vole,
Épouvanté d'une aveugle terreur
Se fait rebelle à la divine erreur,
Qui brouille ainsi mon sens et ma parole.

There is the joy which all spirits desire, there the repose to which all men aspire, love is there, and pleasure still.

There, O my soul, guided to the highest heaven, you will be able to recognize the Idea (ideal pattern) of the beauty which I adore in this world.

Sonnets of Virtuous Love

Not otherwise than the demented priestess, muttering with a fearful abhorrence, tries in vain to shake off the irresistible frenzy of the Cynthian (Apollo) who suddenly maddens her:

My stomach, big with this flying god, stricken with a blind terror, revolts against the divine madness, which confuses thus my senses and my speech.

(The reference in the first four lines is to the oracle at Delphi.)

Mais c'est en vain: car le dieu qui m'étreint
De plus en plus m'aiguillonne, et contraint
De le chanter, quoique mon cœur en gronde.

Chantez-le donc, chantez mieux que devant,
O vous mes vers! qui volez par le monde,
Comme feuillards éparpillés du vent.

J'AI entassé moi-même tout le bois
Pour allumer cette flamme immortelle,
Par qui mon âme avecques plus haute aile
Se guinde au ciel, d'un égal contrepoids.

Jà mon esprit, jà mon cœur, jà ma voix,
Jà mon amour conçoit forme nouvelle
D'une beauté plus parfaitement belle
Que le fin or épuré par sept fois.

Rien de mortel ma langue plus ne sonne:
Jà peu à peu moi-même j'abandonne
Par cette ardeur, qui me fait sembler tel

But it is in vain: for the god who clasps me spurs me on more
and more and forces me to sing him, although my heart murmurs
against it.

Sing him then, sing better than before, O my verses which flutter
through the world, like dead leaves scattered by the wind.

I MYSELF have piled up all the wood to light this immortal flame,
by which my soul with loftier wing hoists itself to heaven with
equal counter-force.

Now my mind, now my heart, now my voice, now my love con-
ceives a new form of beauty more perfectly beautiful than pure gold
seven times refined.

No longer does my tongue utter anything mortal: now little by
little I lose myself in this fire, which makes me appear even as

Que se montrait l'indompté fils d'Alcmène,
Qui, dédaignant notre figure humaine,
Brûla son corps, pour se rendre immortel.

Divers Jeux rustiques

D'un vanneur de blé aux vents

A vous, troupe légère,
Qui d'aile passagère
Par le monde volez,
Et d'un sifflant murmure
L'ombrageuse verdure
Doucement ébranlez,

J'offre ces violettes,
Ces lis et ces fleurettes,
Et ces roses ici,
Ces vermeillettes roses,
Tout fraîchement écloses,
Et ces œillets aussi.

the unconquered son of Alcmena showed himself – he who, disdaining our human form, burnt his body to make himself immortal.

(Alcmena's son, Hercules, built his own funeral-pyre, then mounted on it and set it alight. See Chénier's poem on page 286.)

Rustic Diversions

From a Winnower of Corn to the Winds

To you, airy troop, who on passing wing fly over the world, and with a whistling whisper softly shake the shady foliage,

I offer these violets, these lilies and these flowerets and these roses here, these reddening roses all freshly blooming, and these carnations too.

De votre douce haleine
Éventez cette plaine,
Éventez ce séjour:
Cependant que j'ahane
A mon blé, que je vanne
A la chaleur du jour.

A Vénus

AYANT après long désir
Pris de ma douce ennemie
Quelques arrhes du plaisir
Que sa rigueur me dénie,
　　Je t'offre ces beaux œillets,
Vénus, je t'offre ces roses,
Dont les boutons vermeillets
Imitent les lèvres closes
　　Que j'ai baisé par trois fois,
Marchant tout beau dessous l'ombre
De ce buisson, que tu vois:
Et n'ai su passer ce nombre,
　　Pource que la mère était
Auprès de là, ce me semble,
Laquelle nous aguettait:
De peur encore j'en tremble.

With your soft breath fan this plain, fan this farmstead; while I toil away at my corn which I winnow in the heat of the day.

To Venus

HAVING, after long desire, taken from my sweet enemy some small advance of the pleasure which her cruelty refuses me, I offer you these fine carnations, Venus, I offer you these roses whose ruby buds imitate the pouting lips which I kissed three times, walking softly in the shade of that bush which you see. And I was not able to exceed that number because the mother was near at hand – it seemed to me – and she was spying on us: I still tremble with fear at the thought.

Or je te donne des fleurs:
Mais si tu fais ma rebelle
Autant piteuse à mes pleurs
Comme à mes yeux elle est belle,
Un myrte je dédierai
Dessus les rives de Loire
Et sur l'écorce écrirai
Ces quatre vers à ta gloire:
 Thenot sur ce bord ici,
A Vénus sacre et ordonne
Ce myrte, et lui donne aussi
Ces troupeaux, et sa personne.

Épitaphe d'un chat

A Olivier de Magny

MAINTENANT le vivre me fâche:
Et afin, Magny, que tu saches
Pourquoi je suis tant éperdu,
Ce n'est pas pour avoir perdu
Mes anneaux, mon argent, ma bourse:
Et pourquoi est-ce donques? Pource
Que j'ai perdu depuis trois jours

Now I give you flowers; but if you make my rebel as compassionate to my tears as she is lovely in my eyes, I will dedicate a myrtle to you on the banks of the Loire, and on the bark I will write these four lines in your honour:

Thenot here on this bank to Venus consecrates and dedicates this myrtle, and gives her also these flocks and his own person.

Epitaph on a Cat

To Olivier de Magny *

LIFE irks me now: and in order, Magny, that you should know why I am so disconsolate, it is not because I have lost my rings, my money, my purse. Why is it, then? Because three days ago I lost

---

* A fellow-poet, who was Du Bellay's companion in Rome.

Mon bien, mon plaisir, mes amours.
Et quoi? O souvenance grève!
A peu que le cœur ne me crève
Quand j'en parle ou quand j'en écris:
C'est Belaud mon petit chat gris,
Belaud, qui fut paraventure
Le plus bel œuvre que nature
Fît onc en matière de chats;
C'était Belaud la mort aux rats,
Belaud, dont la beauté fut telle
Qu'elle est digne d'être immortelle.
    Donques Belaud premièrement
Ne fut pas gris entièrement,
Ni tel qu'en France on les voit naître,
Mais tel qu'à Rome on les voit être,
Couvert d'un poil gris argentin,
Ras et poli comme satin,
Couché par ondes sur l'échine,
Et blanc dessous comme une ermine.
Petit museau, petites dents,
Yeux qui n'étaient point trop ardents,
Mais desquels la prunelle perse
Imitait la couleur diverse
Qu'on voit en cet arc pluvieux
Qui se courbe au travers des cieux.

my joy, my pleasure, my love. What then? O grievous memory! My heart almost breaks when I speak or write of it. It was Belaud, my little grey cat, Belaud who was perhaps the finest work that nature ever produced in the way of cats, Belaud who was death to rats, Belaud whose beauty was such that it deserves to be immortal.

Now, first of all Belaud was not completely grey, nor such as they are bred in France, but such as they are seen in Rome, covered with a silvery grey fur, smooth and sleek like satin, lying in waves on the back, and white underneath like ermine. A small muzzle, little teeth, eyes which were not too fiery, but whose sea-green pupils were like the varied colour which ones sees in that rainy bow which curves across the skies.

La tête à la taille pareille,
Le col grasset, courte d'oreille,
Et dessous un nez ébenin
Un petit mufle léonin,
Autour duquel était plantée
Une barbelette argentée,
Armant d'un petit poil folet
Son musequin damoiselet.

Jambe grêle, petite patte
Plus qu'une moufle délicate,
Sinon alors qu'il dégainait
Cela dont il égratignait;
La gorge douillette et mignonne,
La queue longue à la guenonne,
Mouchetée diversement
D'un naturel bigarrement;
Le flanc haussé, le ventre large,
Bien retroussé dessous sa charge,
Et le dos moyennement long,
Vrai sourian, s'il en fut onc.

... Belaud n'était pas ignorant;
Il savait bien, tant fut traitable,
Prendre la chair dessus la table,

The head like the body, with a plumpish neck and short in the
ear, and beneath an ebony-black nose a little lion-like mouth,
around which was set a small silvery beard, equipping with little
twitching hairs his small dainty muzzle.

Slender leg, small paw softer than a mitten, except when he un-
sheathed the things with which he scratched; the throat soft and
dainty, the tail long like a monkey's, variously mottled with natural
streakings; high flanks, broad belly curving up boldly beneath its
load, and a back of medium length, a real mouser if there ever was
one.

Belaud was no uncouth cat. He was so well-mannered that he
could quite well take his meat off the table – I mean, when it was

J'entends, quand on lui présentait,
Car autrement il vous grattait
Et avec la patte friande
De loin muguetait la viande.
  Belaud n'était point malplaisant,
Belaud n'était point malfaisant,
Et ne fit onc plus grand dommage
Que de manger un vieux fromage,
Une linotte et un pinson
Qui le fâchaient de leur chanson.
Mais quoi, Magny, nous-mêmes hommes
Parfaits de tous points nous ne sommes.

Les Antiquités de Rome

TELLE que dans son char la Bérécynthienne,
Couronnée de tours et joyeuse d'avoir
Enfanté tant de dieux, telle se faisait voir
En ses jours plus heureux cette ville ancienne:

Cette ville, qui fut plus que la Phrygienne
Foisonnante en enfants, et de qui le pouvoir
Fut le pouvoir du monde, et ne se peut revoir
Pareille à sa grandeur, grandeur sinon la sienne.

offered him, for if not, he scratched at you and with a gourmet's paw made love to the meat from a distance.

Belaud was never displeasing, Belaud was never naughty and never did any greater harm than to eat an old cheese, a linnet and a finch which annoyed him with their song. But then, Magny, we men ourselves are not perfect on every point.

The Antiquities of Rome

As in her chariot the Berecynthian, crowned with towers and joyful at having given birth to so many gods, so in its happier days appeared this ancient city:

This city, which was more than the Phrygian abounding in children, and whose power was world-wide, and the like of whose greatness cannot be seen again, since no greatness approaches hers.

Rome seule pouvait à Rome ressembler,
Rome seule pouvait Rome faire trembler:
Aussi n'avait permis l'ordonnance fatale

Qu'autre pouvoir humain, tant fût audacieux,
Se vantât d'égaler celle qui fit égale
Sa puissance à la terre, et son courage aux cieux.

Pâles esprits et vous, ombres poudreuses,
Qui, jouissant de la clarté du jour,
Fîtes sortir cet orgueilleux séjour
Dont nous voyons les reliques cendreuses:

Dites, esprits – ainsi les ténébreuses
Rives de Styx non passable au retour,
Vous enlaçant d'un trois fois triple tour,
N'enferment point vos images ombreuses –

Dites-moi donc – car quelqu'une de vous
Possible encor se cache ici dessous –
Ne sentez-vous augmenter votre peine,

Rome alone could resemble Rome, Rome alone could make
Rome tremble. Therefore the decree of fate had not allowed

Any other human power, however ambitious, to boast that it
could equal her who made her sway equal to the earth and her
courage to the heavens.

(The Berecynthian was Cybele, mother of the gods. By the
Phrygian city, Du Bellay probably meant Troy.)

Pale spirits and you, dusty ghosts, who, when you enjoyed the
light of day, raised up this proud city whose crumbling remains we
see:

Say, spirits – unless the dark banks of un-recrossable Styx, en-
twining you in a ninefold circle, imprison your shadowy phantoms –

Tell me, then – for one of you is perhaps still hidden underneath
here – do you not feel your sorrow increase

Quand quelquefois de ces coteaux romains
Vous contemplez l'ouvrage de vos mains
N'être plus rien qu'une poudreuse plaine?

COMME l'on voit de loin sur la mer courroucée
Une montagne d'eau d'un grand branle ondoyant,
Puis, traînant mille flots, d'un gros choc aboyant
Se crever contre un roc, où le vent l'a poussée:

Comme on voit la fureur par l'Aquilon chassée
D'un sifflement aigu l'orage tournoyant,
Puis d'une aile plus large en l'air s'ébanoyant
Arrêter tout à coup sa carrière lassée:

Et comme on voit la flamme ondoyant en cent lieux
Se rassemblant en un, s'aiguiser vers les cieux,
Puis tomber languissante: ainsi parmi le monde

Erra la Monarchie: et croissant tout ainsi
Qu'un flot, qu'un vent, qu'un feu, sa course vagabonde
Par un arrêt fatal s'est venu' perdre ici.

When sometimes from these Roman slopes you contemplate the work of your hands and see that it is no more than a dusty plain?

As one sees from afar on the angry sea a mountain of water swaying up with a great heave, then, drawing countless waves after it, burst with a huge barking crash against a rock on which the wind has driven it:
As one sees the fury (of the elements) pursued by the north wind stirring up the storm with a shrill whistling, then, sporting in the air on more leisurely wing, suddenly halt in its wearied course:
As one sees the flame which curls up in many places coming together in one to point against the skies, then falling back languidly: so through the world
The Roman Empire roved: and, swelling up like a wave, a wind, a flame, by an immutable decree its wandering course came to die out here.

Quand ce brave séjour, honneur du nom latin,
Qui borna sa grandeur d'Afrique et de la Bise,
De ce peuple qui tient les bords de la Tamise,
Et de celui qui voit éclore le matin,

Anima contre soi d'un courage mutin
Ses propres nourrissons, sa dépouille conquise,
Qu'il avait par tant d'ans sur tout le monde acquise,
Devint soudainement du monde le butin:

Ainsi quand du grand Tout la fuite retournée
Où trente-six mil ans ont sa course bornée,
Rompra des éléments le naturel accord,

Les semences qui sont mères de toutes choses,
Retourneront encor à leur premier discord,
Au ventre du Chaos éternellement closes.

Les Regrets

France, mère des arts, des armes et des lois,
Tu m'as nourri longtemps du lait de ta mamelle:

When this proud city, the glory of the Latin name, whose greatness was bounded by Africa and by the farthest North, by that
nation which holds the banks of the Thames and by the one which
sees the morning break,

Excited against itself with rebellious heart its own nurslings, its
conquered spoil, which over so many years it had won from the
entire world, it suddenly became the world's plunder.

So when the flow of the great Whole, in which thirty-six thousand years have confined its course, is reversed and breaks the
natural harmony of the elements,

The germs which are the mothers of all things will return again
to their original discord, pent up for eternity in the womb of chaos.

Ores, comme un agneau qui sa nourrice appelle,
Je remplis de ton nom les antres et les bois.

Si tu m'as pour enfant avoué quelquefois,
Que ne me réponds-tu maintenant, ô cruelle?
France, France, réponds à ma triste querelle:
Mais nul, sinon Écho, ne répond à ma voix.

Entre les loups cruels j'erre parmi la plaine;
Je sens venir l'hiver, de qui la froide haleine
D'une tremblante horreur fait hérisser ma peau.

Las, tes autres agneaux n'ont faute de pâture,
Ils ne craignent le loup, le vent, ni la froidure:
Si ne suis-je pourtant le pire du troupeau.

CEPENDANT que Magny suit son grand Avanson,
Panjas son Cardinal, et moi le mien encore,
Et que l'espoir flatteur, qui nos beaux ans dévore,
Appâte nos désirs d'un friand hameçon,

FRANCE, mother of the arts, of arms, and of laws, you have long
fed me with the milk from your breast; now, like a lamb calling for
its mother, I fill the caves and the woods with your name.

If at one time you owned me as your child, why do you not
answer me now, O cruel one? France, France, answer my plaintive
cry: but none, except Echo, replies to my voice.

Among the cruel wolves I stray over the plain; I feel the winter
coming and its cold breath makes my hair rise in trembling horror.

Alas, your other lambs have food in plenty, they do not fear the
wolf, the wind, or the cold: and yet I am not the worst of the
flock.

WHILE Magny follows his great Avanson,* Panjas his Cardinal,*
and I mine, too, and deceitful hope, consuming our best years, lures
on our desires with a tempting bait,

* Patrons of Du Bellay's friends in Rome, the poets Olivier de
Magny and Jean de Panjas.

Tu courtises les rois, et d'un plus heureux son
Chantant l'heur de Henri, qui son siècle décore,
Tu t'honores toi-même et celui qui honore
L'honneur que tu lui fais par ta docte chanson.

Las, et nous cependant nous consumons notre âge
Sur le bord inconnu d'un étrange rivage,
Où le malheur nous fait ces tristes vers chanter,

Comme on voit quelquefois, quand la mort les appelle,
Arrangés flanc à flanc parmi l'herbe nouvelle,
Bien loin sur un étang trois cygnes lamenter.

HEUREUX qui, comme Ulysse, a fait un beau voyage,
Ou comme cestui-là qui conquit la toison,
Et puis est retourné, plein d'usage et raison,
Vivre entre ses parents le reste de son âge!

Quand reverrai-je, hélas, de mon petit village
Fumer la cheminée, et en quelle saison

You (Ronsard) pay court to kings, and with more fortunate strains singing the fortune of Henry,* who adorns his age, you bring honour to yourself and to him who honours the honour which you bring him by your learned song.

Meanwhile we, alas, consume our days on the unknown brink of a foreign shore, where sorrow makes us sing these sad verses,

As one sees sometimes, when death is summoning them, drawn up side by side on the young grass, far across a pond three swans lamenting.

HAPPY the man who, like Ulysses, has had a good journey, or like that man who won the fleece (Jason – the golden fleece), and then came home full of experience and wisdom to live the rest of his days among his family.

Alas, when shall I see the chimneys of my little village smoking,

---

* Henri II, King of France.

Reverrai-je le clos de ma pauvre maison,
Qui m'est une province, et beaucoup d'avantage?

Plus me plaît le séjour qu'ont bâti mes aïeux
Que des palais romains le front audacieux;
Plus que le marbre dur me plaît l'ardoise fine,

Plus mon Loire gaulois que le Tibre latin,
Plus mon petit Liré que le Mont Palatin,
Et plus que l'air marin la douceur angevine.

Tu ne me vois jamais, Pierre, que tu ne die
Que j'étudie trop, que je fasse l'amour,
Et que d'avoir toujours ces livres à l'entour
Rend les yeux éblouis, et la tête alourdie.

Mais tu ne l'entends pas, car cette maladie
Ne me vient du trop lire ou du trop long séjour,
Ains de voir le bureau qui se tient chacun jour:
C'est, Pierre mon ami, le livre où j'étudie.

and in what season shall I see the garden of my humble house, which is a province, and much more, to me?

The home which my ancestors built pleases me more than the lofty front of the Roman palaces: delicate slate pleases me more than hard marble, my Gallic Loire more than the Latin Tiber, my little Liré more than the Palatine Hill, and more than the sea air the mildness of Anjou.

You never see me, Peter,* without telling me that I study too much, that I should do some love-making, and that having these books always around makes the eyes dull and the head heavy.

But you don't understand, for this sickness comes, not from reading too much or staying indoors too long, but from seeing how people behave in the daily round. That, Peter my friend, is the book in which I study.

---

* His Roman barber.

Ne m'en parle donc plus, autant que tu as cher
De me donner plaisir et de ne me fâcher:
Mais bien en ce pendant que d'une main habile

Tu me laves la barbe et me tonds les cheveux,
Pour me désennuyer, conte-moi si tu veux,
Des nouvelles du Pape, et du bruit de la ville.

J𝖤 hais du Florentin l'usurière avarice,
Je hais du fol Siénois le sens mal arrêté,
Je hais du Genevois la rare vérité,
Et du Vénitien la trop caute malice:

Je hais le Ferrarois pour je ne sais quel vice,
Je hais tous les Lombards pour l'infidélité,
Le fier Napolitain pour sa grand' vanité,
Et le poltron Romain pour son peu d'exercice:

Je hais l'Anglais mutin, et le brave Écossais,
Le traître Bourguignon, et l'indiscret Français,
Le superbe Espagnol, et l'ivrogne Tudesque:

So stop talking about it, if you really want to give me pleasure and not annoy me. Instead, while with skilful hand you are washing my beard and trimming my hair, tell me if you will, to cheer me up, the news of the Pope and the rumours of the town.

I HATE the Florentine's usurious greed, I hate the witlessness of the mad Siennese, I hate the scant truthfulness of the Genoese and the Venetian's over-cunning guile.

I hate the Ferrarese for a certain vice, I hate all Lombards for untrustworthiness, the proud Neapolitan for his great vanity, and the cowardly Roman for his unwarlike sloth.

I hate the unruly Englishman and the foolhardy Scot, the treacherous Burgundian and the indiscreet Frenchman, the haughty Spaniard and the drunken German.

Bref, je hais quelque vice en chaque nation,
Je hais moi-même encor mon imperfection,
Mais je hais par sur tout un savoir pédantesque.

MARCHER d'un grave pas, et d'un grave sourcil
Et d'un grave souris à chacun faire fête,
Balancer tous ses mots, répondre de la tête,
Avec un *Messer non*, ou bien un *Messer sì*:

Entremêler souvent un petit: *È così*,
Et d'un *son Servitor* contrefaire l'honnête,
Et comme si l'on eût sa part en la conquête,
Discourir sur Florence, et sur Naples aussi:

Seigneuriser chacun d'un baisement de main,
Et, suivant la façon du courtisan romain,
Cacher sa pauvreté d'une brave apparence:

Voilà de cette cour la plus grande vertu,
Dont souvent, mal monté, malsain, et mal vêtu,
Sans barbe et sans argent on s'en retourne en France.

In short, I hate some fault in each nation, I hate even myself for
my imperfection, but above all I hate a pedantic display of learning.

To walk with a solemn step, and with a solemn look and a solemn
smile to greet all and sundry, to weigh all one's words, to reply with
a nod, uttering a *Messer non*,* or else a *Messer sì*†:
　　To slip in often a little *È così*,‡ and to imitate good manners with
a *Son Servitor*,§ and – as if one had taken part in the conquest – to
discourse about Florence, and about Naples also:
　　To Mylord everyone with a kissing of hands, and, copying the
ways of the Roman courtier, to hide one's poverty under a brave
appearance:
　　That is the greatest virtue of this Court, from which often, with
poor horse, poor health, and poor clothes, without beard or money
one returns to France.

---

* No, sir.	† Yes, sir.
‡ So it is.	§ Your humble servant.

Voici le Carnaval, menons chacun la sienne,
Allons baller en masque, allons nous pourmener,
Allons voir Marc-Antoine, ou Zany bouffonner
Avec son Magnifique à la Vénitienne:

Voyons courir le pal à la mode ancienne,
Et voyons par le nez le sot buffle mener:
Voyons le fier taureau d'armes environner,
Et voyons au combat l'adresse italienne:

Voyons d'œufs parfumés un orage grêler,
Et la fusée ardent' siffler menu par l'air.
Sus donc, dépêchons-nous, voici la pardonnance.

Il nous faudra demain visiter les saints lieux;
Là nous ferons l'amour, mais ce sera des yeux,
Car passer plus avant c'est contre l'ordonnance.

La terre y est fertile, amples les édifices,
Les poêles bigarrés, et les chambres de bois,

The Carnival is here, let's each take his girl, let us dance in masks,
let us walk about the town, let us go and see Mark Antony, or
Zanny * clowning, with his Venetian magnifico character.

Let us go and see them racing for the *palio* (banner) in the old
style, and see the stupid buffalo led around by the nose; let us see
the fierce bull hemmed in with weapons, and see the Italian skill in
fighting.

Let us see a shower of scented eggs raining down and the fiery
rockets hissing thick and fast through the air. Come on, let's hurry,
the pardoning has started.

Tomorrow we must visit the holy places; there we will make
love, but it will be with our eyes, for to go any further is against the
regulation.

The soil there is fertile, the buildings large, the stoves mottled,
and the rooms built of wood, the magistrates incorruptible, in-

---

* Stock names of Italian comic actors.

La police immuable, immuables les lois,
Et le peuple ennemi de forfaits et de vices.

Ils boivent nuit et jour en Bretons et en Suisses,
Ils sont gras et refaits, et mangent plus que trois:
Voilà les compagnons et correcteurs des rois,
Que le bon Rabelais a surnommés Saucisses.

Ils n'ont jamais changé leurs habits et façons,
Ils hurlent comme chiens leurs barbares chansons,
Ils comptent à leur mode, et de tout se font croire:

Ils ont force beaux lacs et force sources d'eau,
Force prés, force bois: j'ai du reste, Belleau,
Perdu le souvenir, tant ils me firent boire.

LOUISE LABÉ

CLAIRE VÉNUS, qui erres par les cieux,
Entends ma voix qui en plaints chantera,
Tant que ta face au haut du ciel luira,
Son long travail et souci ennuyeux.

corruptible the laws, and the population opposed to crime and vice.*
They drink day and night like Bretons and Switzers, they are fat and hearty and eat enough for three: such are the peers and correctors of kings, whom the good Rabelais nicknamed Sausages.

They have never changed their habits and customs, they howl their barbarous songs like dogs, they count in their own way, and think the world of themselves.

They have many fine lakes and many springs, many meadows, many woods: the rest, Belleau, has slipped my memory, for they made me drink so much.

BRIGHT Venus, roving through the skies, hear my voice which, as long as your face shines in the height of heaven, will sing in plaintive tones of its long torment and heavy care.

_____
* In Switzerland.

Mon œil veillant s'attendrira bien mieux,
Et plus de pleurs te voyant jettera.
Mieux mon lit mol de larmes baignera,
De ses travaux voyant témoins tes yeux.

Donc des humains sont les lassés esprits
De doux repos et de sommeil épris.
J'endure mal tant que le soleil luit:

Et quand je suis quasi toute cassée,
Et que me suis mise en mon lit lassée,
Crier me faut mon mal toute la nuit.

LUTH, compagnon de ma calamité,
De mes soupirs témoin irréprochable,
De mes ennuis contrôleur véritable,
Tu as souvent avec moi lamenté: /

Et tant le pleur piteux t'a molesté,
Que, commençant quelque sort délectable,
Tu le rendais tout soudain lamentable,
Feignant le ton que plein avait chanté.

My wakeful eye will be more easily grieved and will shed more
tears for seeing you. It will bathe my soft bed more freely with
tears when it sees that your eyes witness its sufferings.

Now the wearied spirits of men are overcome by sweet rest and
sleep. I endure pain as long as the sun shines.

And when I am almost wholly broken and have lain down
wearily on my bed, I must cry my pain the whole night through.

LUTE, companion of my distress, irrefutable witness of my sighs,
faithful recorder of my sorrows, you have often lamented with me;

And my pitiful tear has so much moved you that, after beginning
some delightful strain, you suddenly made it sorrowful, muting the
note which it had sung full and clear.

Et si te veux efforcer au contraire,
Tu te détends, et si me contrains taire:
Mais, me voyant tendrement soupirer,

Donnant faveur à ma tant triste plainte,
En mes ennuis me plaire suis contrainte,
Et d'un doux mal douce fin espérer.

Oh, si j'étais en ce beau sein ravie
De celui-là pour lequel vais mourant,
Si avec lui vivre le demeurant
De mes courts jours ne m'empêchait envie:

Si m'accolant me disait: «Chère amie,
Contentons-nous l'un l'autre,» s'assurant
Que jà tempête, Euripe, ni courant
Ne nous pourra disjoindre en notre vie:

Si, de mes bras le tenant accolé,
Comme du lierre est l'arbre encercelé,
La mort venait, de mon aise envieuse,

And if I try to force you to the contrary, your strings grow slack
and so you oblige me to be silent; but when you see me tenderly
sighing and approve my sad grieving, I am obliged (by you) to take
pleasure in my sorrows, and to hope for a sweet outcome of a sweet
pain.

Oh, if I were ravished in that sweet breast of him for whom I languish, if the spiteful world did not prevent me from living the re-
mainder of my short days with him,

If, clasping me, he said: 'Dear love, let us content one another,'
swearing that now neither tempest, Euripus * nor current would be
able to separate us in our lives:

If, while I held him clasped in my arms as the tree is entwined by
the ivy, death came, envious of my pleasure,

---

* A narrow strait in Greece.

Lorsque, souef, plus il me baiserait
Et mon esprit sur ses lèvres fuirait,
Bien je mourrais, plus que vivante, heureuse.

Baise-m'encor, rebaise-moi et baise:
Donne-m'en un de tes plus savoureux,
Donne-m'en un de tes plus amoureux:
Je t'en rendrai quatre plus chauds que braise.

Las, te plains-tu? ça, que ce mal j'apaise
En t'en donnant dix autres doucereux.
Ainsi, mêlant nos baisers tant heureux,
Jouissons-nous l'un de l'autre à notre aise.

Lors double vie à chacun ensuivra.
Chacun en soi et son ami vivra.
Permets-m'Amour penser quelque folie:

Toujours suis mal, vivant discrètement,
Et ne me puis donner contentement,
Si hors de moi ne fais quelque saillie.

While softly he kissed me the more and my spirit fled upon his lips, I could well die, better than alive – happy.

Kiss me again, re-kiss me and kiss: give me one of your most delicious, give me one of your most amorous: I will give you back four hotter than coals.

There, is it hurting? Come, let me soothe that pain by giving you ten more sweet ones. So, mingling our happy kisses, let us enjoy each other at our ease.

Then a double life will follow for both. Each will live in himself and in his dear. Allow me, Love, to think a little wildly:

I am always unhappy, living discreetly, and I can find no contentment if I do not sometimes sally out of myself.

PIERRE DE RONSARD

MIGNONNE, allons voir si la rose
Qui ce matin avait déclose
Sa robe de pourpre au soleil,
A point perdu cette vêprée,
Les plis de sa robe pourprée,
Et son teint au vôtre pareil.

Las! voyez comme en peu d'espace
Mignonne, elle a dessus la place
Las! las! ses beautés laissé choir!
O vraiment marâtre Nature,
Puisqu'une telle fleur ne dure
Que du matin jusques au soir!

Donc, si vous me croyez, mignonne,
Tandis que votre âge fleuronne
En sa plus verte nouveauté,
Cueillez, cueillez votre jeunesse:
Comme à cette fleur, la vieillesse
Fera ternir votre beauté.

My sweet, let us go and see if the rose, which this morning opened its crimson robe to the sun, has not lost this evening the folds of its crimson dress and its colour like yours.

Ah! see how in so short a time, my sweet, it has, ah me, shed its beauties upon the ground! O truly stony-hearted Nature, since such a flower lasts only from the morning till the evening.

So, if you will heed me, sweet, while your young years bloom in their freshest newness, gather, gather your youth: as with this flower, age will wither your beauty.

Ode

PLUSIEURS de leurs corps dénués
Se sont vus en diverse terre
Miraculeusement mués,
L'un en serpent et l'autre en pierre;

L'un en fleur, l'autre en arbrisseau,
L'un en loup, l'autre en colombelle:
L'un se vit changer en ruisseau,
Et l'autre devint arondelle.

Mais je voudrais être miroir
Afin que toujours tu me visses:
Chemise je voudrais me voir,
Afin que souvent tu me prisses.

Volontiers eau je deviendrais,
Afin que ton corps je lavasse:
Être du parfum je voudrais,
Afin que je te parfumasse.

Je voudrais être le ruban
Qui serre ta belle poitrine:
Je voudrais être le carcan
Qui orne ta gorge ivoirine.

MANY, divested of their bodies, have seen themselves in various lands miraculously transformed, one into a serpent and another into a stone;

One into a flower, another into a shrub, another into a wolf, another into a dove: one saw himself changed into a stream and another became a swallow.

But I would like to be a mirror, so that you should always see me: I would like to be a shift, so that you should often take me up.

Gladly would I become water, so that I should wash your body: I would like to be perfume, so that I should perfume you.

I would like to be the ribbon which clasps your lovely breast: I would like to be the necklace which adorns your ivory throat.

Je voudrais être tout autour
Le corail qui tes lèvres touche,
Afin de baiser nuit et jour
Tes belles lèvres et ta bouche.

Ah! je voudrais, richement jaunissant,
En pluie d'or goutte à goutte descendre
Dans le giron de ma belle Cassandre,
Lorsqu'en ses yeux le somme va glissant;

Puis je voudrais en taureau blanchissant
Me transformer pour finement la prendre,
Quand en avril par l'herbe la plus tendre
Elle va, fleur, mille fleurs ravissant.

Ah! je voudrais, pour alléger ma peine,
Être un Narcisse, et elle une fontaine,
Pour m'y plonger une nuit à séjour;

Et si voudrais que cette nuit encore
Fût éternelle, et que jamais l'aurore
D'un feu nouveau ne rallumât le jour.

I would like to be the coral which colours your lips all around, so as to kiss night and day your lovely lips and your mouth.

Ah, I would like, richly yellowing, to fall down drop by drop in golden rain into the bosom of my sweet Cassandra, when sleep goes gliding into her eyes.

Then I would like to transform myself into a white bull to seize her subtly when she goes in April over the tenderest grass, a flower delighting a thousand flowers.

Ah, I would like, to assuage my pain, to be a Narcissus and she a pool, to plunge myself in a whole night long;

And I would like, too, that night to be eternal and the dawn never to re-kindle the day with a new fire.

Or que Jupin, époint de sa semence,
Hume à longs traits les feux accoutumés,
Et que du chaud de ses reins allumés
L'humide sein de Junon ensemence;

Or que la mer, or que la véhémence
Des vents fait place aux grands vaisseaux armés,
Et que l'oiseau parmi les bois ramés
Du Thracien les tensons recommence:

Or que les prés et ore que les fleurs
De mille et mille et de mille couleurs
Peignent le sein de la terre si gaie,

Seul et pensif, aux rochers plus secrets,
D'un cœur muet je conte mes regrets,
Et par les bois je vais celant ma plaie.

Ah! Bel Accueil, que ta douce parole
Vint traîtrement ma jeunesse offenser,
Quand au verger tu la menas danser
Sur mes vingt ans l'amoureuse carole!

Now that Jove, spurred on by his seed, snuffs in long draughts the familiar fires, and with the heat of his kindled loins makes fertile the moist bosom of Juno;

Now that the sea, now that the violence of the winds makes way for the great rigged vessels, and the bird among the branchy woods pipes the Thracian's (Orpheus') madrigals anew:

Now that the fields and now that the flowers, with thousand, thousand, and thousand colours paint the breast of the earth so gay,

Alone and pensive, to the most secret rocks I tell my sorrows with a silent heart and wander through the woods hiding my wound.

Ah, Fair Welcome, how treacherously your soft words came to attack my young heart, when in the orchard towards my twentieth year you led it to dance the amorous round.

Amour adonc me mit à son école,
Ayant pour maître un peu sage penser,
Qui sans raison me mena commencer
Le chapelet de la danse plus folle.

Depuis cinq ans hôte de ce verger,
Je vais ballant avecque Faux Danger,
Tenant la main d'une dame trop caute.

Je ne suis seul par amour abusé;
A ma jeunesse il faut donner la faute:
En cheveux gris je serai plus rusé.

MARIE, levez-vous, vous êtes paresseuse:
Jà la gaie alouette au ciel a fredonné,
Et jà le rossignol doucement jargonné,
Dessus l'épine assis, sa complainte amoureuse.

Sus debout! allons voir l'herbelette perleuse,
Et votre beau rosier de boutons couronné,

Love then put me to his school, (I) having a far from prudent thought for master, who without reason led me to begin the measure of the maddest dance.

For five years now a dweller in this orchard, I go dancing with False Danger, holding the hand of too artful a lady.

I am not misled by love only; it is my youth which must bear the blame; when my hair is grey I shall be more wily.

(This sonnet looks back to the medieval *Roman de la Rose*, in which Bel Accueil is a character. Others are Faux Semblant and Danger, but in line 10 Ronsard seems to have confused the two.)

GET up, Marie, you lazy girl: the gay lark has already trilled in the sky and the nightingale, sitting on the hawthorn, has already sweetly warbled its amorous lay.

Get up! Get up! Let us go and see the pearly lawn and your

Et vos œillets mignons auxquels aviez donné
Hier au soir de l'eau d'une main si soigneuse.

Harsoir en vous couchant vous jurâtes vos yeux
D'être plus tôt que moi ce matin éveillée:
Mais le dormir de l'aube aux filles gracieux

Vous tient d'un doux sommeil encor les yeux sillée.
Ça! ça! que je les baise, et votre beau tétin
Cent fois pour vous apprendre à vous lever matin.

COMME on voit sur la branche, au mois de mai, la rose
En sa belle jeunesse, en sa première fleur,
Rendre le ciel jaloux de sa vive couleur,
Quand l'aube de ses pleurs au point du jour l'arrose:

La grâce dans sa feuille et l'amour se repose,
Embaumant les jardins et les arbres d'odeur:
Mais, battue ou de pluie ou d'excessive ardeur,
Languissante elle meurt feuille à feuille déclose.

pretty rose-bush crowned with buds, and your pretty pinks to
which last night you gave water with so loving a hand.
　　Last night when you went to bed you swore by your eyes that
you would be awake earlier than me this morning; but the slumber
of dawn, so gracious to girls,
　　Keeps your eyes still sealed with a gentle sleep. There, there, let
me kiss them, and your pretty breast, a hundred times to teach you
to get up early.

As the rose appears on the branch, in May, in its lovely youth, in
its newest bloom, making the sky jealous of its brilliant hue, when
the dawn waters it with its tears at daybreak:
　　Grace in its leaves and love lies hidden, filling the gardens and
the trees with scent: but, beaten down by the rain or by excessive
heat, it languishes and dies, laid open leaf by leaf.

Ainsi en ta première et jeune nouveauté,
Quand la terre et le ciel honoraient ta beauté,
La Parque t'a tuée, et cendre tu reposes.

Pour obsèques reçois mes larmes et mes pleurs,
Ce vase plein de lait, ce panier plein de fleurs,
Afin que vif et mort ton corps ne soit que roses.

La Chanson de Perrot

... JE veux faire un beau lit d'une verte jonchée
De pervenche feuillue en contre-bas couchée,
De thym qui fleure bon, et d'aspic porte-épi,
D'odorant poliot contre terre tapi,
De neufard toujours vert qui la froideur incite,
Et de jonc qui les bords des rivières habite.
   Je veux jusques au coude avoir l'herbe, et je veux
De roses et de lis couronner mes cheveux.
Je veux qu'on me défonce une pipe angevine,
Et en me souvenant de ma toute divine,
De toi, mon doux souci, épuiser jusqu'au fond
Mille fois ce jourd'hui mon gobelet profond,

So in your early and youthful freshness, when earth and heaven acclaimed your beauty, Fate slew you and ashes you lie.

For your funeral receive my sobs and my tears, this vase full of milk, this basket full of flowers, so that living and dead your body may be only roses.

Perrot's Song

I WANT to make a fine bed from a green pile of leafy periwinkle laid at the bottom, of sweet-smelling thyme and of eared spike-lavender, of fragrant mint pressed close against the ground, of the always green water-lily which induces coolness, and of the rush which grows on the banks of rivers.

I want to have grass elbow-deep and to crown my hair with roses and lilies. I want them to broach me a cask of Angevin wine and, while I think of my wholly divine one – of you, my sweet burden – to drain my deep goblet to the bottom a thousand times

Et ne partir d'ici jusqu'à tant qu'à la lie
De ce bon vin d'Anjou la liqueur soit faillie.
    Melchior Champenois et Guillaume Manceau,
L'un d'un petit rebec, l'autre d'un chalumeau,
Me chanteront comment j'eus l'âme dépourvue
De sens et de raison sitôt que je t'eus vue,
Puis chanteront comment pour fléchir ta rigueur
Je t'appelai ma vie et te nommai mon cœur,
Mon œil, mon sang, mon tout; mais ta haute pensée
N'a voulu regarder chose tant abaissée,
Ains en me dédaignant tu aimas autre part
Un qui son amitié chichement te départ.
Voilà comme il te prend pour mépriser ma peine,
Et le rustique son de mon tuyau d'aveine...

Remontrance au Peuple de France

... Vous ne combattez pas, soldats, comme autrefois
Pour borner plus avant l'empire de vos rois:
C'est pour l'honneur de Dieu et sa querelle sainte
Qu'aujourd'hui vous portez l'épée au côté ceinte.

on this day, and not to leave here until the juice of this good wine of Anjou is exhausted to the dregs.

Melchior from Champagne and William from Maine, one with a little rebeck and the other with a shepherd's pipe, will sing how my soul was bereft of sense and of reason as soon as I saw you, then they will sing how, to move you to relent, I called you my life and named you my heart, my eye, my blood, my all; but your lofty mind would not stoop to notice so lowly a thing; rather, disdaining me, you gave your love elsewhere, to one who doles out his affection stingily to you. You see how it has served you to despise my moan and the rustic sound of my oaten pipe.

Exhortation to the People of France

You are not fighting, soldiers, as in other times, to extend the domains of your kings: it is for the glory of God and his holy cause that you have your swords girded to your sides today.

Je dis pour ce grand Dieu qui bâtit tout de rien,
Qui jadis affligea le peuple égyptien
Et nourrit d'Israël la troupe merveilleuse
Quarante ans aux déserts de manne savoureuse,
Qui d'un rocher sans eaux les eaux fit ondoyer,
Fit de nuit la colonne ardente flamboyer
Pour guider ses enfants par monts et par vallées,
Qui noya Pharaon sous les ondes salées
Et fit passer son peuple ainsi que par bateaux
Sans danger, à pied sec par le profond des eaux.
Pour ce grand Dieu, soldats, les armes avez prises
Qui favorisera vous et vos entreprises,
Comme il fit Josué par le peuple étranger,
Car Dieu ne laisse point ses amis au danger.
    Dieu tout grand et tout bon qui habites les nues,
Et qui connais l'auteur des guerres advenues,
Dieu qui regardes tout, qui vois tout et entends!
Donne, je te suppli', que l'herbe du printemps
Si tôt parmi les champs nouvelle ne fleurisse,
Que l'auteur de ces maux au combat ne périsse,
Ayant le corselet d'outre en outre enfoncé

I say, for that great God who made all from nothing, who of old afflicted the people of Egypt and who fed the wondrous squadrons of Israel for forty years in the desert on sweet-tasting manna, who from a waterless rock made the waters flow out, by night made the fiery pillar blaze to guide his children over hills and dales, who drowned Pharaoh in the salt waves and brought his people across as though on boats, in safety and dryfoot through the depths of the waters. You have taken up arms, soldiers, for this great God who will prosper you and your undertakings, as He did for Joshua among the alien people, for God does not leave his friends in peril.

God all-great and all-good who dwell in the clouds and who know the author of the present wars, You who look on all, who see all and hear! Grant, I beseech You, that the spring grass should no sooner have sprung up newly in the fields than the author of these woes should perish in battle, with his breastplate pierced through and through with a pike or with lead fired with

D'une pique ou d'un plomb fatalement poussé.
Donne que de son sang il enivre la terre,
Et que ses compagnons au milieu de la guerre,
Renversés à ses pieds, haletants et ardents,
Mordent dessus le champ la poudre entre leurs dents
Étendus l'un sur l'autre, et que la multitude
Qui s'assure en ton nom, franche de servitude,
De fleurs bien couronnée, à haute voix, Seigneur,
Tout à l'entour des morts célèbre ton honneur,
Et d'un cantique saint chante de race en race
Aux peuples à venir tes vertus et ta grâce ...

Les Démons

... Tout ainsi les Démons, qui ont le corps habile,
Aisé, souple et dispos, à se muer facile,
Changent bientôt de forme, et leur corps agile est
Transformé tout soudain en tout ce qu'il leur plaît :
Ores, en un tonneau grossement s'élargissent,
Ores, en peloton rondement s'étrécissent,
Ores, en un chevron les verriez allonger,
Ores mouvoir les pieds, et ores ne bouger.

deadly aim. Grant that he should sate the earth with his blood and that his companions in the thick of the battle, overthrown at his feet, panting and raging, should bite the dust of the field with their teeth, lying heaped upon each other, and that the multitude which trusts in your name, freed from oppression, crowned with flowers, and with loud voices, around the dead, Lord, should hymn your glory, and with a holy canticle should sing your virtues and your mercies from generation to generation of the peoples to come.

Demons

In the same way demons, which have nimble bodies, lithe, supple, and alert, easily able to transform themselves, quickly change their shape, and their agile bodies are rapidly turned into whatever they please: now into a barrel they swell out fatly, now into a ball they contract roundly, now into a rafter you would see them lengthening,

Bien souvent on les voit se transformer en bête
Tronque par la moitié: l'une n'a que la tête,
L'autre n'a que les yeux, l'autre n'a que les bras,
Et l'autre que les pieds tout velus par là-bas.
... Les autres sont nommés par divers noms, Incubes,
Larves, Lares, Lémurs, Pénates et Succubes,
Empouses, Lamiens, qui ne vaguent pas tant
Que font les aérins; sans plus vont habitant
Autour de nos maisons, et de travers se couchent
Dessus notre estomac, et nous tâtent et touchent;
Ils remuent de nuit bancs, tables et tréteaux,
Clefs, huis, portes, buffets, lits, chaires, escabeaux,
Ou comptent nos trésors, ou jettent contre terre
Maintenant une épée, et maintenant un verre;
Toutefois au matin on ne voit rien cassé,
Ni meuble qui ne soit en sa place agencé.
　　On dit qu'en Norovègue ils se louent à gages
Et font comme valets des maisons les ménages,
Ils pansent les chevaux, ils vont tirer le vin,
Ils font cuire le rôt, ils serencent le lin,
Ils filent la fusée, et les robes nettoient

now moving their feet, and now not stirring. Often they are seen
turning into a beast with only part of a body: one has only a head,
another only eyes, another only arms, another only feet all hairy
underneath.

The others are called by various names, Incubi, Larvae, Lares,
Lemures, Penates and Succubi, Night-Walkers, Lamians, which do
not roam so much as the aerial spirits do; they are content to live
round our homes and lie across our chests and prod and touch
us; at night they move benches, tables and trestles, keys, doors,
presses, beds, chairs, stools, or count our treasures, or sometimes
fling down a sword, sometimes a glass. Yet in the morning nothing
is found broken, nor any furniture disturbed from its place.

They say that in Norway they hire themselves out and do the
work of the house like servants, they groom the horses, they draw
the wine, they cook the roast, they rinse the washing, they spin the

Au lever de leurs maîtres, et les places baloient.
Or' qui voudrait narrer les contes qu'on fait d'eux,
De tristes, de gaillards, d'horribles, de piteux,
On n'aurait jamais fait, car homme ne se treuve
Qui toujours n'en raconte une merveille neuve.

Les autres moins terrains sont à part habitants
Torrents, fleuves, ruisseaux, les lacs et les étangs,
Les marais endormis et les fontaines vives,
Or' paraissant sur l'eau et ores sur les rives.

Tant que les aérins ils n'ont d'affections,
Aussi leur corps ne prend tant de mutations:
Ils n'aiment qu'une forme, et volontiers icelle
Est du nombril en haut d'une jeune pucelle
Qui a les cheveux longs, et les yeux verts et beaux,
Contre-imitant l'azur de leurs propres ruisseaux.
Pour ce ils se font nommer Naïades, Néréides,
Les filles de Téthys, les cinquante Phorcydes,
Qui errent par la mer sur le dos des dauphins,
Bridant les esturbots, les fouches et les thins,
Aucunefois vaguant tout au sommet des ondes,
Aucunefois au bas des abîmes profondes ...

wool and brush the clothes when their masters rise, and sweep the rooms. If one tried to relate all the stories that are told of them, sad, comic, gruesome, or pitiful, one would never have finished, for every man you meet will always tell some wonderful new tale about them.

The other, less earthy, kind are dwellers apart in torrents, rivers, streams, lakes and ponds, stagnant marshes and gushing springs, appearing now on the water and now on the banks.

They have not such lively affections as the aerial ones, and so their bodies do not take on so many different shapes. They like a single form, and usually that is from the navel up the form of a young maiden with long hair and fair green eyes, resembling the azure of their own streams. Therefore they are called naiads, nereids, daughters of Tethys, the fifty daughters of Phorcys (sirens), who roam the seas on the backs of dolphins, bridling the turbots, the seals, and the tunnies, sometimes moving on the crest of the waves, sometimes at the bottom of the deep gulfs.

Le Chat

A Rémy Belleau, poète

... MAIS par-sus tous l'animal domestique
Du triste chat a l'esprit prophétique,
Et faisaient bien ces vieux Égyptiens
De l'honorer, et ces dieux qui de chiens
Avaient la face et la bouche aboyante.
L'âme du ciel en tout corps tournoyante
Les pousse, anime, et fait aux hommes voir
Par eux les maux auxquels ils doivent choir.
Homme ne vit qui tant haïsse au monde
Les chats que moi d'une haine profonde;
Je hais leurs yeux, leur front et leur regard,
Et les voyant je m'enfuis d'autre part,
Tremblant de nerfs, de veines et de membre',
Et jamais chat n'entre dedans ma chambre,
Abhorrant ceux qui ne sauraient durer
Sans voir un chat auprès d'eux demeurer.
Et toutefois cette hideuse bête
Se vint coucher tout auprès de ma tête,

The Cat

To Rémy Belleau, Poet

BUT above all the domestic animal, the mournful cat, has the spirit of prophecy, and those old Egyptians did well to honour it, with those gods which had the faces and the barking mouths of dogs.

The divine spirit, which circulates in all bodies, moves them and animates them and shows men through them the evils into which they are to fall. No man living hates cats as profoundly as I do; I hate their eyes, their face, their look, and when I see them I escape to some other place, with my nerves, my veins and my limbs quivering, and never does a cat enter my room, for I abhor those who cannot bear to be without a cat somewhere near them. And in spite of that this hideous beast came and lay down near my head,

Cherchant le mol d'un plumeux oreiller
Où je soulais à gauche sommeiller;
Car volontiers à gauche je sommeille
Jusqu'au matin que le coq me réveille.

    Le chat cria d'un miauleux effroi;
Je m'éveillai comme tout hors de moi
Et en sursaut mes serviteurs j'appelle;
L'un allumait une ardente chandelle,
L'autre disait qu'un bon signe c'était
Quand un blanc chat son maître reflattait;
L'autre disait que le chat solitaire
Était la fin d'une longue misère.

    Et lors, fronçant les plis de mon sourcil,
La larme à l'œil je leur réponds ainsi:
«Le chat devin miaulant signifie
Une fâcheuse et longue maladie,
Et que longtemps je gard'rai la maison,
Comme le chat qui en toute saison
De son seigneur le logis n'abandonne,
Et soit printemps, soit été, soit automne,
Et soit hiver, soit de jour soit de nuit,

attracted by the softness of a downy pillow on which I was sleeping as usual on my left side; for I sleep for choice on the left until the morning when the cock wakes me.

The cat cried out with a horrible miaow; I woke up beside myself with fear and, leaping up, I called my servants; one lit a blazing candle, another said that it was a good omen when a white cat caressed his master; another said that a solitary cat meant the end of some long misery.

And then, frowning heavily, with tears in my eyes I answered them thus:

'The prophetic cat miaowing means a painful and long illness, and that I shall keep to the house for a long time, like the cat which in all seasons does not abandon his master's house, and whether it is spring, summer, autumn, or winter, whether night or day, remains

Ferme s'arrête et jamais ne s'enfuit,
Faisant la ronde et la garde éternelle
Comme un soldat qui fait la sentinelle» …

Odelette

A son laquais

J'ai l'esprit tout ennuyé
D'avoir trop étudié
Les Phœnomènes d'Arate;
Il est temps que je m'ébatte
Et que j'aille aux champs jouer.
Bons dieux! qui voudrait louer
Ceux qui collés sus un livre
N'ont jamais souci de vivre?

Que nous sert d'étudier,
Sinon de nous ennuyer
Et soin dessus soin accroître,
A nous, qui serons peut-être
Ou ce matin, ou ce soir,
Victime de l'Orque noir,
De l'Orque qui ne pardonne,
Tant il est fier, à personne!

there fixedly and never runs away, keeping watch and eternal guard, like a soldier on sentry-duty.'

Odelet to his lackey

My mind is quite wearied by too much study of the *Phaenomena* of Aratus; it is time for me to amuse myself and go and frolic in the fields. Ye gods! Who would praise those who, hunched over a book, never think of living?

What good does it do us to study, except to make us weary and pile care on care upon us, we who perhaps this morning, or this evening, will fall victim to black Fate – Fate which is so cruel that it spares no man?

Corydon, marche devant;
Sache où le bon vin se vend;
Fais après à ma bouteille
Des feuilles de quelque treille
Un tapon pour la boucher;
Ne m'achète point de chair,
Car, tant soit-elle friande,
L'été je hais la viande.

Achète des abricots,
Des pompons, des artichauts,
Des fraises et de la crème;
C'est en été ce que j'aime,
Quand sur le bord d'un ruisseau
Je la mange au bruit de l'eau,
Étendu sur le rivage
Ou dans un antre sauvage.

Ores que je suis dispos,
Je veux boire sans repos,
De peur que la maladie
Un de ces jours ne me die,
Me happant à l'imprévu:
Meurs, galant, c'est assez bu.

Corydon, go on ahead. Find out where they sell good wine.
Then make for my bottle, from the leaves of some climbing vine, a
stopper to close it. Do not buy me meat, for, however delicate it is,
I hate meat in summer.

Buy some apricots, some melons, some artichokes, some strawberries, and some cream. That is what I like in summer, when on
the edge of a stream I eat it to the sound of the water, lying on the
bank or in some wild cave.

While I am still hale and hearty I mean to drink without ceasing,
for fear that sickness should say to me one of these days, as it seizes
me unawares, 'Die, fellow, you've drunk enough.'

Épitaphe de François Rabelais

... J AMAIS le soleil ne l'a vu,
Tant fût-il matin, qu'il n'eût bu,
Et jamais au soir la nuit noire,
Tant fût tard, ne l'a vu sans boire,
Car altéré sans nul séjour
Le galant buvait nuit et jour.
... Il chantait la grande massue
Et la jument de Gargantue,
Le grand Panurge, et le pays
Des Papimanes ébahis,
Leurs lois, leurs façons et demeures,
Et frère Jean des Antoumeures,
Et d'Epistème les combats;
Mais la Mort qui ne buvait pas
Tira le buveur de ce monde,
Et ores le fait boire en l'onde
Qui fuit trouble dans le giron
Du large fleuve d'Achéron.
    Or toi quiconque sois qui passes
Sur sa fosse répands des tasses,

Epitaph on François Rabelais

NEVER did the sun see him, however early it was, before he had drunk, and never in the evening did dark night, however late it was, see him *not* drinking, for - thirsty without respite – the fellow drank night and day.

He hymned the great club and the mare of Gargantua, great Panurge, and the country of the gaping Papimanes, their laws, their customs, and their dwellings, and Friar Jean des Entommeures and the battles of Epistemon; but Death, who did not drink, dragged the drinker from this world and now makes him drink in the water which flows muddily in the bosom of the wide River Acheron.

Now, passer-by, whoever you be, spread cups upon his grave,

Répands du bril et des flacons,
Des cervelas et des jambons,
Car si encor dessous la lame
Quelque sentiment a son âme,
Il les aime mieux que des lis
Tant soient-ils fraîchement cueillis.

Sonnet pour Sinope

Si j'étais Jupiter, maîtresse, vous seriez
Mon épouse Junon; si j'étais roi des ondes,
Vous seriez ma Téthys, reine des eaux profondes,
Et pour votre palais le monde vous auriez;

Si le monde était mien, avec moi vous tiendriez
L'empire de la terre aux mamelles fécondes,
Et dessus un beau coche, en longues tresses blondes,
Par le peuple en honneur déesse vous iriez.

Mais je ne suis pas dieu, et si ne le puis être;
Le ciel pour vous servir seulement m'a fait naître.
De vous seule je prends mon sort aventureux.

spread foliage and flagons, saveloys and hams, for if his soul beneath the sod still has any feeling, he loves them better than lilies, however freshly gathered.

Sonnet for Sinope

If I were Jupiter, mistress, you would be my spouse Juno; if I were king of the waves, you would be my Tethys, queen of the deep waters, and for your palace you would have the world.

If the world were mine, you would hold sway with me over the earth with its fertile breasts, and in a splendid coach, with your long fair tresses, you would ride among the people honoured as a goddess.

But I am not a god, and I cannot be one; heaven gave me life only to serve you. My hazardous fate depends on you alone.

Vous êtes tout mon bien, mon mal, et ma fortune;
S'il vous plaît de m'aimer, je deviendrai Neptune,
Tout Jupiter, tout roi, tout riche et tout heureux.

Sonnets pour Hélène

Je liai d'un filet de soie cramoisie
Votre.bras l'autre jour, parlant avecques vous;
Mais le bras seulement fut captif de mes nouds,
Sans vous pouvoir lier ni cœur ni fantaisie.

Beauté que pour maîtresse unique j'ai choisie,
Le sort est inégal: vous triomphez de nous;
Vous me tenez esclave, esprit, bras et genoux,
Et Amour ne vous tient ni prise ni saisie.

Je veux parler, maîtresse, à quelque vieil sorcier,
Afin qu'il puisse au mien votre vouloir lier,
Et qu'une même plaie à nos cœurs soit semblable.

You are my whole pleasure, my pain, and my fortune. If it pleases you to love me, I shall become Neptune, wholly Jupiter, wholly king, wholly rich, and wholly happy.

Sonnets for Helen

I bound a ribbon of crimson silk to your arm the other day while I was talking to you; but only the arm was captured by my knots, I could not bind your heart or your fancy.

Beauty whom I have chosen as my sole mistress, the chances are not even, you triumph over us; you hold me enslaved – mind, arms, and knees – and Love has neither hold nor grip upon you.

I mean to speak, mistress, to some old sorcerer, in order that he should bind your will to mine, and that the same shaft should pierce our two hearts.

Je faux: l'amour qu'on charme est de peu de séjour.
Être beau, jeune, riche, éloquent, agréable,
Non les vers enchantés, sont les sorciers d'amour.

Qu'il me soit arraché des tétins de sa mère,
Ce jeune enfant Amour, et qu'il me soit vendu:
Il ne fait que de naître et m'a déjà perdu!
Vienne quelque marchand, je le mets à l'enchère.

D'un si mauvais garçon la vente n'est pas chère,
J'en ferai bon marché. Ah! j'ai trop attendu.
Mais voyez comme il pleure, il m'a bien entendu.
Apaise-toi, mignon, j'ai passé ma colère,

Je ne te vendrai point: au contraire je veux
Pour page t'envoyer à ma maîtresse Hélène,
Qui toute te ressemble et d'yeux et de cheveux,

Aussi fine que toi, de malice aussi pleine.
Comme enfants vous croîtrez, et vous jou'rez tous deux:
Quand tu seras plus grand, tu me pay'ras ma peine.

I deceive myself: conjured love does not last long. To be handsome, young, rich, eloquent, agreeable, not enchanted verses, are
the sorcerers of love.

Let him be torn for me from his mother's breasts, that young child
Love, and sold to me: he has only just been born and has already
undone me. When some merchant comes, I'll auction him.

Of such a young rascal the price is not high, I'll let him go cheap.
Ah, I have waited too long. But look how he weeps, he has understood me quite well. Dry your tears, pretty boy, I have got over
my anger,

I won't sell you: on the contrary, I mean to send you as a page
to my mistress Helen, who has eyes and hair exactly like yours;
she is as sharp as you and as full of mischief. You will grow as
children do and you will play together. When you are bigger, you
will repay me for my pains.

Vous me dîtes, maîtresse, étant à la fenêtre,
Regardant vers Montmartre et les champs d'alentour:
«La solitaire vie et le désert séjour
Valent mieux que la Cour; je voudrais bien y être.

«A l'heure mon esprit de mes sens serait maître,
En jeûne et oraison je passerais le jour,
Je défierais les traits et les flammes d'Amour;
Ce cruel de mon sang ne pourrait se repaître.»

Quand je vous répondis: «Vous trompez de penser
Qu'un feu ne soit pas feu pour se couvrir de cendre;
Sur les cloîtres sacrés la flamme on voit passer;

«Amour dans les déserts comme aux villes s'engendre;
Contre un dieu si puissant, qui les dieux peut forcer,
Jeûnes ni oraisons ne se peuvent défendre.»

You said to me, mistress, as you stood at the window, looking towards Montmartre and the fields around: 'A cloistered life and a solitary existence are better than the Court; I wish I were there.

'Even now my mind would be master of my senses, I should pass my days in fasting and prayer, I should defy the arrows and the flames of Love; that cruel god would not be able to batten on my blood.'

Then I answered you: 'You are mistaken to think that a fire is not fire when it is covered with ashes; one sees the flame pass over the holy cloisters.

'Love breeds in desert places as it breeds in towns; against so powerful a god, who can command the gods, neither fasts nor prayers are of any avail.'

Le soir qu'Amour vous fit en la salle descendre
Pour danser d'artifice un beau ballet d'amour,
Vos yeux, bien qu'il fût nuit, ramenèrent le jour,
Tant ils surent d'éclairs par la place répandre.

Le ballet fut divin, qui se soulait reprendre,
Se rompre, se refaire, et tour dessus retour
Se mêler, s'écarter, se tourner à l'entour,
Contre-imitant le cours du fleuve de Méandre.

Ores il était rond, ores long, or étroit,
Or en pointe, en triangle en la façon qu'on voit
L'escadron de la grue évitant la froidure.

Je faux, tu ne dansais, mais ton pied voletait
Sur le haut de la terre; aussi ton corps s'était
Transformé pour ce soir en divine nature.

That evening when Love brought you down into the hall to
dance so skilfully a fine ballet of love, your eyes, though it was
night, brought back the day, so much light did they shed upon that
scene.

The ballet was divine, as it went on linking up, breaking back,
coming together again and, turning this way and that, mingling,
drawing away, wheeling around, imitating the course of the river
Meander.

Now it was round, now long, now narrow, now pointed, tri-
angular in the shape of a flight of cranes fleeing south from the cold.

I am wrong, sweet, you did not dance, but your foot fluttered
over the ground; and so your body took on for that evening a
divine quality.

Te regardant assise auprès de ta cousine
Belle comme une aurore, et toi comme un soleil,
Je pensai voir deux fleurs d'un même teint pareil,
Croissantes en beauté sur la rive voisine.

La chaste, sainte, belle et unique Angevine,
Vite comme un éclair sur moi jeta son œil;
Toi, comme paresseuse et pleine de sommeil,
D'un seul petit regard tu ne m'estimas digne.

Tu t'entretenais seule au visage abaissé,
Pensive toute à toi, n'aimant rien que toi-même,
Dédaignant un chacun d'un sourcil ramassé,

Comme une qui ne veut qu'on la cherche ou qu'on l'aime.
J'eus peur de ton silence et m'en allai tout blême,
Craignant que mon salut n'eût ton œil offensé.

As I watched you sitting beside your cousin, she lovely as the dawn and you as the sun, I seemed to see two flowers of the same hue, growing in beauty on the bank nearby.

The chaste, virtuous, lovely, and peerless Angevine girl turned her eyes towards me as swift as a flash: you, as though indolent and full of sleep, did not count me worthy of a single little glance.

You communed with yourself with your head bent low, wholly self-absorbed, loving nothing but yourself, disdaining each and all with knitted brow,

Like one who does not want to be sought out or loved. I was frightened by your silence and went away very pale, fearing that my greeting had offended your eye.

Quand vous serez bien vieille, au soir, à la chandelle,
Assise auprès du feu, dévidant et filant,
Direz, chantant mes vers, en vous émerveillant:
«Ronsard me célébrait du temps que j'étais belle.»

Lors vous n'aurez servante oyant telle nouvelle,
Déjà sous le labeur à demi sommeillant,
Qui au bruit de mon nom ne s'aille réveillant,
Bénissant votre nom de louange immortelle.

Je serai sous la terre et, fantôme sans os,
Par les ombres myrteux je prendrai mon repos;
Vous serez au foyer une vieille accroupie,

Regrettant mon amour et votre fier dédain.
Vivez, si m'en croyez, n'attendez à demain:
Cueillez dès aujourd'hui les roses de la vie.

Élégie à Philippe Desportes

Nous devons à la Mort et nous et nos ouvrages;
Nous mourrons les premiers, le long repli des âges

When you are very old, at evening, by candlelight, sitting near the fire spooling and spinning the wool, you will say, in wonder, as you sing my verses: 'Ronsard praised me in the days when I was beautiful.'

Then not one of your servants who hears that news, though already half asleep over her work, but will start awake at the sound of my name, and bless your name of immortal renown.

I shall be under the ground, a boneless ghost, taking my rest in the myrtles' shade; you will be an old woman crouching by the hearth, regretting my love and your own proud scorn. Heed me and live now, do not wait till tomorrow. Gather today the roses of life.

Elegy to Philippe Desportes

We owe to Death both ourselves and our works; we shall die first;

En roulant engloutit nos œuvres à la fin;
Ainsi le veut Nature et le puissant Destin.
    Dieu seul est éternel; de l'homme élémentaire
Ne reste après la mort ni veine ni artère;
Qui pis est, il ne sent, il ne raisonne plus,
Locatif décharné d'un vieil tombeau reclus.
... L'heur de l'âme est de Dieu contempler la lumière;
La contemplation de la cause première
Est sa seule action; contemplant elle agit,
Mais au contemplement l'heur de l'homme ne gît.
    Il gît à l'œuvre seul, impossible à la cendre
De ceux que la Mort fait sous les ombres descendre.
C'est pourquoi de Pluton les champs déshabités
N'ont polices ni lois, ni villes, ni cités.
    Or l'ouvrage et l'ouvrier font un même voyage,
Leur chemin est la Mort. Athènes et Carthage,
Et Rome qui tenait la hauteur des hauteurs,
Sont poudre maintenant comme leurs fondateurs.

●

the long swell of the ages, rolling on, engulfs our works in the end. So Nature decrees it and powerful Fate.

Only God is eternal; of the elemental man neither vein nor artery remains after death; worse, he no longer feels or reasons, the fleshless tenant of an old and lonely tomb.

The joy of the soul is to contemplate the light of God; contemplation of the prime cause is its only action; in contemplating it acts, but the joy of man does not lie in contemplation.

It lies in works alone, impossible for the dust of those whom death sends down among the shades. That is why Pluto's uninhabited realms have neither government nor laws, nor towns nor cities.

Now the work and the workman make the same journey; death is their road. Athens and Carthage, and Rome which stood on the height of heights, are dust now like their founders.

… Quant à moi, j'aime mieux trente ans de renommée
Jouissant du soleil, que mille ans de renom
Lorsque la fosse creuse enfouira mon nom,
Et lorsque notre forme en une autre se change,
L'homme qui ne sent plus n'a besoin de louange …

Aн, longues nuits d'hiver, de ma vie bourrelles,
Donnez-moi patience et me laissez dormir ;
Votre nom seulement et suer et frémir
Me fait par tout le corps, tant vous m'êtes cruelles.

Le sommeil tant soit peu n'évente de ses ailes
Mes yeux toujours ouverts, et ne puis affermir
Paupière sur paupière, et ne fais que gémir,
Souffrant comme Ixion des peines éternelles.

Vieille ombre de la terre, ainçois l'ombre d'enfer,
Tu m'as ouvert les yeux d'une chaîne de fer,
Me consumant au lit, navré de mille pointes.

For my part, I prefer thirty years of fame in the light of the sun
to a thousand years of renown when the hollow tomb has swallowed up my name, for when our form changes into another, the
man who no longer feels has no need of praise.

Aн, long winter nights, my life's tormentors, give me respite and
let me sleep; your very name makes me sweat and shiver all over
my body, so cruel you are to me.

Never in the least does sleep fan my ever-open eyes with its
wings, I cannot press eyelid upon eyelid, and I do nothing but
groan, suffering like Ixion eternal torments.

Old shadow of the earth, or rather shadow of hell, you have
bound open my eyes with an iron chain, consuming me on my bed,
pierced with a thousand sharp points.

Pour chasser mes douleurs amène-moi la mort:
Ha mort, le port commun, des hommes le confort,
Viens enterrer mes maux, je t'en prie à mains jointes.

Il faut laisser maisons et vergers et jardins,
Vaisselles et vaisseaux que l'artisan burine,
Et chanter son obsèque en la façon du cygne
Qui chante son trépas sur les bords Méandrins.

C'est fait, j'ai dévidé le cours de mes destins,
J'ai vécu, j'ai rendu mon nom assez insigne:
Ma plume vole au ciel pour être quelque signe,
Loin des appâts mondains qui trompent les plus fins.

Heureux qui ne fut onc, plus heureux qui retourne
En rien comme il était, plus heureux qui séjourne,
D'homme fait nouvel ange, auprès de Jésus-Christ,

Laissant pourrir çà-bas sa dépouille de boue,
Dont le sort, la fortune et le destin se joue,
Franc des liens du corps pour n'être qu'un esprit.

Bring me death to drive away my pains. Ah, death, the common haven, the comforter of men, come and bury my sufferings, I beg you with clasped hands.

It is time to leave houses and orchards and gardens, vessels and plate which the craftsman engraves, and to sing one's passing as does the swan, when it sings its death on the banks of the Meander.

It is over, I have unravelled the course of my destiny, I have lived, I have made my name famous enough; my quill flies to heaven to become some sign there, far from the worldly lures which deceive the most subtle.

Happy is he who never was, happier he who returns to the nothingness which he was, happier (still) he who dwells, transformed from man into a new angel, at the side of Jesus Christ,

Leaving to rot down here his body of clay, with which fate and fortune and destiny sport, free from the bonds of flesh to be nothing but a spirit.

RÉMY BELLEAU

Le Ver luisant de nuit

JAMAIS ne se puisse lasser
Ma Muse de chanter la gloire
D'un Ver petit, dont la mémoire
Jamais ne se puisse effacer :
D'un Ver petit, d'un Ver luisant,
D'un Ver sous la noire carrière
Du ciel, qui rend une lumière
De son feu le ciel méprisant –
Une lumière qui reluit
Au soir sur l'herbe rousoyante
Comme la tresse rayonnante
De la courrière de la nuit –
D'un Ver tapi sous les buissons,
Qui au laboureur prophétise,
Qu'il faut que pour faucher aiguise
Sa faux, et fasse les moissons.
Gentil prophète et bien appris,
Appris de Dieu qui te fait naître
Non pour néant, ains pour accroître
Sa grandeur dedans nos esprits.

The Glow-worm

MAY my Muse never grow weary of singing the renown of a little Worm, and may its memory never be blotted out: a little Worm, a Glow-Worm, a Worm beneath the dark wheel of heaven, which gives out a light disdaining heaven in its brightness – a light which shines out in the evening on the rosy grass like the gleaming tresses of the courier of the night (the moon) – a Worm lurking under the bushes which gives warning to the farmer that it is time to sharpen his scythe for reaping and to begin the harvest. Pretty and well-trained prophet, trained by God who does not give you life for nothing, but to increase his greatness in our minds.

Et pour montrer au laboureur
Qu'il a son ciel dessus la terre,
Sans que son œil vaguement erre
En haut, pour apprendre le heur
Ou de la tête du Taureau,
Ou du Cancre, ou du Capricorne,
Ou du Bélier qui de sa corne
Donne ouverture au temps nouveau.

Vraiment tu te dois bien vanter
Être seul ayant la poitrine
Pleine d'une humeur cristalline
Qui te fait voir, et souhaiter
Des petits enfants seulement,
Ou pour te montrer à leur père,
Ou te pendre au sein de leur mère
Pour lustre, comme un diamant.

Vis donc, et que le pas divers
Du pied passager ne t'offense,
Et pour ta plus sûre défense
Choisis le fort des buissons verts.

And to show the farmer that he has his heaven upon this earth,
without his eye vaguely roving above him to learn his fortune
either from the head of Taurus, or of Cancer, or of Capricorn, or
of the Ram, which butts open the new season with its horn.

Truly you should be very proud to be the only creature to have
your breast full of a crystalline liquid which makes you visible, and
coveted only by little children – either to show you to their father
or to hang you on their mother's breast as a shining ornament, like
a diamond.

Live then, and may the casual steps of passing feet do you no
harm, and for your safest refuge choose the heart of the green
bushes.

Le Béril

LE Béril que je chante est une pierre fine,
Imitant le vert gai des eaux de la marine,
Quand les fiers Aquilons mollement accoisés
Ont fait place aux Zéphyrs sur les flots reposés.
Quelquefois le Béril a la face dorée
Comme liqueur de miel fraîchement épurée,
Dont le lustre est faiblet s'il n'est fait à biseau,
Car le rebat de l'angle hausse son lustre beau:
Autrement languissant, morne et de couleur paille,
Sans les rayons doublés que lui donne la taille.
      Le meilleur est celui dont le visage peint
De l'Émeraude fine imite le beau teint:
Seul le rivage Indois le Béril nous envoie,
Soit ou vert ou doré: pour les durtés du foie
Et pour le mal des yeux il est fort souverain,
Les soupirs trop hâtés il appaise soudain,
Le hoquet et les rots: entretient le ménage
De l'homme et de la femme ès lois de mariage:
Il chasse la paresse, et d'un pouvoir ami
Il rabaisse l'orgueil d'un cruel ennemi.

The Beryl

THE Beryl of which I sing is a precious stone, resembling the gay green of the waters of the sea when the stormy blasts, gently appeased, have given place to the zephyrs on the calmed waves. Sometimes the Beryl has a golden surface like newly-strained liquid honey, but its lustre is feeble if it is not bevelled, for the blow of the tool's edge heightens its fine lustre which is otherwise sickly, dull, and straw-coloured, lacking the double gleams which cutting gives to it.

The best is the sort whose tinted surface resembles the lovely hue of fine emeralds. Only the Indian shore sends us the Beryl, either green or golden. For hardenings of the liver and for eye diseases it is a sovereign remedy, it immediately calms panting, hiccups, and belching. It maintains the union of man and woman within the laws of marriage. It drives away sloth and with its friendly influence humbles the pride of a cruel enemy.

Béril, je te suppli', si telle est ta puissance,
Chasse notre ennemi hors les bornes de France;
Trop de peuple français a senti les efforts
De son bras enivré du sang de tant de morts.

Prière

TES mains m'ont fait et repétri de chair,
Comme un potier qui de grâce gentille
Tourne en vaisseau une masse d'argille:
Puis tout soudain tu me fais trébucher.

Souvienne-toi avant que me damner
Que de limon et de bourbe fangeuse
Tu m'as formé, et qu'en terre poudreuse
Après ma mort me feras retourner.

Tu m'as coulé comme le lait nouveau,
Qui s'épaissit et se caille en présure,
De nerfs et d'os assemblé ma figure,
Puis, revêtu et de chair et de peau,

Beryl, I beg you, if such is your power, drive our enemy beyond the frontiers of France; too many Frenchmen have felt the weight of his arm made drunk by the blood of so many dead.

Prayer

YOUR hands have made me and modelled me from flesh, like a potter who with delicate skill turns a lump of clay into a vessel: then suddenly You make me stumble.

Remember before You damn me that You formed me from mire and slimy mud, and that after my death You will make me return to dusty earth.

You poured me like new milk, which thickens and curdles in rennet, You put together my body from nerves and bones, then, clothed with flesh and skin,

Tu m'as donné et la vie et les ans,
Me conduisant au sentier de ta grâce,
Et aux rayons de ta divine face
Guidé mes pas, mon esprit et mes sens.

ÉTIENNE JODELLE

Des astres, des forêts, et d'Achéron l'honneur,
Diane au monde haut, moyen et bas préside,
Et ses chevaux, ses chiens, ses Euménides guide,
Pour éclairer, chasser, donner mort et horreur.

Tel est le lustre grand, la chasse et la frayeur
Qu'on sent sous ta beauté claire, prompte, homicide,
Que le haut Jupiter, Phébus, et Pluton cuide
Son foudre moins pouvoir, son arc, et sa terreur.

Ta beauté par ses rais, par son rets, par la crainte,
Rend l'âme éprise, prise, et au martyre étreinte:
Luis-moi, prends-moi, tiens-moi, mais hélas, ne me perds

You gave me life and years, leading me in the way of your grace, and by the light of your divine face have guided my steps, my spirit, and my senses.

The pride of the heavens, of the forests, and of Acheron, Diana presides over the upper, middle, and lower worlds, and guides her horses, her hounds, and her Furies to illumine, hunt, sow death and horror.

Such is the bright lustre, the hunt, and the fear which springs from your clear, swift, murderous beauty, that mighty Jupiter, Phoebus Apollo, and Pluto think they can do less with thunder, with bow, and with terror.

Your beauty by its beams, by its snares, by fear, leaves the heart captivated, captured, and martyred. Shine on me, seize me, hold me, but ah, do not destroy me

Des flambeaux forts et griefs, feux, filets et encombres,
Lune, Diane, Hécate, aux cieux, terre et enfers
Ornant, quêtant, gênant nos dieux, nous, et nos ombres.

QUELQUE lieu, quelque amour, quelque loi qui
   t'absente,
Et ta déité tâche ôter de devant moi,
Quelque oubli qui, contraint de lieu, d'amour, de loi,
Fasse qu'en tout absent de ton cœur je me sente:

Tu m'es, tu me seras sans fin pourtant présente
Par le nom, par l'effet fatal qui est en toi;
Par tout tu es Diane, en tout rien je ne vois
Qui mon œil, qui mon cœur de ta présence exempte.

En la terre, et non pas seulement aux forêts,
De moi vivant l'objet continuel tu es,
Étant Diane: et puis, si le ciel me rappelle,

O Lune, ton bel œil mon heur malheurera:
Si je tombe aux enfers, mon seul tourment sera
De souffrir sans fin l'œil d'une Hécate tant belle.

with your bright and hurtful torches, fires, nets, and pitfalls –
Moon, Diana, Hecate, in heaven, earth, and hell gracing, harrying,
tormenting our gods, us, and our ghosts.

WHATEVER place, whatever love, whatever law keeps you absent,
and strives to remove your divinity from before me, whatever for-
getfulness, imposed by place, love, law, causes me to feel wholly
absent from your heart:
   You are, you will yet be ceaselessly present to me by your name,
by the fatal power which is in you; by all things you are Diana,
in all things I see nothing which dispenses my eye or my heart from
your presence.
   Upon earth, and not in the forests alone, you are my continual
object while I live, being Diana: and then, if heaven recalls me, O
Moon, your fair eye will ill-star my fortune: if I drop down to hell,
my sole torment will be to endure endlessly the eye of so lovely a
Hecate.

JEAN-ANTOINE DE BAÏF

L'Hippocrène

Vers baïfins

MUSE, reine d'Hélicon, fille de mémoire, ô déesse,
O des poètes l'appui, favorise ma hardiesse.
Je veux donner aux Français un vers de plus libre
    accordance,
Pour le joindre au luth sonné d'une moins contrainte
    cadence.
Fais qu'il oigne doucement des oyants les pleines oreilles,
Dedans dégouttant flatteur un miel doucereux à mer-
    veilles.
Je veux d'un nouveau sentier m'ouvrir l'honorable
    passage
Pour aller sur votre mont m'ombroyer sous votre bocage,
Et ma soif désaltérer en votre fontaine divine
Qui sourdit du mont cavé dessous la corne Pégasine,
Lorsque le cheval ailé bondit en l'air hors de l'ondée
Du sang qui coulait du col de la Méduse outrecuidée.

The Horse's Fountain

(In Baïfin verse – a name coined by de Baïf for the fifteen-foot
line of his own invention.)

MUSE, Queen of Helicon, Daughter of Memory, O Goddess, O
protectress of poets, prosper my adventurous undertaking; I wish
to give the French a line of freer harmony, to be linked to the lute
played with a less constrained cadence. Make it anoint sweetly the
open ears of its hearers, caressingly dropping in a marvellously
suave honey. I want to blaze for myself a glorious new path, by
which to go up to your mountain and sit in the shade of your grove
and quench my thirst at your divine spring which gushed from the
hollow mount beneath the hoof of Pegasus, when the winged horse
bounded skywards out of the torrent of blood which flowed from
the neck of the overweening Medusa.

84

... Et nulle bête depuis n'a touché cette onde argentine,
Qu'en mémoire du cheval ils surnommèrent chevaline,
Fors les chantres oisillons qui par le laurierin bocage
Fredonnetant leurs chansons dégoisent un mignot
    ramage.
Mais les corbeaux croassants ni les corneilles jaseresses
Ni les criards chats-huants ni les agaces jangleresses
Ne touchent à la belle eau, qui, coulant de la nette source,
Sur un sablon argentin crêpe sa tournoyante course
Alentour de cent préaux et cent verdoyantes îlettes,
Là où la fraîche moiteur abreuve dix mille fleurettes...

Chansonnette mesurée

A LA fontaine je voudrais
    Avec ma belle aller jouer.
Là dedans l'eau nous irions tous deux rafraîchir
    Notre amour trop ardent.

    Mille douceurs, mille bons mots, mille plaisirs,
    Mille gentils amoureux jeux se feraient là,

And no creature since has touched that silvery water, which in memory of the horse they dubbed the Horse's Fountain, except the fledgling songsters which, warbling their songs through the laurelled grove, pour out a pretty twittering. But neither the cawing crows nor the chattering rooks nor the screeching owls nor the noisy magpies touch the fine water which, as it flows from the clear spring, winds its twisting course over silvery sand around a hundred meadows and a hundred green islets, upon which the cool moisture waters ten thousand flowers.

Rhythmic Song *

IN the pool I would like to go and sport with my fair love. There in the water we would both go to cool our too ardent passion.

    A thousand caresses, a thousand loving words, a thousand pleasures, a thousand sweet amorous games would we have there,

* Written in unrhymed quantitative verse, for music.

Mille baisers, mille doux embrassements là nous nous
    donn'rions.

    – A la fontaine ...

    Nous irions par le fleuri pré courir aux fleurs,
    Cueillerions l'orfin et l'argent et le pourprin,
Chapelets ronds et bouquets, chaînes et tortils nous y
    li'rions.

    – A la fontaine ...

    Si le destin le nous permet que feignons-nous,
    Que n'allons-nous jouir heureux de si beaux dons?
Et le printemps nous y convie et de notre âge la saison.

    – A la fontaine ...

    Pèse bien : Qu'est-ce du monde, ô mon amour doux?
    Si l'amour manque et la plaisance, ce n'est rien :
Du désir donc et du plaisir recueillons, belle, le doux
    fruit.

    – A la fontaine ...

a thousand kisses, a thousand soft embraces would we exchange
there.

    We would go through the flowery meadow running from flower
to flower; we would pick the golden, the silver, and the crimson;
garlands and posies, chains and coronals we would weave there.

    If fate allows us this, why do we linger, why do we not go
happily to enjoy such sweet gifts? The spring invites us to them
and this season of our life.

    Consider this: What is the world's use, O my sweet love? If love
lacks and enjoyment, it is nothing. So, fair maid, let us gather
desire's and pleasure's sweet fruit.

A l'hirondelle

Vers mesurés

BABILLARDE, qui toujours viens
Le sommeil et songe troubler
Qui me fait heureux et content,
Babillarde aronde, tais-toi.

Babillarde aronde, veux-tu
Que, coupant ton aile et ton bec,
Je te fasse pis que Térée?
Babillarde aronde, tais-toi.

Si tu ne veux te taire, crois-moi,
Je me vengerai de tes cris,
Punissant ou toi ou les tiens.
Babillarde aronde, tais-toi.

Crie contre tel qui heureux
En amour, veillant, à cœur soûl
De sa belle prend le plaisir.
Babillarde aronde, tais-toi.

The Swallow

Rhythmic Verse

YOU chatterer, who always come to disturb sleep and dreams
which make me happy and content, chattering swallow, quiet then.

Chattering swallow, would you like me, cutting your wing and
your beak off, to do worse to you than Tereus? * Chattering swallow, quiet then.

If you will not be quiet, believe me, I will pay you out for your
cries, punishing you or your children. Chattering swallow, quiet
then.

Cry against him who, happy in love, wakeful, enjoys his darling
to his heart's content. Chattering swallow, quiet then.

---

* In the Greek myth, Tereus cut out the tongue of his wife
Procne, who was later turned into a swallow.

Ne sois envieuse sur moi
Qui ne peut jouir que dormant
Et ne suis heureux que songeant.
Babillarde aronde, tais-toi.

Épitaphe

[*des protestants tués le jour de la Saint-Barthélemy*]

PAUVRES corps où logeaient ces esprits turbulents,
Naguère la terreur des princes de la terre,
Même contre le ciel osant faire la guerre,
Déloyaux, obstinés, pervers et violents :

Aujourd'hui le repas des animaux volants
Et rampants charogniers, et de ces vers qu'enserre
La puante voirie, et du peuple qui erre
Sous les fleuves profonds en la mer se coulant :

Pauvres corps, reposez ; si vos malheureux os,
Nerfs et veines et chair, sont dignes de repos,
Qui ne purent souffrir le repos de la France.

Do not rail against me, who can find my pleasure only in sleep
and am happy only in dreams. Chattering swallow, quiet then.

Epitaph

[*On the Protestants killed on St Bartholomew's Day*]

POOR bodies in which those turbulent spirits lodged, once the
terror of the princes of the earth, presuming to make war even
against heaven, disloyal, stubborn, perverse, and violent:

Today the pasture of the flying creatures and the creeping
carrion-beasts, and of those worms which the stinking sewers contain, and of the nation which roams under the deep rivers flowing
down to the sea:

Poor bodies, rest in peace; if your unhappy bones, nerves, veins,
and flesh are worthy of peace which could not allow France to
be at peace.

Esprits dans les carfours toutes les nuits criez:
O mortels avertis, et voyez et croyez
Que le forfait retarde et ne fuit la vengeance.

JEAN PASSERAT

Sur la mort de Thulène, fou du roi

SIRE, Thulène est mort: j'ai vu sa sépulture,
Mais il est presque en vous de le ressusciter;
Faites de son état un poète héritier;
Le poète et le fou sont de même nature.

L'un fuit l'ambition et l'autre n'en a cure:
Tous deux ne font jamais leur argent profiter;
Tous deux sont d'une humeur aisée à irriter;
L'un parle sans penser, et l'autre à l'aventure.

L'un a la tête verte, et l'autre va couvert
D'un joli chaperon fait de jaune et de vert;
L'un chante des sonnets, l'autre danse aux sonnettes;

Spirits every night cry at the crossroads: O mortals now warned,
see and believe that crime delays vengeance, but does not escape it.

On the Death of Thulène, the King's Fool

SIRE, Thulène is dead: I have seen his tomb, but it is almost
within your power to restore him to life. Let a poet inherit his post;
the poet and the fool are of the same nature.

One flees ambition and the other takes no heed of it; both never
make their money prosper; both are of an easily irritable temper;
one speaks without thinking and the other at random.

One is green in the head and the other wears a pretty cap of
yellow and green; one sings sonnets and the other dances to the
sound of *sonnettes* (bells);

Le plus grand différend qui se trouve entre nous,
C'est qu'on dit que toujours fortune aime les fous,
Et qu'elle est peu souvent favorable aux poètes.

La Journée de Senlis

A CHACUN nature donne
Des pieds pour le secourir :
Les pieds sauvent la personne ;
Il n'est que de bien courir.

Ce vaillant prince d'Aumale,
Pour avoir fort bien couru,
Quoiqu'il ait perdu sa malle,
N'a pas la mort encouru.

Ceux qui étaient à sa suite
Ne s'y endormirent point,
Sauvant par heureuse fuite
Le moule de leur pourpoint.

Quand ouverte est la barrière,
De peur de blâme encourir,
Ne demeurez point derrière :
Il n'est que de bien courir.

The chief difference to be found between us is that they say that
fortune always loves fools, but she is rarely favourable to poets.

The Day of Senlis *

To each man nature gives feet to help him out: the feet save the
person; the only thing is to run fast.

That valiant Prince of Aumale, through having run so well,
avoided death although he lost his baggage.

The people of his following were not caught napping; they
saved by a timely flight the creases of their doublets.

When the barrier is down, for fear of incurring blame, do not lag
behind: the only thing is to run fast.

* Battle fought in 1589, at which the Leaguers were defeated by
the supporters of Henri IV.

... Souvent celui qui demeure
Est cause de son méchef :
Celui qui fuit de bonne heure
Peut combattre derechef.

Il vaut mieux des pieds combattre
En fendant l'air et le vent,
Que se faire occire ou battre
Pour n'avoir pris le devant.

Qui a de l'honneur envie
Ne doit pourtant en mourir :
Où il y va de la vie
Il n'est que de bien courir.

Villanelle

J'AI perdu ma tourterelle :
Est-ce point celle que j'ois ?
Je veux aller après elle.

Tu regrettes ta femelle.
Hélas ! aussi fais-je, moi.
J'ai perdu ma tourterelle.

Often those who lag behind are the cause of their own undoing: he who runs away early can fight another time.

It is better to fight with one's feet, cleaving the air and the wind, than to let oneself be slain or beaten for not having got ahead.

He who covets honour must all the same not die for it: when life is in danger, the only thing is to run fast.

Villanelle

I HAVE lost my turtle-dove: Is that not she whom I hear? I want to go after her.

You pine for your mate. So, alas, do I. I have lost my turtle-dove.

Si ton amour est fidèle,
Aussi est ferme ma foi;
Je veux aller après elle.

Ta plainte se renouvelle,
Toujours plaindre je me dois;
J'ai perdu ma tourterelle.

En ne voyant plus la belle,
Plus rien de beau je ne vois;
Je veux aller après elle.

Mort, que tant de fois j'appelle,
Prends ce qui se donne à toi!
J'ai perdu ma tourterelle;
Je veux aller après elle.

Ode

(*Vers mesurés rimés*)

CE petit dieu, colère archer, léger oiseau,
    A la parfin ne me lairra que le tombeau,
Si du grand feu que je nourris ne s'amortit la vive ardeur.
    Un été froid, un hiver chaud, me gèle et fond,

If your love is faithful, so is my faith constant; I want to go after her.

Your grieving is renewed, I must grieve always; I have lost my turtle-dove.

No longer seeing my fair one, nothing fair can I see; I want to go after her.

Death, on whom I call so often, take what is offered you. I have lost my turtle-dove; I want to go after her.

Ode

(*Rhymed rhythmic verse*)

THIS little god, angry archer, light-winged bird, in the end will leave me only the tomb, if the sharp heat of the great fire which I feed is not cooled. A cold summer, a hot winter, freezes and melts

Mine mes nerfs, glace mon sang, ride mon front:
Je me meurs vif, ne mourant point: je sèche au temps de
    ma verdeur.
Sotte, trop tard à repentir tu te viendras:
  De m'avoir fait ce mal à tort tu te plaindras.
Tu t'attends donc à me chercher remède au jour que je
    mourrai?
D'un amour tel méritait moins la loyauté
  Que de goûter du premier fruit de ta beauté?
Je le veux bien, tu ne veux pas, tu le voudras, je ne
    pourrai.

JEAN DE LA TAILLE

Chanson

En avril où naquit Amour,
J'entrai dans son jardin un jour,
Où la beauté d'une fleurette
Me plut sur celles que je vis:
Ce ne fut pas la pâquerette,
L'œillet, la rose, ni le lis;
Ce fut la belle Marguerite,
Qu'au cœur j'aurai toujours écrite.

me, saps my nerves, ices my blood, furrows my brow: I am dying alive, not dying: I wither in the time of my greenness. Fool, too late will you come to repent: you will complain wrongly that you have done this harm to me. Are you waiting until the day of my death to find me a remedy? Did the constancy of such a love deserve less than to taste the first-fruits of your beauty? I am willing, you are not willing, you will be willing, I shall not be able.

Song

In April when love was born, I went into his garden one day, and there the beauty of a floweret pleased me above the others which I saw. It was not the daisy, the carnation, the rose, or the lily; it was the sweet Marguerite which I shall always have written on my heart.

Elle ne commençait encor
Qu'à s'éclore, ouvrant son fond d'or;
C'est des fleurs la fleur plus parfaite,
Qui plus dure en son teint naïf
Que le lis, ni la violette,
La rose, ni l'œillet plus vif.
J'aurai toujours au cœur écrite,
Sur toutes fleurs, la Marguerite.

Les uns lou'ront le teint fleuri
D'autre fleur, dès le soir flétri,
Comme d'une rose tendrette
Qu'on ne voit qu'en un mois fleurir;
Mais, par moi, mon humble fleurette
Fleurira toujours sans flétrir.
J'aurai toujours au cœur écrite,
Sur toutes fleurs, la Marguerite.

Plût à Dieu que je pusse un jour
La baiser mon saoul, et qu'Amour
Cette grâce et faveur m'eût faite,
Qu'en saison je pusse cueillir

It was only just beginning to bloom, opening its golden cup; it
is of all flowers the most perfect, lasting longer in its simple hue
than the lily or the violet, the rose, or the more vivid carnation. I
shall always have written on my heart, above all flowers, the
Marguerite.

Some will praise the bloom of some other flower, withered by
evening-time, such as that of the delicate rose, which is seen in
bloom for one month only; but, through me, my humble floweret
will always bloom without withering. I shall always have written
on my heart, above all flowers, the Marguerite.

Would to God that I might one day kiss it to my heart's content,
and that Love should grant me this grace and favour, that in its

Cette jeune fleur vermeillette
Qui, croissant, ne fait qu'embellir:
J'aurai toujours au cœur écrite,
Sur toutes fleurs, la Marguerite.

NICOLAS RAPIN

Sur la bataille d'Ivry

(*Vers anapestiques rimés*)

Chevaliers généreux, qui avez le courage françois,
Accourez, accourez secourir l'héritier de vos rois,
Secourez votre roi naturel, si vaillant, si guerrier,
A la peine, à la charge, à l'assaut le premier, le dernier:
    Un roi ne s'est jamais vu
    De tant de grâce pourvu.

A cheval, à cheval, casaniers, tout affaire laissé;
Le loyal coutelas à la main et le casque baissé,
Débattez courageux votre honneur, votre vie et vos
    biens;

season I might pick that young rosy flower which, as it grows,
grows only more lovely: I shall always have written on my heart,
above all flowers, the Marguerite.

The Battle of Ivry

(*Anapaestic verse with rhymes*)

Noble knights, brave French hearts, ride up, ride up and rally to
the heir of your Kings, rally to your natural King, so brave, so
soldierly, in the thick of the battle, in the charge, in the assault the
first and the last (to remain); no king has ever been seen endowed
with so much grace.
    To horse, to horse, home-keepers, leaving all (other) business;

Ne souffrez ce tyran, qui s'accroît de la perte des siens,
    Ravir le sceptre et les lois
    Du grand royaume françois.

Ne craignez de donner la bataille et le choc commencer,
Attaquez et donnez à ce gros qui se veut avancer;
Ce ne sont que mutins, maladroits à la guerre et aux
      coups,
Qui jamais ne sauront soutenir ni tenir devant vous:
    Au traître, lâche et trompeur,
    L'écharpe blanche fait peur.

De clairons, de tambours et de voix, animez le combat,
Côtoyez votre roi, qui premier à la presse combat,
Désireux de trouver ce voleur que l'Érynne poursuit;
Il a honte, il a peur, je le vois, le renard, qui s'enfuit:
    Io péan! s'en est fait,
    Io! triomphe parfait.

with your faithful swords in hand and your helms lowered, fight bravely for your honour, your lives, and possessions; do not allow that tyrant who grows fat on the woes of his countrymen to usurp the sceptre and the rule of the great kingdom of France.

Do not fear to give battle and to begin the clash, attack, and charge on that main body which offers to advance; they are only rebels, unskilled in war and at blows, who will never be able to stand or hold fast before you: into the traitor, cowardly and deceitful, the white scarf strikes fear.

Stir up the fight with bugles, drums, and cries, advance beside your King, fighting in the forefront of the fray, bent on finding that brigand whom the vengeful Fury pursues; he is ashamed, he is afraid, I see him, the fox, slipping away:

Io pæan! the day is won. *Io!* victory is complete.

ROBERT GARNIER

Élégie sur la mort de Ronsard

... ADIEU, mon cher Ronsard; l'abeille en votre tombe
    Fasse toujours son miel;
Que le baume arabic à tout jamais y tombe,
    Et la manne du ciel,
Le laurier y verdisse avecque le lierre
    Et le myrte amoureux;
Riche en mille boutons, de toutes parts l'enserre
    Le rosier odoreux,
Le thym, le basilic, la franche marguerite,
    Et notre lis françois,
Et cette rouge fleur où la plainte est écrite
    Du malcontent Grégeois.
Les nymphes de Gâtine et les naïades saintes
    Qui habitent le Loir,
Le venant arroser de larmettes épreintes,
    Ne cessent de douloir.
Las! Cloton a tranché le fil de votre vie
    D'une piteuse main,
La voyant de vieillesse et de goutte suivie,
    Torturage inhumain;

Elegy on the Death of Ronsard

FAREWELL, my dear Ronsard, may the bee always make its honey in your tomb; may gum Arabic drip for ever in there and the heavenly manna, may the laurel grow green there with the ivy and the amorous myrtle; rich with a thousand buds, may the fragrant rosebush enclose it on every side, with thyme, basil, the simple daisy, and our French lily, and that red flower on which the complaint of the discontented Greek is written.* May the nymphs of Gâtine and the sacred naiads who dwell in the Loir, coming to water it with flowing tears, not cease to mourn. Alas, Clotho has snipped the thread of your life with a merciful hand, seeing it pursued by old age and gout, an inhuman torture; seeing poor France,

---

* A kind of hyacinth which sprang from the blood of Ajax.

Voyant la pauvre France, en son corps outragée
    Par le sanglant effort
De ses enfants qui l'ont tant de fois ravagée,
    Soupirer à la mort;
Le Suisse aguerri, qui aux combats se loue,
    L'Anglais fermé de flots,
Ceux qui boivent le Pô, le Tage et la Danoue
    Fondre dessus son dos,
Ainsi que le vautour, qui de griffes bourrelles
    Va sans fin tirassant
De Prométhé' le foie, en pâtures nouvelles
    Coup sur coup renaissant.
Les meurtres inhumains se font entre les frères,
    Spectacle plein d'horreur,
Et déjà les enfants courent contre leurs pères
    D'une aveugle fureur;
Le cœur des citoyens se remplit de furies;
    Les paysans écartés
Meurent contre une haie; on ne voit que tûries
    Par les champs désertés.
Et puis allez chanter l'honneur de notre France
    En siècles si maudits!
Attendez-vous qu'aucun vos labeurs récompense
    Comme on faisait jadis?

outraged in her body by the murderous assault of her children who have ravaged her so often, sighing for death; (seeing) the warlike Switzer, who hires himself for fighting, the Englishman fenced with waves, those who drink of the Po, the Tagus, and the Danube swooping down upon her like the vulture, which with racking claws endlessly tears out the liver of Prometheus, time after time reborn as new food for it. Inhuman killings take place between brothers – a sight full of horror – and already children leap upon their fathers in blind fury; the citizens' hearts are filled with rage; the isolated peasants die against a hedge; only slaughters are seen in the deserted fields. And then go and sing the glory of our France in such accursed times! Do you think that any will reward your

La triste pauvreté nos chansons accompaigne;
    La Muse, les yeux bas,
Se retire de nous, voyant que l'on dédaigne
    Ses antiques ébats.
Vous êtes donc heureux, et votre mort heureuse,
    O Cygne des François;
Ne lamentez que nous, dont la vie ennuyeuse
    Meurt le jour mille fois.
Vous errez maintenant aux campaignes d'Élise,
    A l'ombre des vergers,
Où chargent en tout temps, assurés de la bise,
    Les jaunes orangers,
Où les prés sont toujours tapissés de verdure,
    Les vignes de raisins,
Et les petits oiseaux gazouillant au murmure
    Des ruisseaux cristallins ...

Chœur des Juives

PAUVRES filles de Sion,
Vos liesses sont passées;
La commune affliction
Les a toutes effacées.

labours as they used to do? Sad poverty accompanies our songs; the Muse, with eyes downcast, withdraws from us, seeing that her ancient revels are despised. So you are happy, and your death is happy, O Swan of the French; mourn only for us, whose dismal lives die a hundred deaths a day. You wander now in the fields of Elysium in the shade of the orchards, where in all seasons, secure from the storm, the yellow orange-trees are laden with fruit, where the meadows are always covered with green, the vines with grapes, and the little birds twittering to the murmur of the crystalline streams.

Chorus from The Jewish Woman

POOR daughters of Zion, your joys are over; the general affliction has effaced them all.

Ne luiront plus vos habits
De soie avec l'or tissue;
La perle avec le rubis
N'y sera plus aperçue.

La chaîne qui dévalait
Sur vos gorges ivoirines
Jamais comme elle soulait
N'embellira vos poitrines.

Vos seins, des cèdres plorants
En mainte larme tombée
Ne seront plus odorants,
Ni des parfums de Sabée,

Et vos visages, déteints
De leur naturel albâtre,
N'auront souci que leurs teints
Soient peinturés de cinabre.

L'or crêpé de vos cheveux,
Qui sur vos tempes se joue,
De mille folâtres nœuds
N'ombragera votre joue.

Your clothes will gleam no longer with silk spun with gold; the
pearl with the ruby will be seen no more.

The chain which swept down over your ivory throats will never,
as it used to, adorn your breasts.

Your breasts will no longer smell of the cedars which weep in
many a down-dropping tear nor be fragrant with the perfumes of
Sheba,

And your faces, having lost their natural alabaster, will not
trouble for their complexions to be rouged with cinnabar.

The wavy gold of your hair which sports on your temples will
not shade your cheeks with countless wanton curls.

Nous n'entendrons plus les sons
De la soupireuse lyre
Qui s'accordait aux chansons
Que l'amour vous faisait dire,

Quand les cuisantes ardeurs
Du jour étant retirées,
On dansait sous les tiédeurs
Des brunissantes soirées,

Et que ceux-là dont l'amour
Tenait les âmes malades,
Faisaient aux dames la cour
De mille douces aubades,

Contant les affections
De leurs amitiés fidèles
Et les dures passions
Qu'ils souffraient pour l'amour d'elles.

Las! que tout est bien changé!
Nous n'avons plus que tristesse.
Tout plaisir s'est étrangé
De nous, et toute liesse.

We shall hear no more the sound of the soft-sighing lyre which tuned with the songs love caused you to sing,
When, the burning heat of the day having gone, you danced in the cool of the darkening evenings,
And when those whose hearts were sick with love paid their court to the ladies with a thousand sweet madrigals,
Singing of the feelings of their faithful affection and of the grievous passions which they suffered for love of them.
Alas, how changed all things are! Now we have only sadness. All pleasure has been banished from us, and all joy.

Notre orgueilleuse Cité,
Qui les cités de la terre
Passait en félicité,
N'est plus qu'un monceau de pierre.

Dessous ses murs démolis,
Comme en communs cimetières,
Demeurent ensevelis
La plus grand' part de nos frères.

Et nous, malheureux butin,
Allons soupirer captives,
Bien loin dessous le matin,
Sur l'Euphrate aux creuses rives,

Où, confites en tourment,
Toute liberté ravie,
En pleurs et gémissement
Nous finirons notre vie.

Our proud city, which excelled in felicity the cities of the earth,
is now only a heap of stones.

Under its razed walls, as in a common grave, the greater number
of our brothers lie buried.

And we, unhappy booty, go to sigh in captivity, far off, towards
the sunrise on the hollow-banked Euphrates,

Where, filled with anguish, with all freedom torn from us, with
sobs and moaning we shall end our lives.

GUILLAUME DE SALLUSTE DU BARTAS

Les Semaines

[*Puissance de Dieu*]

Toi qui guides le cours du ciel porte-flambeaux,
Qui, vrai Neptune, tiens le moite frein des eaux,
Qui fais trembler la terre, et de qui la parole
Serre et lâche la bride aux postillons d'Éole,
Élève à toi mon âme, épure mes esprits,
Et d'un docte artifice enrichis mes écrits.
O Père, donne-moi que d'une voix faconde
Je chante à nos neveux la naissance du monde.
O grand Dieu, donne-moi que j'étale en mes vers
Les plus rares beautés de ce grand univers;
Donne-moi qu'en son front ta puissance je lise,
Et, qu'enseignant autrui, moi-même je m'instruise.
    De toujours le clair feu n'environne les airs,
Les airs d'éternité n'environnent les mers,
La terre de tout temps n'est ceinte de Neptune;
Tout ce Tout fut bâti, non des mains de fortune

[*The Power of God*]

You, who guide the course of the torch-bearing sky, you, the true
Neptune, who hold the moist bridle of the waters, who shake the
earth, and whose command tightens and slackens the rein of the
riders of the winds, raise my soul up towards you, purify my
spirit, and enrich my writings with learned art. O Father, grant that
with ready tongue I may sing to our descendants of the birth of the
world. O great God, grant that I may show in my verses the
choicest beauties of this great universe; grant that I may read your
power on its face and that, teaching others, I may instruct myself.
    The bright fire has not always surrounded the air, the air has not
surrounded the seas for all eternity, the earth has not been girdled
by Neptune since all time; all this Whole was made, (and) not by

Faisant entrechoquer par discordants accords
Du rêveur Démocrit les invisibles corps.
    L'immuable décret de la bouche divine
Qui causera sa fin, causa son origine.
Non en temps, avant temps, ains même avec le temps,
J'entends un temps confus, car les courses des ans,
Des siècles, des saisons, des mois et des journées,
Par le bal mesuré des astres sont bornées.
    Or donc, avant tout temps, matière, forme et lieu,
Dieu tout en tout était, et tout était en Dieu,
Incompris, infini, immuable, impassible,
Tout-esprit, tout-lumière, immortel, invisible,
Pur, sage, juste et bon. Dieu seul régnait en paix:
Dieu de soi-même était et l'hôte et le palai...

the hand of chance clashing together in unharmonious harmonies
the invisible atoms of Democritus the dreamer.*
    The immutable decree of the divine voice which will cause its
end, caused its origin. Not in time, (but) before time, or rather
exactly with time (was it created), I mean a confused time, for the
courses of the years, of the centuries, of the seasons, of the months,
and of the days, are marked out by the measured dance of the stars.
    So then, before all time, matter, form, and place, God was all in
everything and everything was in God, uncomprehended, infinite,
unchangeable, immovable, all-spirit, all-light, immortal, invisible,
pure, wise, just, and good. God reigned alone in peace: God was
his own guest and his own dwelling-place.

---

* According to the theory of Democritus, worlds were formed
by unexplained conjunctions of atoms – minute bodies perpetually
moving in infinite numbers in space. Against this, Du Bartas insists
on a divine and deliberate act of creation.

[*Louanges de la terre*]

Je te salue, ô Terre, ô Terre porte-grains,
Porte-or, porte-santé, porte-habits, porte-humains,
Porte-fruits, porte-tours, alme, belle, immobile,
Patiente, diverse, odorante, fertile,
Vêtue d'un manteau tout damassé de fleurs,
Passementé de flots, bigarré de couleurs.
Je te salue, ô cœur, racine, base ronde,
Pied du grand animal qu'on appelle le Monde,
Chaste épouse du Ciel, assuré fondement
Des étages divers d'un si grand bâtiment.
Je te salue, ô sœur, mère, nourrice, hôtesse
Du Roi des Animaux. Tout, ô grande princesse,
Vit en faveur de toi. Tant de cieux tournoyants
Portent pour t'éclairer leurs astres flamboyants.
Le feu, pour t'échauffer, sur les flottantes nues
Tient ses pures ardeurs en arcade étendues.
L'air, pour te raffraîchir, se plaît d'être secous
Or d'un âpre Borée, or d'un Zéphyre doux.
L'eau, pour te détremper, de mers, fleuves, fontaines,
Entrelace ton corps tout ainsi que de veines.

[*In Praise of the Earth*]

Hail to you, O Earth, grain-bearer, gold-bearer, health-bearer, clothes-bearer, man-bearer, fruit-bearer, tower-bearer, kindly, beautiful, immovable, patient, various, sweet-smelling, fertile, clad with a mantle all damasked with flowers, braided with waters, motley with colours. Hail to you, O heart, root, round base, foot of the great creature which is called the Universe, chaste spouse of heaven, sure foundation of the different storeys of so great an edifice. Hail to you, O sister, mother, nurse, hostess of the King of the Animals. Everything, O great princess, exists for your benefit. So many wheeling heavens bear their flaming stars to give light to you. To warm you, the fire stretches its pure ardours arch-like above the floating clouds. To refresh you, the air is content to be shaken, now by a biting north wind, now by a gentle zephyr. To bathe you, the water interlaces your body with seas, rivers, springs,

Hé! que je suis marri que les plus beaux esprits
T'ayent pour la plupart, ô Terre, en tel mépris;
Et que les cœurs plus grands abandonnent superbes
Le rustique labeur et le souci des herbes
Aux hommes plus brutaux, aux hommes de nul prix,
Dont les corps sont de fer et de plomb les esprits ...

[*La Création des oiseaux*]

LE céleste Phénix commença son ouvrage
Par le Phénix terrestre, ornant d'un tel plumage
Ses membres revivants que l'annuel flambeau
De Cairan jusqu'en Fez ne voit rien de plus beau.
Il fit briller ses yeux, il lui planta pour crête
Un astre flamboyant au sommet de sa tête:
Il couvrit son col d'or, d'écarlate son dos
Et sa queue d'azur, puis voulut qu'Atropos
Lui servît de Vénus, et qu'une mort féconde
Rendît son âge égal au long âge du monde.

as though with veins. Ah, it grieves me to think that the finest minds hold you, in general, O Earth, in such disdain; and that the noblest hearts contemptuously leave rustic toil and the care of the plants to the most sottish men, men of no account, whose bodies are of iron and whose minds are of lead.

[*The Creation of the Birds*]

THE heavenly Phoenix began his work with the earthly Phoenix, adorning his constantly resurrected members with such plumage that the yearly torch (of the sun) from Cairo to Fez sees nothing more beautiful.

He made his eyes shine, he planted a flaming star as a crest for him on the top of his head: he covered his neck with gold, his back with scarlet and his tail with azure, then ordained that Death should do him the service of Love, and that a fertile death should make his life equal to the long life of the world.*

* The Phoenix of the legend was the sole bird of its species and so could not mate. On ageing, it plunged into fire and was reborn periodically from its own ashes.

... L'unique oiseau ramant par des sentes nouvelles
Se voit bientôt suivi d'une infinité d'ailes,
Diverses en grandeur, couleur et mouvement,
Ailes que l'Éternel engendre en un moment.
La flairante Arondelle à toutes mains bricole,
Tournoie, virevolte, et plus raide s'envole
Que la flèche d'un Turc, qui voulant décocher,
Fait la corde au tétin et l'arc au fer toucher.
Jà volant elle chante, et chantant, elle pense
D'employer en lieu sûr plus d'art que de dépense
A bâtir un palais, qui, rond par le devant,
Servira de modèle au maçon plus savant.
Elle charge déjà son bec de pailles frêles,
Et ses ongles de terre et d'eau ses noires ailes;
Elle en fait un mortier, et jette proprement
D'un logis demi-rond l'assuré fondement.
    La gentille Alouette avec son tire-lire
Tire l'ire à l'iré, et tire-lirant tire
Vers la voûte du ciel: puis son vol vers ce lieu
Vire, et désire dire: adieu Dieu, adieu Dieu.
Le peint Chardonneret, le Pinson, la Linotte

The sole bird of its kind, soaring on new paths, soon sees itself
followed by an infinite number of wings, various in size, colour,
and motion, wings which the Almighty engenders in a moment. The
scenting swallow casts to and fro, wheels, swoops back, and
darts off more swiftly than the arrow of a Turk who, about to let
fly, makes the bowstring touch his breast and the barb touch the
bow. Now flying, she sings, and as she sings she plans to exercise in
some safe place more skill than extravagance by building a house
which, rounded in front, will serve as a model to the most cunning
mason. Already she loads her beak with slender straws, her claws
with earth and her dark wings with water; she makes mortar from
this and neatly throws up the firm foundation of a half-round
dwelling.

The pretty lark with its *tirra-lirra* draws the wrath from the
wrathful and, carolling, draws towards the vault of heaven, then
turns its flight towards this place (the earth) and tries to say: Goodbye God, goodbye God. The bright-painted goldfinch, the chaf-

Jà donnent aux frais vents leur plus mignarde note.
... Le Colchide Faisan, le fécond Étourneau,
La chaste Tourterelle et le lascif Moineau,
Le Tourt becque-raisin, la Pie babillarde,
La friande Perdrix, la Palombe grisarde,
Le petit Benarric, mets digne des grands rois,
Et le vert Papegai, singe de notre voix,
Font la cour au Phénix, son divin chant admirent,
Et dans l'or et l'azur de ses plumes se mirent ...

[La Création avant la chute]

O MERVEILLEUX effet de la dextre divine!
La plante a chair et sang, l'animal a racine;
La plante comme en rond de soi-même se meut;
L'animal a des pieds et si marcher ne peut.
La plante est sans rameaux, sans fruit, et sans feuillage,
L'animal sans amour, sans sexe et vif lignage:
La plante à belles dents paît son ventre affamé
Du fourrage voisin; l'animal est semé.

finch, the linnet, now give to the fresh winds their prettiest notes.

The pheasant of Colchis, the fast-breeding starling, the chaste turtle-dove and the wanton sparrow, the grape-pecking blackbird, the talkative magpie, the dainty partridge, the greyish wood-pigeon, the little blackcap – a dish fit for great kings – and the green parakeet, the aper of our voice, pay court to the Phoenix, admire his divine song, and see themselves reflected in the gold and azure of his feathers.

[Creation before the Fall]

O MARVELLOUS work of the divine right hand. The plant has flesh and blood, the animal has roots; the plant moves, as it were, around itself; the animal has feet and yet cannot walk. The plant has no branches, no fruit, and no foliage, the animal no love, no sex, or living progeny. The plant voraciously fills its hungry belly with the fodder near it; the animal is sown.

[*La Tour de Babel*]

Ici pour dur ciment nuit et jour on amasse
Des étangs bitumeux l'eau gluantement grasse.
Le tuilier cuit ici dans ses fourneaux fumants
En brique la poussière. Ici les fondements
Jusqu'aux enfers on creuse, et les impures âmes
Revoyent contre espoir du beau soleil les flammes.
Tout le ciel retentit au dur son des marteaux,
Et les poissons du Tigre en tremblent sous les eaux.
De tour et de longueur les murs rougeâtres croissent;
Leur ombre s'étend loin, jà de loin ils paroissent;
Tout bouillonne d'ouvriers, et les faibles humains
Pensent au premier jour toucher le ciel des mains.
    Quoi voyant, l'Éternel renfrogne son visage,
Et d'un son qui, grondant, roule comme un orage
Par les champs nuageux, déracine les monts,
Et fait crouler du ciel les immobiles gonds:
    «Voyez (dit-il) ces nains, voyez cette racaille,
Ces fils de la poussière. Oh, la belle muraille!

[*The Tower of Babel*]

HERE for hard cement they collect night and day the glutinously
greasy water of the bituminous lakes. Here the tiler bakes the dust
into bricks in his smoking kilns. Here they dig the foundations
down to hell and, against all hope, the impure souls see the flames
of the sweet sun again.

The whole sky rings with the hard sound of the hammers, and
the fishes of the Tigris tremble to hear it beneath the waters. In circuit and length the reddish walls grow; their shadow stretches far,
now from afar they can be seen; the whole place seethes with work-
men, and those weak human beings expect daily to touch the sky
with their hands.

Seeing this, the Almighty puckers his brow and, with a noise
which, rumbling, rolls like a storm over the cloudy fields (of the
sky), uproots the mountains and bursts open the fixed hinges of
heaven:

'Look,' he says, 'at these dwarfs, look at this rabble, these sons
of the dust. Oh, the marvellous wall! Oh, the impregnable tower!

Oh, l'imprenable tour! Oh, que ce fort est seur
Contre tant de canons braqués par ma fureur!
Je leur avais juré que la terre féconde
Ne craindrait désormais la colère de l'onde;
Ils s'en font un rempart. Je voulais qu'épandus
Ils peuplassent le monde; et les voici rendus
Prisonniers en un parc. Je désirais seul être
Leur loi, leur protecteur, leur pasteur, et leur maître;
Ils choisissent pour prince un voleur inhumain,
Un tyran qui veut faire à leurs dépens sa main,
Qui dépite mon bras; et qui, plein de bravade,
A ma sainte maison présente l'escalade.
Sus, rompons leur dessein; et puisqu'unis de voix
Aussi bien que de sang, de vouloir et de lois,
Ils s'obstinent au mal et d'un hardi langage
S'animent, forcenés, nuit et jour à l'ouvrage,
Mettons un enrayoir à leur courant effort;
Frappons-les vivement d'un esprit de discord;
Confondons leur parole, et faisons que le père
Soit barbare à son fils, et sourd le frère au frère.»

Oh, how secure is this fortress against so many cannons trained (against it) by my wrath! I swore to them that the fertile earth should not fear the fury of the waters again; they take that (my promise) as a rampart. I wished them to disperse and people the earth, and here they are imprisoned in a pen. I desired to be their sole law, protector, shepherd, and master; they choose for their prince an inhuman bandit, a tyrant who means to profit at their expense, who defies my arm and who, full of bravado, sets scaling-ladders against my holy house. Up, let us confound their plan; and since, united in tongue, as well as in blood, intention, and laws, they persist in evil and with rash words urge each other wildly on day and night to the task, let us put a curb on their galloping onslaught; let us strike them swiftly with a spirit of discord; let us confuse their speech and cause the father to be foreign to his son and the brother deaf to his brother.'

Les Pyrénées

FRANÇAIS, arrête-toi, ne passe la campagne
Que Nature mura de roches d'un côté,
Que l'Ariège entrefend d'un cours précipité:
Campagne qui n'a point en beauté de compagne.

Passant, ce que tu vois n'est point une montagne,
C'est un grand Briarée, un géant haut monté,
Qui garde ce passage et défend, indompté,
De l'Espagne la France, et de France l'Espagne.

Il tend à l'une l'un, à l'autre l'autre bras;
Il porte sur son chef l'antique faix d'Atlas;
Dans deux contraires mers il pose ses deux plantes;

Les épaisses forêts sont ses cheveux épais,
Les rochers sont ses os, les rivières bruyantes
L'éternelle sueur que lui cause un tel faix.

The Pyrenees

FRENCHMAN, halt, do not pass beyond the region which nature walled off on one side with rocks and which the Ariège cleaves with its rapid current: a region which has no peer in beauty.

Traveller, what you see is not a mountain, it is a great Briareus, a giant high-uplifted, who guards this way across and, invincible, bars France from Spain and Spain from France.

To one he holds out one arm, to the second, the other; he bears on his head the ancient burden of Atlas; in two opposite seas he sets his two footsoles;

The thick forests are his thick hair, the rocks are his bones, and the roaring rivers the eternal sweat which such a burden causes him.

PHILIPPE DESPORTES

Si la foi plus certaine en une âme non feinte,
Un honnête désir, un doux languissement,
Une erreur variable et sentir vivement,
Avec peur d'en guérir, une profonde atteinte:

Si voir une pensée au front toute dépeinte,
Une voix empêchée, un morne étonnement,
De honte ou de frayeur naissant soudainement,
Une pâle couleur de lis et d'amour teinte:

Bref, si se mépriser pour une autre adorer,
Si verser mille pleurs, si toujours soupirer,
Faisant de sa douleur nourriture et breuvage,

Si de loin se voir flamme, et de près tout transi,
Sont cause que je meurs par défaut de merci,
L'offense en est sur vous, et sur moi le dommage.

If the most constant faithfulness in an unfeigning heart, virtuous desire, a gentle languishing, a bemused uncertainty, and the keen sensing – with fear of healing – of a deep wound,

If to see a mind openly depicted in a face, a stammering tongue, a dull bewilderment, suddenly arising from timidity or misgiving, a pale complexion tinted with lilies and love:

In short, if to despise oneself in order to adore another, if to shed a thousand tears, if to sigh continually, making food and drink of one's distress,

If to find oneself flame afar off and be benumbed when near, are the causes of my dying deprived of pity, the blame falls upon you and the hurt on me.

(This is a fairly close translation of Petrarch's sonnet beginning:
　　S'una fede amorosa, un cor non finto ...

Cf. Wyatt's English version of the same original:
　　If amorous faith, or if an heart unfeigned ...)

Par vos grâces, ma Dame, et par le dur martyre
Qui me rend en aimant triste et désespéré,
Par tous les lieux secrets où j'ai tant soupiré,
Et par le plus grand bien qu'un amoureux désire;

Par ces beaux traits qu'Amour dedans vos yeux retire,
Par les lis de vos mains, par votre poil doré,
Et où rien de plus grand pourrait être juré,
Je l'appelle à témoin de ce que je veux dire.

Jamais d'autres beautés mon œil ne sera pris,
Doux espoir de mes maux, cher feu de mes esprits,
Vous serez ma recherche et première et dernière;

Et mon cœur cessera d'idolâtrer vos yeux
Lorsqu'on ne verra plus au soleil de lumière,
D'eaux en mer, d'herbe aux prés, et d'étoiles aux cieux.

By your graces, my lady, and by the cruel martyrdom which makes
me, while loving, sad and despairing, by all the secret places where
I have signed so much, and by the greatest bliss which a lover
desires;

By those sweet shafts which Love conceals in your eyes, by the
lilies of your hands, by your golden hair, and – if there were anything greater that could be sworn by – I summon it to be witness
of my meaning.

Never will my eye be caught by other beauties, sweet hope of
my sufferings, dear fire of my spirits; you shall be my first and my
last concern;

And my heart shall cease to worship your eyes when no more
light is seen in the sun, waters in the sea, grass in the meadows, and
stars in the sky.

ICARE est chu ici, le jeune audacieux,
Qui pour voler au ciel eut assez de courage:
Ici tomba son corps dégarni de plumage,
Laissant tous braves cœurs de sa chute envieux.

O bienheureux travail d'un esprit glorieux,
Qui tire un si grand gain d'un si petit dommage!
O bienheureux malheur plein de tant d'avantage
Qu'il rende le vaincu des ans victorieux!

Un chemin si nouveau n'étonna sa jeunesse,
Le pouvoir lui faillit mais non la hardiesse,
Il eut pour le brûler des astres le plus beau.

Il mourut poursuivant une haute aventure,
Le ciel fut son désir, la mer sa sépulture:
Est-il plus beau dessein, ou plus riche tombeau?

AUTOUR des corps, qu'une mort avancée
Par violence a privés du beau jour,
Les ombres vont, et font maint et maint tour,
Aimant encor leur dépouille laissée.

ICARUS fell here, the daring youth, who had the courage to fly up
to heaven; here fell his body shorn of its plumage, leaving all gallant hearts envious of his fall.

O blessed anguish of a proud spirit, which extracts such gain
from so small a hurt! O fortunate misfortune so full of benefits that
it makes the vanquished a victor over the years!

So new a road did not daunt his youth, his power failed him but
not his daring, he had the loveliest of the stars to burn him.

He died pursuing a noble quest, heaven was his desire, the sea his
sepulchre. Is there a finer purpose or a richer tomb?

AROUND bodies which a premature death has violently robbed of
the light of day, the ghosts go and turn and twist, loving still their
abandoned remains.

Au lieu cruel où j'eus l'âme blessée
Et fus meurtri par les flèches d'Amour,
J'erre, je tourne et retourne à l'entour,
Ombre maudite, errante et déchassée.

Légers esprits plus que moi fortunés,
Comme il vous plaît vous allez et venez
Au lieu qui clôt votre dépouille aimée.

Vous la voyez, vous la pouvez toucher,
Où las! je crains seulement d'approcher
L'endroit qui tient ma richesse enfermée.

Offrande au Sommeil

Je t'apporte, ô Sommeil, du vin de quatre années,
Du lait, des pavots noirs aux têtes couronnées.
Veuille tes ailerons en ce lieu déployer,
Tant qu'Alizon la vieille, accroupie au foyer,
(Qui, d'un pouce retors et d'une dent mouillée,

In that cruel spot in which my heart was stricken and I was slain
by the arrows of Love, I roam, I turn and turn around it, a ghost
accursed, wandering and expelled.

Aery spirits more happy than I, as you please you come and go
in the place which encloses your beloved remains.

You see them, you can touch them, while I, alas, fear even to
approach the place in which my treasure is contained.

Offering to Sleep

O Sleep, I bring you wine four years old, milk, dark poppies with
crowned heads: graciously open your wings in this place, until old
Alison, crouching before the hearth (Alison who, with curved
thumb and moistened tooth, has stripped her loaded distaff almost

Sa quenouille chargée a quasi dépouillée),
Laisse choir le fuseau, cesse de babiller,
Et de toute la nuit ne se puisse éveiller:
Afin qu'à mon plaisir j'embrasse ma rebelle,
L'amoureuse Isabeau, qui soupire auprès d'elle.

GABRIELLE DE COIGNARD

LA crainte de la mort incessamment me trouble:
En enfer il n'y a nulle rédemption,
Je n'ai de mes péchés nulle contrition,
Tant plus je vais avant, plus ma peine redouble.

Tu me consommeras comme une sèche étouble
A ce terrible jour de tribulation;
Laisse-moi repentir de ma transgression,
Car l'amère douleur en mon âme s'accouple.

Tu as bâti mon corps de chair, d'os et tendons,
De peau, veines et sang, rate, foie et poumons;
Souvienne-toi, Seigneur, que je suis poudre et cendre;

bare), drops the spindle, ceases chattering, and cannot open her eyes for the rest of the night – so that at my pleasure I may embrace my rebel, the amorous Isabel who sits sighing beside her.

THE fear of death troubles me incessantly; in hell there is no redemption; I feel no contrition for my sins; the further I go, the more my anguish increases.

You will consume me like dry stubble on that terrible day of tribulation. Let me repent of my transgression, for bitter grief fastens on my soul.

You have formed my body of flesh, bones, and tendons, of skin, veins, and blood, spleen, liver, and lungs; remember, Lord, that I am dust and ashes.

Comme un fétu poussé par la rigueur du vent,
Tu me peux balayer et réduire à néant:
Hé! ne me laisse pas aux abîmes descendre.

CES jours me sont si doux en ce beau lieu champêtre,
Voyant d'un fer tranchant fendre le long guéret,
Et enterrer le blé jaunissant, pur et net,
Puis le voir tôt après tout verdoyant renaître.

Mon Dieu, le grand plaisir de voir sur l'herbe paître
La frisée brebis portant son agnelet,
Et le cornu bélier, qui marche tout seulet
Au devant du troupeau, comme patron et maître.

L'air est délicieux, sans pluies ni chaleurs,
Un petit vent mollet fait ondoyer les fleurs,
Les bois portent encor leur superbe couronne;

L'on n'oit point la rumeur d'un vulgaire babil,
Sinon des oiselets le ramage gentil:
Loué soit l'Éternel qui tous ces biens nous donne.

Like a straw driven by the violence of the wind, you can sweep
me away and reduce me to nothing. Ah, do not let me go down to
the gulf.

THESE days are so sweet to me in this lovely country spot, where I
see the long furrow laid open by the sharp ploughshare and the yellow grain buried, pure and clean, then see it soon after all greenly
reborn.

My God, what pleasure to see grazing on the grass the curly ewe
big with her lamb, and the horned ram walking all alone at the head
of the flock, as its leader and master.

The air is delicious, without rain or heat, a soft breeze ripples the
flowers, the woods wear once again their splendid crown;

No noise of trivial prattling is heard, but only the pretty warbling
of the birds. Praised be Almighty God who gives us all these good
things.

JEAN DE LA CEPPÈDE

Théorèmes Spirituels

Aux monarques vainqueurs la rouge cotte d'armes
Appartient justement. Ce Roi victorieux
Est justement vêtu par ces moqueurs gens d'armes
D'un manteau qui le marque et prince et glorieux.

O pourpre, emplis mon têt de ton jus précieux
Et lui fais distiller mille pourprines larmes,
A tant que, méditant ton sens mystérieux,
Du sang trait de mes yeux j'ensanglante ces carmes.

Ta sanglante couleur figure nos péchés
Au dos de cet Agneau par le Père attachés:
Et ce Christ t'endossant se charge de nos crimes.

O Christ, ô saint Agneau, daigne-toi de cacher
Tous mes rouges péchés, brindelles des abîmes,
Dans les sanglants replis du manteau de ta chair.

To conquering monarchs the red coat-of-arms (tunic) belongs of right. This victorious King is rightly clad by these mocking men-at-arms in a cloak which stamps Him both a prince and glorious.

O (royal) purple, fill my head with your precious liquid and make it distil a myriad crimson tears, until at last, contemplating your mysterious meaning, I stain these songs with the blood milked from my eyes.

Your blood-red colour symbolizes our sins, bound by the Father on the back of this Lamb; and this Christ, putting you on, takes our offences upon Himself.

O Christ, holy Lamb, deign to hide all my red sins, kindling-twigs of hell, in the bleeding folds of the cloak of your flesh.

L'AMOUR l'a de l'Olympe ici-bas fait descendre :
L'amour l'a fait de l'homme endosser le péché :
L'amour lui a déjà tout son sang fait épandre :
L'amour l'a fait souffrir qu'on ait sur lui craché :

L'amour a ces halliers à son chef attaché :
L'amour fait que sa Mère à ce bois le voit pendre :
L'amour a dans ces mains ces rudes clous fiché :
L'amour le va tantôt dans le sépulcre étendre.

Son amour est si grand, son amour est si fort
Qu'il attaque l'Enfer, qu'il terrasse la mort,
Qu'il arrache à Pluton sa fidèle Eurydice.

Belle pour qui ce beau meurt en vous bien-aimant,
Voyez s'il fut jamais un si cruel supplice,
Voyez s'il fut jamais un si parfait amant.

LOVE has brought Him down here from Olympus: love has made Him take the sin of man upon Himself; love has already made Him pour out all his blood: love has made Him suffer them to spit upon Him:

Love has bound these thorns on his head: love causes his Mother to see Him hanging on this tree: love has driven these hard nails into these hands: love will presently lay Him in the sepulchre.

His love is so great, his love is so strong, that He attacks Hell, that He lays death low, that He snatches his faithful Eurydice from Pluto.

Fair one for whom this fair groom dies adoring you, consider if there was ever so cruel a death, consider if there was ever so perfect a lover.

Il est donc monté, belle, au gibet ordonné
Pour vous faire monter à son trône suprême;
Il a son tendre chef de ronces couronné
Pour ceindre votre chef d'un brillant diadème.

Il pâtit des tourments le tourment plus extrême
Pour satisfaire au mal qu'il vous a pardonné,
Il vide ores de sang son corps livide et blême
Pour le prix dont prodigue il vous a rançonné.

Il souffre patient qu'à ce jour on fabrique
Des logettes pour vous dans la pierre mystique
De son corps, et sa voix vous semond d'y venir.

Belle, venez-y donc, votre Époux le commande:
Et pour tant de bienfaits dont il peut vous bénir,
Donnez-lui votre cœur, c'est tout ce qu'il demande.

So, fair one,* He has gone up to the appointed gallows to take you
up to his supreme throne; He has crowned his tender head with
thorns to encircle your head with a sparkling diadem.

He suffers the most extreme of torments to atone for the evil
which He has forgiven you, now He drains his pale and livid body
of blood as the price for which He has prodigally ransomed you.

On this day He patiently suffers them to fashion dwelling-places
for you in the mystic stone of his body, and his voice summons you
to come into them.

Come then, fair one, your Spouse commands it: and for so many
boons with which He can bless you, give Him your heart, that is all
He asks.

---

* In a note on this and the preceding sonnet, La Ceppède explains 'the fair one' ('la belle') as a metaphor for the faithful soul,
or the Church.

L'AUTEL des vieux parfums dans Solyme encensé
Fait or' d'une voirie un temple vénérable,
Où du Verbe incarné l'Hypostase adorable
S'offre très-odorante à son Père offensé.

Le vieux pal, sur lequel jadis fut agencé
En Édom le serpent aux mordus secourable,
Élève ores celui qui piteux a pansé
Du vieux serpent d'Éden la morsure incurable.

Le pressoir de la vigne en Calvaire est dressé,
Où ce fameux raisin ce pressoir a pressé
Pour noyer dans son vin nos léthales vipères.

L'échelle Israëlite est posée en ce lieu,
Sur laquelle aujourd'hui s'appuyant l'homme-Dieu,
Nous fait jouir des biens qu'il promit à nos pères.

THE altar censed with the old perfumes in Solyma now makes of a place of slaughter a temple to be venerated, in which the adorable hypostasis of the Word Incarnate (the person of Christ) is offered sweet-smelling to his offended Father.

The old stake, on which the serpent helpful to the bitten was once set in Edom, now raises up Him who has compassionately tended the incurable bite of the old serpent of Eden.

The press of the vine is set up on Calvary, where that press has pressed that famous grape to drown our deadly vipers in its wine.

Jacob's ladder is put up in this place, and the Man-God supported on it today makes us enjoy the blessings He promised to our fathers.*

---

* The key to the first two lines is in Numbers 16, in which a rebellious faction of the Israelites offer incense to the altar and are 'swallowed up by the earth' as a sign of Jehovah's refusal. The second quatrain refers first to the brazen serpent set up by Moses as a cure for snake-bite (Numbers 21, ix) and then to the serpent of the Garden of Eden.

O Croix naguère infâme, horrible, épouvantable,
Ton antique scandale est ores aboli,
Christ a de l'Éternel par son sang ramolli
Le courroux qui te fit jadis si redoutable.

Ce nectar, par qui seul le monde est rachetable,
T'arrosant, a changé ton absinthe en moly,
Et ton bois raboteux si doucement poli
Qu'il est or' des élus le séjour délectable.

Belle tour de David, forte de deux remparts
Où pendent mille écus: à toi de toutes parts
Accourent les mortels. Hé! sois donc ma retraite.

Tu brises aujourd'hui les portes des enfers;
Fais que ta sainte image en mon âme portraite
Brise ainsi quelque jour ma prison et mes fers.

O Cross formerly shameful, horrible, fearful, your old ignominy
is now abolished; by his blood Christ has appeased the wrath of
the Almighty which made you so much to be feared of old.

That nectar (Christ's blood), by which alone the world is re-
deemable, by watering you has changed your wormwood into
moly; * and has so smoothly polished your knotty wood that it is
now the delightful abode of the elect.

Fair tower of David, strong with a double rampart on which
hang a thousand shields, mortal men flock to you from all sides. Be
then my refuge!

Today you break the gates of hell; let your holy image,
stamped upon my soul, break one day in like manner my captivity
and my chains.

---

* A fabulous plant credited with magical properties. In the
Odyssey, Hermes gives it to Ulysses as a protection against Circe.

CE grand Soleil, de qui l'autre n'est qu'une flamme,
Par quatre des maisons du grand Cercle a passé :
Par celle de la Vierge, où neuf mois sa belle âme
A de son corps égal l'organe compassé :

Par celle du Verseau, quand son œil a tracé
Sa douleur par son pleur, en maint acte sans blâme :
Par celle du Taureau, quand son corps terrassé
S'est pour victime offert sur le gibet infâme.

Or à ce jour il entre en celle du Lion.
Perruqué de lumière, il darde un million
De rayons flamboyants sur les deux hémisphères,

Et sa voix rugissante et son frémissement
Au sortir de la tombe épouvantent les fères
Et les rangent au joug de leur amendement.

THAT great Sun (Christ), of which the other is only a flame, has
passed through four of the houses of the great Circle (of the
Zodiac) : through that of the Virgin, in which during nine months
his fair soul formed the organism of his matching body ;

Through that of the Waterbearer, when his eye portrayed his
sorrow with its tears in many a blameless act ; through that of the
Bull, when his body was pulled down and offered itself as a victim
on the shameful gallows.

Now on this day He enters the house of the Lion. Bemaned with
light, He darts a million fiery beams on the two hemispheres,

and his bellowing voice and his roar as he comes out from the
grave strike terror into the beasts and bring them to the yoke of
their reclaiming.

LE cerf que le veneur relance au bois sauvage
Voit un fleuve, s'y jette, nage et gagne le bord.
Christ poursuivi des Juifs nage aux eaux de la mort,
Les passe, et vient surgir à l'immortel rivage.

Le cerf hait le serpent, l'attaque, le ravage,
Le mord et l'engloutit: Christ mortellement mord
Le serpent qui fournit à la mort son breuvage,
Cette mort engloutit et détruit son effort.

Il a (pour ce qu'il est le vivant et la vie)
Cette mort dévorée à son être asservie,
Comme l'estomac change en lait son aliment.

A ce victorieux la trompe prophétique
Comme au cerf matineux a chanté son cantique,
Et nous semond fidèle au même compliment.

THE stag which the huntsman starts in the wild wood sees a river, plunges in, swims, and reaches the bank. Christ pursued by the Jews swims in the waters of death, passes through, and clambers out on the immortal shore.

The stag hates the serpent, attacks it, mangles it, bites it, and swallows it: Christ mortally bites the serpent which provides death with its poison, swallows up that death, and destroys its power.

He has (because He is the living one and life) subjected this eaten death to his being, as the stomach transforms its food into milk.

To this victor, as to the morning stag, the prophetic trumpet has sung its canticle, and faithfully summons us to the same act of praise.

L'Oiseau dont l'Arabie a fait si grande fête
Est de ce grand Héros le symbole assuré.
Le Phénix est tout seul. Le Christ est figuré
Seul libre entre les morts par son royal prophète.

Le Phénix courageux se porte à sa défaite
Sur du bois parfumé : l'amour démesuré
Fait que Christ a la mort sur ce bois enduré,
Qui parfume le ciel d'une odeur très-parfaite.

De sa moüelle après le Phénix renaissant
Enlève tout son bois et l'emporte puissant
Sur un autel voisin des arènes brûlées.

Par sa divinité le Christ ressuscitant,
Sur l'azuré lambris des voûtes étoilées
Élèvera son bois de rayons éclatant.

The bird which Arabia cherished so highly is the certain symbol of this great Hero. The Phoenix is alone of its kind. Christ is represented by his royal prophet (David) as alone unenslaved among the dead.

The Phoenix bravely goes to its destruction on scented wood: measureless love led Christ to suffer death on the wood of that tree which sweetens heaven with its most excellent perfume.

Reborn afterwards from its ashes (marrow), the Phoenix takes up all its wood and carries it powerfully to an altar near to the burnt sands.

Christ, resurrected by his divine essence, against the azure ceiling of the starry vaults will raise up his tree resplendent with light.

Paraphrase sur le Premier Psaume de David

Beatus non abiit

BIENHEUREUX qui s'abstient du conseil des iniques,
Qui sage ne suit point leurs sentiers Plutoniques,
Qui ne sied avec eux en leurs sièges pestés;
Mais qui ses volontés range aux lois éternelles,
Qui discourt du Seigneur les décrets attestés,
Sous l'un et l'autre jour des célestes prunelles.

Il sera tel qu'on voit sur le moite rivage
D'un ruisseau doux-coulant à couvert du ravage
Des bruyants Aquilons un arbre toujours vert:
Que le Lion ne sèche aux plus chaudes journées,
Que l'Arcture n'effeuille, et qui paraît couvert
De son fruit dès qu'il sent les saisons retournées.

Ainsi Dieu bénira du juste les services:
Mais celui qui se vautre en la bourbe des vices,
Qui méprise le Ciel, n'atteindra pas ce bien.

Paraphrase of the First Psalm of David

Blessed is the man that walketh not …

BLESSED is the man who abstains from the counsel of the wicked, who wisely does not follow their Plutonic ways, who does not sit with them in their pestiferous seats; but bends his will to the eternal laws and converses of the proven decrees of the Lord beneath the two beams of the divine eyeballs.

He will be as on the moist bank of a softly flowing river an evergreen tree is seen sheltered from the ravages of the roaring winds; which the Lion does not wither in the hottest days, nor Arcturus unleaf, and which appears laden with its fruit as soon as it feels the seasons declining.

So God will bless the works of the righteous; but the man who wallows in the slough of the vices, who scorns heaven, will not obtain that blessing. He will be like fine dust in the wind and quick-

Il sera comme au vent la poussière menue,
Et le mercure au feu, qui s'envolent en rien,
Et comme la vapeur, qui se perd dans la nue.

A ce grand dernier jour qui jugera le monde
Son âme criminelle et sa dépouille immonde
Se musseront aux yeux du Juge criminel,
Et n'approcheront point des blanches colombelles
Echues en partage à ce Juge éternel,
Qui perdra des méchants les escadres rebelles.

AGRIPPA D'AUBIGNÉ

[*Sonnet pour Diane*]

Un clairvoyant faucon en volant par rivière
Planait dedans le ciel, à se fondre apprêté
Sur son gibier blotti. Mais voyant à côté
Une corneille, il quitte une pointe première.

Ainsi de ses attraits une maîtresse fière
S'élevant jusqu'au ciel m'abat sous sa beauté,
Mais son vouloir volage est soudain transporté
En l'amour d'un corbeau pour me laisser arrière.

silver in the fire, which are gone in an instant, and like a vapour which is lost in the clouds.

On that great final day which will judge the world, his sinful soul and his vile body will hide from the eyes of the Criminal Judge, and they will not come near the white doves who belong to the share of that Eternal Judge, who will destroy the rebellious squadrons of the wicked.

A keen-eyed falcon flying over riverland was hovering in the sky, ready to swoop on its crouching prey. But seeing a crow at one side, it abandons its first aim.

So a cruel mistress, raised to heaven by her charms, strikes me down beneath her beauty, but her fickle fancy is suddenly transferred to the love of a crow, leaving me behind.

Ha! beaux yeux obscurcis qui avez pris le pire,
Plus propres à blesser que discrets à élire,
Je vous crains abattu, ainsi que fait l'oiseau

Qui n'attend que la mort de la serre ennemie :
Fors que le changement lui redonne la vie,
Et c'est le changement qui me traîne au tombeau.

Stances

[*Misères de l'amour*]

... Si quelquefois poussé d'une âme impatiente
Je vais précipitant mes fureurs dans les bois,
M'échauffant sur la mort d'une bête innocente,
Ou effrayant les eaux et les monts de ma voix,

Milles oiseaux de nuit, mille chansons mortelles
M'environnent, volant par ordre sur mon front :
Que l'air en contrepoids fâché de mes querelles
Soit noirci de hiboux et de corbeaux en rond.

Ah, sweet clouded eyes which have picked the worse, more fitted
to wound than skilled to choose, I fear you cowering here, as does
the bird which expects only death from the hostile talons: except that
the change gives it back its life, and the change is what draws me
towards the grave.

Stanzas

[*Miseries of Love*]

If sometimes, driven by my impatient heart, I go and vent my
frenzy in the woods, waxing hot over the death of some innocent
beast, or startling the waters and the hills with my voice,
  A thousand night birds, a thousand baleful songs (bird-cries) surround me, flying in order across my face: let the sky, grieved in
sympathy by my lamentations, be darkened all around with owls
and crows.

Les herbes sècheront sous mes pas, à la vue
Des misérables yeux dont les tristes regards
Feront tomber les fleurs et cacher dans la nue
La lune et le soleil et les astres épars.

Ma présence fera dessécher les fontaines
Et les oiseaux passants tomber morts à mes pieds,
Étouffés de l'odeur et du vent de mes peines :
Ma peine, étouffe-moi, comme ils sont étouffés !

... Il reste qu'un démon connaissant ma misère
Me vienne un jour trouver aux plus sombres forêts,
M'essayant, me tentant pour que je désespère,
Que je suive ses arts, que je l'adore après.

Moi je résisterai, fuyant la solitude
Et des bois et des rocs, mais ce cruel, suivant
Mes pas, assiégera mon lit et mon étude,
Comme un air, comme un feu, et léger comme un vent.

The grass will wither under my footsteps, at the sight of these
miserable eyes whose sad looks will cause the flowers to droop and
the moon and the sun and the scattered stars to hide in the clouds.
My presence will make the springs run dry and the passing birds
fall dead at my feet, choked with the stench and the wind of my
sorrows; my sorrow, choke me, as they are choked.
It remains for a demon who knows my misery to seek me out one
day in the darkest forests, trying me, tempting me to make me
despair, to obey his arts and worship him afterwards.
I shall resist, fleeing from the solitude of woods and rocks, but
that cruel being, dogging my steps, will beset my bed and my study,
like a draught, like a fire, and light as a breeze.

Il m'offrira de l'or, je n'aime la richesse;
Des états, des faveurs, je méprise les cours;
Puis me promettera le corps de ma maîtresse:
A ce point Dieu viendra soudain à mon secours.

Le menteur, empruntant la même face belle,
L'idée de mon âme et de mon doux tourment,
Viendra entre mes bras apporter ma cruelle,
Mais je n'embrasserai pour elle que du vent.

Tantôt une fumée épaisse, noire ou bleue,
Passant devant mes yeux me fera tressaillir;
En bouc et en barbet, en fascinant ma veue,
Au lit de mon repos il viendra m'assaillir.

Neuf gouttes de pur sang naîtront sur ma serviette,
Ma coupe brisera sans coup entre mes mains,
J'oirai des coups en l'air, on verra des bluettes
De feu que pousseront les démons inhumains.

He will offer me gold – I do not love wealth; estates, favours – I despise courts; then he will promise me the body of my mistress: at that point God will come quickly to my help.

The deceiver, putting on the same lovely face, the ideal of my soul and of my sweet torments, will come and place my cruel one in my arms, but instead of her I shall embrace only air.

Sometimes a thick smoke, black or blue, will make me start as it drifts before my eyes; in the form of a he-goat or a spaniel, bewitching my sight, he will come to assail me on my couch.

Nine drops of pure blood will appear on my napkin, my glass will break untouched in my hands, I shall hear thuds in the air, flashes of fire given out by inhuman demons will be seen.

... Et lorsque mes rigueurs auront fini ma vie
Et que par le mourir finira mon souffrir,
Quand de me tourmenter la fortune assouvie
Voudra mes maux, ma vie et son ire finir,

Nymphes qui avez vu la rage qui m'affole,
Satyres que je fis contrister à ma voix,
Baptisez en pleurant quelque pauvre mausole
Aux fonds plus égarés et plus sombres des bois ...

Les Tragiques

[Les Ministres de Dieu]

Au palais flamboyant du haut ciel empyrée
Reluit l'Éternité en présence adorée
Par les anges heureux: trois fois trois rangs de vents,
Puissance du haut ciel, y assistent servants.
Les saintes légions, sur leurs pieds toutes prêtes,
Lèvent aux pieds de Dieu leurs précieuses têtes
Sous un grand pavillon d'un grand arc de couleurs.
Au moindre clin de l'œil du Seigneur des Seigneurs

And when my afflictions have brought my life to a close and
death puts an end to my suffering, when fortune, sated with tormenting me, is willing to end my woes, my life, and its own
wrath –
Nymphs who have seen the frenzy which maddens me, satyrs
whom I have saddened by my cries, baptise with your tears some
humble tomb in the most hidden and darkest depths of the woods.

[God's Ministers]

In the fiery palace of the high Empyrean, Eternal God shines out,
adored in his presence by the happy angels. Three times three
ranks of winds, the power of high heaven, stand there to serve Him.
The heavenly legions, all ready afoot, raise their magnificent heads
at the feet of God under the vast canopy of a great rainbow. At the
least flicker of the eye of the Lord of Lords they are off like a flash;

Ils partent de la main: ce troupeau sacré vole
Comme vent décoché au vent de la parole,
Soit pour être des saints les bergers curieux,
Les préserver de mal, se camper autour d'eux,
Leur servir de flambeaux en la nuit plus obscure,
Les défendre d'injure, et détourner l'injure
Sur le chef des tyrans: soit pour, d'un bras armé,
Déployer du grand Dieu le courroux animé.

    D'un coutelas ondé, d'une main juste et forte,
L'un défend aux pécheurs du Paradis la porte;
Un autre fend la mer; par l'autre sont chargés
Les pauvres de trésors, d'aise les affligés,
De gloire les honteux, l'ignorant de science,
L'abattu de secours, le transi d'espérance;
Quelqu'autre va trouver un monarque en haut lieu,
Bardé de mille fers, et, au nom du grand Dieu,
Assuré, l'épouvante; élevé, l'extermine;
Le fait vif dévorer à la sale vermine.
L'un veille un règne entier, une ville, un château,
Une personne seule, un pasteur, un troupeau.

that holy band flies like a wind unleashed by the wind of the word, either to be the watchful shepherds of the saints, to preserve them from evil, to encamp round them, to serve as torches for them in the darkest night, to defend them from harm, and to divert the harm upon the heads of the tyrants; or else, weapon in hand, to loose the active wrath of mighty God.

With a curving sword, with a strong righteous arm, one bars the gate of Paradise to sinners; another divides the sea; by another the poor are loaded with treasures, the afflicted with comfort, the meek with glory, the ignorant with knowledge, the downtrodden with help, the stricken with hope; another seeks out a monarch on his throne, ringed with a thousand swords, and in the name of mighty God terrifies him though he seems secure, though exalted, exterminates him, causes him to be devoured alive by foul vermin. One watches over a whole kingdom, a town, a castle, a single person, a shepherd, a flock. Appointed guardians of the faithful band,

Gardes particuliers de la troupe fidèle,
De la maison de Dieu ils sentent le vrai zèle,
Portent dedans le ciel les larmes, les soupirs
Et les gémissements des bienheureux martyrs...

[*Prière à Dieu pour venger les Protestants*]

... Tu vois, juste vengeur, les fleaux de ton Église,
Qui, par eux mise en cendre et en masure mise,
A contre tout espoir son espérance en toi,
Pour son retranchement le rempart de la foi.

Tes ennemis et nous sommes égaux en vice,
Si, juge, tu te sieds en ton lit de justice;
Tu fais pourtant un choix d'enfants ou d'ennemis,
Et ce choix est celui que ta grâce y a mis.

Si tu leur fais des biens, ils s'enflent en blasphèmes,
Si tu nous fais du mal, il nous vient de nous-mêmes;
Ils maudissent ton nom quand tu leur es plus doux;
Quand tu nous meurtrirais, si te bénirons-nous.

they discern true zeal for the house of God and bear up to heaven
the tears, the sighs, and the groans of the blessèd martyrs.

Prayer to God to Avenge the Protestants

You see, just avenger, the scourges of your Church, which, reduced to ashes and ruins by them, places against all hope its hope in
you, and has for its bulwark the rampart of faith.

Your enemies and we are equal in sin, if, O judge, you sit on
your judgment-seat; yet you make a choice between children and
foes, and this choice is the choice which your grace has imposed.

If you do good to them they swell out in blasphemies; if you do
evil to us, it comes from ourselves; they curse your name when you
are most kindly to them; if you should slay us, yet will we bless
you.

Cette bande meurtrière à boire nous convie
Le vin de ton courroux: boiront-ils point la lie?
Ces verges qui sur nous s'égayent comme au jeu,
Sales de notre sang, vont-elles pas au feu?

Châtie en ta douceur, punis en ta furie
L'escapade aux agneaux, des loups la boucherie;
Distingue pour les deux, comme tu l'as promis,
La verge à tes enfants, la barre aux ennemis.

Veux-tu longtemps laisser en cette terre ronde
Régner ton ennemi? N'es-tu Seigneur du monde,
Toi, Seigneur, qui abats, qui blesses, qui guéris,
Qui donnes vie et mort, qui tue' et qui nourris?

Les princes n'ont point d'yeux pour voir tes grand'-
    merveilles;
Quand tu voudras tonner, n'auront-ils point d'oreilles?
Leurs mains ne servent plus qu'à nous persécuter;
Ils ont tout pour Satan, et rien pour te porter.

    That murderous band invites us to drink the wine of your wrath: shall they not drink the dregs? Those rods which play upon us, as though it were a sport – stained with our blood, shall they not go into the fire?
    Chastise in your mildness, punish in your fury, the mischief of the lambs, the carnage of the wolves; make distinction for the two, as you have promised, between the rod for your children, the bar * for your foes.
    Will you allow your enemy to reign for long on this round earth? Are you not Lord of the world – you, Lord, who cast down, who smite, who heal, who give life and death, who slay, and who feed?
    The princes have no eyes to see your great marvels; when you decide to thunder, will they have no ears? Their hands now serve no purpose but to persecute us; they have everything for Satan, and nothing to bring you.

    * The iron bar with which criminals were broken on the wheel.

Sion ne reçoit d'eux que refus et rudesses,
Mais Babel les rançonne et pille leurs richesses;
Tels sont les monts cornus qui, avaricieux,
Montrent l'or aux enfers et les neiges aux cieux.

Les temples du païen, du Turc, de l'idolâtre,
Haussent au ciel l'orgueil du marbre et de l'albâtre;
Et Dieu seul, au désert pauvrement hébergé,
A bâti tout le monde et n'y est pas logé!

Les moineaux ont leurs nids, leurs nids les hirondelles;
On dresse quelque fuie aux simples colombelles;
Tout est mis à l'abri par le soin des mortels,
Et Dieu seul, immortel, n'a logis ni autels.

Tu as tout l'univers, où ta gloire on contemple,
Pour marchepied la terre et le ciel pour un temple:
Où te chassera l'homme, ô Dieu victorieux?
Tu possèdes le ciel et les cieux des hauts cieux!

Zion (the Reformed Church) receives only refusals and harshness from them, but Babylon (Rome) holds them to ransom and plunders their wealth; they are like the horny mountains which, in miser-fashion, show gold to the nether regions and snow to the skies.

The temples of the heathen, of the Turk, of the idolater, raise to heaven the pomp of marble and alabaster; and God alone, poorly lodged in the wilderness, has built the whole world and has no dwelling in it.

The sparrows have their nests, their nests the swallows; some cote is put up for the simple doves; everything is given shelter by the care of mortal men, and only God, immortal, has no dwelling nor altars.

You have the whole universe, in which we contemplate your glory, for your footstool the earth and the heavens for a temple: whither will man drive you, O victorious God? You possess heaven and the heaven of high heaven.

Nous faisons des rochers les lieux où on te prêche,
Un temple de l'étable, un autel de la crèche;
Eux, du temple une étable aux ânes arrogants,
De la sainte maison la caverne aux brigands.

Les premiers des chrétiens priaient aux cimetières:
Nous avons fait ouïr aux tombeaux nos prières,
Fait sonner aux tombeaux le nom de Dieu le fort,
Et annoncé la vie aux logis de la mort.

Tu peux faire conter ta louange à la pierre,
Mais n'as-tu pas toujours ton marchepied en terre?
Ne veux-tu plus avoir d'autres temples sacrés
Qu'un blanchissant amas d'os de morts massacrés?

Les morts te loueront-ils? Tes faits grands et terribles
Sortiront-ils du creux de ces bouches horribles?
N'aurons-nous entre nous que visages terreux
Murmurant ta louange aux secrets de nos creux?

We make the rocks places where your name is preached, the stable a temple, the manger an altar; they make of the temple a stable for arrogant asses, of the holy house a robbers' cave.

The earliest Christians prayed in the cemeteries; we have spoken our prayers in the tombs, made the name of mighty God ring in the tombs, and proclaimed the living way in the dwellings of death.

You can have your praises told to the stone, but have you not still your footstool upon earth? Do you no longer wish to have other holy temples than a whitening heap of bones of the slaughtered dead?

Will the dead praise you? Will your great and terrible acts issue from the hollows of those ghastly mouths? Shall we have among us only earthy faces murmuring your praise in the secret of our caves?

En ces lieux caverneux tes chères assemblées,
Des ombres de la mort incessamment troublées,
Ne feront-elles plus résonner tes saints lieux,
Et ton renom voler des terres dans les cieux?

Quoi! Serons-nous muets, serons-nous sans oreilles,
Sans mouvoir, sans chanter, sans ouïr tes merveilles?
As-tu éteint en nous ton sanctuaire? Non,
De nos temples vivants sortira ton renom.

Tel est en cet état le tableau de l'Église:
Elle a les fers aux pieds, sur les gênes assise,
A sa gorge la corde et le fer inhumain,
Un psaume dans la bouche et un luth en la main.

Tu aimes de ses mains la parfaite harmonie:
Notre luth chantera le principe de vie;
Nos doigts ne sont plus doigts que pour trouver tes sons,
Nos voix ne sont plus voix qu'à tes saintes chansons.

Your beloved congregations in these cavernous places, continually haunted by the shadow of death, – shall they never again make your holy places ring, and your praise rise up from the earth to the heavens?

What, shall we be dumb, shall we be without ears, without motion, without singing, without hearing of your wonders? Have you abolished your sanctuary in us? No, your fame shall show forth from our living temples (of flesh).

Such at the present time is the picture of the Church: she has fetters on her feet, she is seated on the rack, at her throat the rope and the cruel steel, a psalm on her lips and a lute in her hand.

You love the perfect harmony which springs from her hands: our lute will sing the source of all life; our fingers are no more fingers but to find your strains, our voices are no more voices but for your holy songs.

Mets à couvert ces voix que les pluies enrouent;
Déchaîne donc ces doigts, que sur ton luth ils jouent;
Tire nos yeux ternis des cachots ennuyeux,
Et nous montre le ciel pour y tourner les yeux.

Soient tes yeux adoucis à guérir nos misères,
Ton oreille propice ouverte à nos prières,
Ton sein déboutonné à loger nos soupirs
Et ta main libérale à nos justes désirs.

Que ceux qui ont fermé les yeux à nos misères,
Que ceux qui n'ont point eu d'oreille à nos prières,
De cœur pour secourir, mais bien pour tourmenter,
Point de mains pour donner, mais bien pour nous ôter,

Trouvent tes yeux fermés à juger leurs misères;
Ton oreille soit sourde en oyant leurs prières;
Ton sein ferré soit clos aux pitiés, aux pardons;
Ta main sèche, stérile aux bienfaits et aux dons.

Give shelter to these voices which the rains make hoarse; unchain then these fingers, that they may play upon your lute; bring out our dimmed eyes from the dismal dungeons and show us the sky that we may turn them towards it.

Let your eyes grow kind to heal our afflictions, your merciful ear be opened to our prayers, your breast be unbuttoned to receive our sighs, and your hand be bountiful to our just desires.

Let those who have shut their eyes to our afflictions, let those who have had no ear for our prayers, no heart to succour but rather to torment, no hands to give but rather to take from us,

Find your eyes shut to judge their afflictions; let your ear be deaf to hear their prayers, let your mailed breast be closed to pity, to pardon, and your dry hand be barren of blessings and gifts.

Soient tes yeux clairvoyants à leurs péchés extrêmes,
Soit ton oreille ouverte à leurs cris de blasphèmes,
Ton sein déboutonné pour s'enfler de courroux,
Et ta main diligente à redoubler tes coups.

Ils ont pour un spectacle et pour jeu le martyre,
Le méchant rit plus haut que le bon n'y soupire;
Nos cris mortels n'y font qu'incommoder leurs ris,
Les ris de qui l'éclat ôte l'air à nos cris.

Ils crachent vers la lune et les voûtes célestes:
N'ont-elles plus de foudre et de feux et de pestes?
Ne partiront jamais du trône où tu te sieds
Et la Mort et l'Enfer qui dorment à tes pieds?

Lève ton bras de fer, hâte tes pieds de laine;
Venge ta patience en l'aigreur de ta peine:
Frappe du ciel Babel: les cornes de son front
Défigurent la terre et lui ôtent son rond!

Let your eyes be keen for their fearful sins, let your ear be open
to their blasphemous cries, your breast be unbuttoned to swell with
anger, your hand be active to multiply your blows.

They have martyrdom for a spectacle and a sport, the wicked
laugh more loudly than the righteous man groans; our dying cries
serve only to disturb their laughter – that laughter whose outbursts
stifle our cries.

They spit towards the moon and the heavenly vaults: have these
no more thunderbolts and fires and plagues? Will Death and Hell
sleeping at your feet never come forth from the throne on which
you sit?

Raise your iron arm, make swift your feet of wool (i.e. too
slow): avenge your long-suffering by the sharpness of the punish-
ment: strike Babylon from heaven; the horns on its brow disfigure
the earth and spoil its round symmetry.

JACQUES DAVY DU PERRON

Cantique de la Vierge Marie

QUAND au dernier sommeil la Vierge eut clos les yeux,
Les anges qui veillaient autour de leur maîtresse
Élevèrent son corps en la gloire des cieux,
Et les cieux furent pleins de nouvelle allégresse.

Les plus hauts Séraphins à son avènement
Sortaient au devant d'elle et lui cédaient la place,
Se sentant tous ravis d'aise et d'étonnement
De pouvoir contempler la splendeur de sa face.

Dessus les Cieux des Cieux elle va paraissant :
Les flambeaux étoilés lui servent de couronne,
La lune est sous ses pieds en forme de croissant,
Et comme un vêtement le soleil l'environne.

Elle est là-haut assise auprès du Roi des Rois,
Pour rendre à nos clameurs ses oreilles propices,
Et sans cesse l'adjure au saint nom de la Croix
De purger en son sang nos erreurs et nos vices.

Song in Praise of the Virgin

WHEN the Virgin had closed her eyes in the last sleep, the angels who were keeping watch round their mistress carried her body up into the glory of heaven, and the heavens were filled with a new joy.

At her coming the highest seraphim came out to meet her and made way for her, all feeling transported with joy and with wonder at being able to contemplate the splendour of her face.

In the Heaven of Heavens she now appears, the starry candles serve as her crown, the moon is under her feet in the shape of a crescent and like a garment the sun enfolds her.

She is seated on high beside the King of Kings, to incline his ear to our entreaties, and she continually beseeches Him in the holy name of the Cross to wash clean our sins and transgressions in his blood.

... C'est celle dont la foi dure éternellement,
C'est celle dont la foi n'eut jamais de pareille,
C'est celle dont la foi pour notre sauvement
Crut à la voix de l'Ange et conçut par l'oreille.

C'est l'astre lumineux qui jamais ne s'éteint,
Où comme en un miroir tout le ciel se contemple;
Le luisant tabernacle et le lieu pur et saint
Où Dieu même a voulu se consacrer un temple.

C'est le palais royal tout rempli de clarté,
Plus pur et transparent que le ciel qui l'enserre,
C'est le beau Paradis vers l'orient planté,
Les délices du ciel et l'espoir de la terre.

C'est cette myrrhe et fleurs et ce baume odorant
Qui rend de sa senteur nos âmes consolées;
C'est ce Jardin reclus suavement flairant:
C'est la Rose des champs et le Lis des vallées;

She it is whose faith endures eternally, she it is whose faith was above all compare, she it is whose faith for our salvation believed in the voice of the Angel and conceived through the ear.

She is the bright star which is never darkened, in which – as in a mirror – all heaven contemplates itself; the shining tabernacle and the pure and holy place in which God Himself chose to consecrate his temple.

She is the royal palace filled full with light, purer and more transparent than the sky which surrounds it, she is the lovely paradise planted towards the east, the delight of heaven and the hope of the earth.

She is that myrrh and flowers and that fragrant balm which comforts our souls with its scent; she is that secluded, sweet-smelling garden; she is the Rose of the Fields and the Lily of the Valleys.

C'est le rameau qui garde en tout temps sa couleur,
La branche de Jessé, la tige pure et sainte,
Qui rapporte son fruit et ne perd point sa fleur,
Qui demeure pucelle et qui se voit enceinte.

C'est l'Aube du matin qui produit le Soleil
Tout couvert de rayons et de flammes ardentes,
L'Astre des navigants, le Phare nonpareil
Qui la nuit leur éclaire au milieu des tourmentes.

Étoile de la mer, notre seul réconfort,
Sauve-nous des rochers, du vent et du naufrage;
Aide-nous de tes vœux pour nous conduire au port,
Et nous montre ton Fils sur le bord du rivage.

FRANÇOIS DE MALHERBE

A la Reine mère du roi, sur sa bienvenue en France

PEUPLES, qu'on mette sur la tête
Tout ce que la terre a de fleurs;

She is the bough which is green in all seasons, the branch of
Jesse, the pure and holy stem, which bears its fruit and does not
lose its flower, which remains a maid and finds itself with child.

She is the dawn of the morning which brings forth the Sun all
covered with beams and with burning flames, the Star of Sailors,
the peerless beacon which lights up the night for them in the midst
of the storms.

Star of the Sea, our only refuge, save us from the rocks, from the
winds and shipwreck; help us with your prayers to come to the
port, and show us your Son on the brink of the shore.

To the Queen Mother, on her happy arrival in France *

LOYAL subjects, let us deck our heads with all the flowers of the

---

* Ode presented to Marie de Médicis in 1600, on the occasion of
her marriage to Henri IV.

Peuples, que cette belle fête
A jamais tarisse nos pleurs;
Qu'aux deux bouts du monde se voie
Luire le feu de notre joie,
Et soient dans les coupes noyés
Les soucis de tous ces orages
Que pour nos rebelles courages
Les dieux nous avaient envoyés.

A ce coup iront en fumée
Les vœux que faisaient nos mutins
En leur âme encor affamée
De massacres et de butins;
Nos doutes seront éclaircis
Et mentiront les prophéties
De tous ces visages pâlis,
Dont la vaine étude s'applique
A chercher l'an climatérique
De l'éternelle fleur de lis.

Aujourd'hui nous est amenée
Cette princesse, que la foi
D'amour ensemble et d'hyménée
Destine au lit de notre Roi.

earth; subjects, may this happy day for ever dry our tears; let the fire of our joy blaze out from end to end of the world, and in the goblets let there be drowned the anxieties of all those storms which the gods sent us to punish our rebel hearts.

On this day will vanish in smoke the prayers which our rebels murmured in their hearts still athirst for massacres and plunder; our doubts will be dispelled and there will prove to be only lies in the prophecies of all those pallid faces, whose vain study it is to discover the climacteric year (critical year in life) of the eternal *fleur de lis*.

Today this princess is brought to us, she whom the pledge of love and of marriage alike destine for the bed of our King. This is

La voici, la belle Marie,
Belle merveille d'Étrurie,
Qui fait confesser au soleil,
Quoi que l'âge passé raconte,
Que du ciel depuis qu'il y monte
Ne vint jamais rien de pareil.

Telle n'est point la Cythérée
Quand, d'un nouveau feu s'allumant,
Elle sort pompeuse et parée
Pour la conquête d'un amant;
Telle ne luit en sa carrière
Des mois l'inégale courrière,
Et telle dessus l'horizon
L'Aurore au matin ne s'étale,
Quand les yeux mêmes de Céphale
En feraient la comparaison.

Le sceptre que porte sa race,
Où l'heur aux mérites est joint,
Lui met le respect en la face,
Mais il ne l'enorgueillit point;
Nulle vanité ne la touche;

she, the lovely Marie, lovely marvel of Etruria, who forces the sun
to confess that, whatever history relates, since he has been in the
heavens nothing came from them equal to her.

The Cytherean (Venus) cannot match her, when, kindling with a
new fire, she goes forth gloriously arrayed to the conquest of a
lover; nor does the irregular harbinger of the months shine so upon
its course, and the dawn above the horizon does not display itself so
to the morning, even if the eyes of Cephalus * were to make the
comparison.

The sceptre borne by her line, in which high fortune joins with
worth, gives dignity to her face but does not make her proud; no
vanity touches her; the graces speak through her mouth, and her

---

* The lover of Aurora, the dawn.

Les Grâces parlent par sa bouche,
Et son front, témoin assuré
Qu'au vice elle est inaccessible,
Ne peut que d'un cœur insensible
Être vu san être adoré.

Quantesfois, lorsque sur les ondes
Ce nouveau miracle flottait,
Neptune en ses caves profondes
Plaignit-il le feu qu'il sentait?
Et quantesfois en sa pensée
De vives atteintes blessée,
Sans l'honneur de la royauté
Qui lui fit celer son martyre,
Eût-il voulu de son empire
Faire échange à cette beauté?

Dix jours ne pouvant se distraire
Du plaisir de la regarder,
Il a par un effort contraire
Essayé de la retarder;
Mais à la fin, soit que l'audace
Au meilleur avis ait fait place,

face, a certain witness that she is inaccessible to evil, can be seen only by a heart of stone without being adored.

How often, when this modern miracle was floating over the waves, did Neptune in his deep caves complain of the fire which he felt. And how often in his secret thoughts, stricken with smarting wounds – but for his kingly honour which made him hide his torments – would he have been ready to exchange his empire for that beauty?

Unable for ten days to tear himself away from the pleasure of looking at her, he tried by an adverse effort to delay her; but at last, either because his boldness yielded to better counsels, or be-

Soit qu'un autre démon plus fort
Aux vents ait imposé silence,
Elle est hors de sa violence
Et la voici dans notre port.

La voici, peuples, qui nous montre
Tout ce que la gloire a de prix :
Les fleurs naissent à sa rencontre
Dans les cœurs et dans les esprits ;
Et la présence des merveilles
Qu'en oyaient dire nos oreilles
Accuse la témérité
De ceux qui nous l'avaient décrite
D'avoir figuré son mérite
Moindre que n'est la vérité.

O toute parfaite Princesse,
L'étonnement de l'univers,
Astre par qui vont avoir cesse
Nos ténèbres et nos hivers ;
Exemple sans autres exemples,
Future image de nos temples :

cause another, stronger, daemon, reduced the winds to silence, she
has escaped from his violence and here she is in our port.*

Here she is, Frenchmen, to show us the full value of her fame:
flowers spring up to greet her in our hearts and minds; and the
presence of this marvel of which our ears had heard condemns the
presumption of those who had described her to us for having represented her at less than her true worth.

O wholly perfect princess, amazement of the universe, star
thanks to whom our darkness and our winters will cease; un-
exampled example, future image in our churches; whatever our

* The arrival of the royal bride in France was delayed by a particularly stormy sea-crossing.

Quoi que notre faible pouvoir
En votre accueil ose entreprendre,
Peut-il espérer de vous rendre
Ce que nous vous allons devoir?

Ce sera vous qui de nos villes
Ferez la beauté refleurir,
Vous, qui de nos haines civiles
Ferez la racine mourir;
Et par vous la paix assurée
N'aura pas la courte durée
Qu'espèrent infidèlement,
Non lassés de notre souffrance,
Ces Français qui n'ont de la France
Que la langue et l'habillement.

Par vous un Dauphin nous va naître,
Que vous-même verrez un jour
De la terre entière le maître,
Ou par armes ou par amour;
Et ne tarderont ses conquêtes
Dans les oracles déjà prêtes
Qu'autant que le premier coton,
Qui de jeunesse est le message,

feeble powers dare to attempt in your welcome, can we hope to
repay you for what we are going to owe you?

It will be you who will make the beauty of our towns flower
again, you who will kill the root of our civil discords; and peace,
ensured by you, will not have the short duration which is treacherously hoped for by those Frenchmen – not yet wearied of our
sufferings – who of France have only the language and the costume.

Through you a prince will be born to us, whom you yourself will
one day see master of the whole earth, by force either of arms or of
love; and his conquests, which the oracles are already preparing to
announce, will be delayed only for as long as the first down, the

Tardera d'être en son visage
Et de faire ombre à son menton.

O combien lors aura de veuves
La gent qui porte le turban!
Que de sang rougira les fleuves
Qui lavent les pieds du Liban!
Que le Bosphore en ses deux rives
Aura de sultanes captives!
Et que de mères à Memphis
En pleurant diront la vaillance
De son courage et de sa lance
Aux funérailles de leurs fils!...

Paraphrase du Psaume VIII

Domine Dominus noster

O SAGESSE éternelle, à qui cet univers
Doit le nombre infini des miracles divers
Qu'on voit également sur la terre et sur l'onde:
Mon Dieu, mon Créateur,
Que ta magnificence étonne tout le monde,
Et que le ciel est bas au prix de ta hauteur!

sign of young manhood, delays to appear on his face and to darken his chin.

Oh, how many widows will the folk who wear the turban have then! How much blood will redden the rivers which wash the feet of the Lebanon! How many captive sultanesses will the Bosphorus have on its two shores! And how many mothers in Memphis will speak in tears of the stoutness of his heart and lance at the funerals of their sons!

Paraphrase of Psalm VIII

'O Lord our Lord'

O ETERNAL wisdom, to which this universe owes the infinite number of various miracles which we see both on the earth and on the waters: my God, my Creator, how your munificence amazes the whole world and how low is heaven beside your glory!

Quelques blasphémateurs, oppresseurs d'innocents,
A qui l'excès d'orgueil a fait perdre le sens,
De profanes discours ta puissance rabaissent;
   Mais la naïveté,
Dont mêmes au berceau les enfants te confessent,
Clôt-elle pas la bouche à leur impiété?

De moi, toutes les fois que j'arrête les yeux
A voir les ornements dont tu pares les cieux,
Tu me sembles si grand, et nous si peu de chose,
   Que mon entendement
Ne peut s'imaginer quel amour te dispose
A nous favoriser d'un regard seulement.

Il n'est faiblesse égale à nos infirmités;
Nos plus sages discours ne sont que vanités,
Et nos sens corrompus n'ont goût qu'à des ordures;
   Toutefois, ô bon Dieu,
Nous te sommes si chers, qu'entre tes créatures,
Si l'ange est le premier, l'homme a le second lieu.

Quelles marques d'honneur se peuvent ajouter
A ce comble de gloire où tu l'as fait monter?

Certain blasphemers, oppressors of the innocent, whom excess of
pride has robbed of their senses, belittle your power with profane
words; but does not the simplicity with which even in their cradles
children confess You, close the mouth of their impiety?

To me, whenever I lift my eyes to see the beauties with which
You adorn the heavens, You seem so great and we so puny, that my
understanding cannot imagine what love moves You to favour us
with so much as a look.

There is no weakness equal to our imperfections; our wisest
words are but vanity and our corrupt senses have taste only for
filth; and yet, O gracious God, we are so dear to You that, among
your creatures, if the angel is the first, man has the second place.

What marks of honour can be added to that height of glory to

Et pour obtenir mieux quel souhait peut-il faire?
Lui que jusqu'au ponant,
Depuis où le soleil vient dessus l'hémisphère,
Ton absolu pouvoir a fait son lieutenant?

Sitôt que le besoin excite son désir,
Qu'est-ce qu'en ta largesse il ne trouve à choisir?
Et par ton règlement l'air, la mer et la terre
N'entretiennent-ils pas
Une secrète loi de se faire la guerre,
A qui de plus de mets fournira ses repas?

Certes je ne puis faire, en ce ravissement,
Que rappeler mon âme, et dire bassement:
O sagesse éternelle, en merveilles féconde,
Mon Dieu, mon Créateur,
Que ta magnificence étonne tout le monde,
Et que le ciel est bas au prix de ta hauteur!

which You have raised him? And to obtain more, what wish can he form? He whom your absolute power has made its lieutenant from the place where the sun comes over the horizon as far as the west?

As soon as need awakens his appetite what does he not find to choose from your bounty? And by your ordinance do not the air, the sea, and the earth obey a secret law to compete with each other (to decide) which will furnish his table with the most kinds of food?

In truth I can do no more, in this ecstatic contemplation, than call back my soul to me and say humbly: O eternal wisdom, rich in wonders, my God, my Creator, how your munificence amazes the whole world and how low is heaven beside your glory!

Imitation du Psaume Lauda anima mea Dominum

N'ESPÉRONS plus, mon âme, aux promesses du monde:
Sa lumière est un verre, et sa faveur une onde,
Que toujours quelque vent empêche de calmer;
Quittons ces vanités, lassons-nous de les suivre:
      C'est Dieu qui nous fait vivre,
      C'est Dieu qu'il faut aimer.

En vain, pour satisfaire à nos lâches envies,
Nous passons près des rois tout le temps de nos vies,
A souffrir des mépris et ployer les genoux;
Ce qu'ils peuvent n'est rien: ils sont comme nous sommes,
      Véritablement hommes,
      Et meurent comme nous.

Ont-ils rendu l'esprit, ce n'est plus que poussière
Que cette majesté si pompeuse et si fière
Dont l'éclat orgueilleux étonne l'univers;
Et dans ces grands tombeaux où leurs âmes hautaines
      Font encore les vaines,
      Ils sont mangés des vers.

Inspired by the Psalm 'Praise the Lord, O my soul' *

LET us trust no more, my soul, in the world's promises: its light is
a glinting glass and its favour a shifting wave which some wind always prevents from calming. Let us renounce these vanities, let us
turn from following them. It is God who gives us life, it is God
whom we must love.

Vainly, to satisfy our base desires, we spend in courts of kings
the whole span of our lives, enduring contempt and bending our
knees. Their power is nothing, they are as we are, in very truth
men, and die as we do.

When they give up the ghost, it is no more than dust – that
majesty so stately and so proud whose pomp and splendour awes
the world. And in those great tombs where their haughty souls still
make a vain display, they are eaten by the worms.

---

* No. 146 in the English Psalter.

Là se perdent ces noms de maîtres de la terre,
D'arbitres de la paix, de foudres de la guerre :
Comme ils n'ont plus de sceptre ils n'ont plus de flatteurs,
Et tombent avec eux d'une chute commune
    Tous ceux que leur fortune
    Faisait leurs serviteurs.

JEAN DE SPONDE

Élégie

Vous languissez, mes vers : les glaçons de l'absence
Éteignant vos fureurs au point de leur naissance,
Vous n'entrebattez plus de soupirs votre flanc,
Vos artères d'esprits, ni vos veines de sang.
Eh quoi, la mort vous tient ? et ce front teint en cendre
Vous marque les tombeaux où vous allez descendre ?
Si vous pouviez encor revoir dedans les cieux
Ce feu qui s'est caché des pointes de vos yeux,
Vous vivriez, dites-vous, mais la clarté ravie
Ravit en même temps l'éclair de votre vie.
Vous ne sauriez passer vos jours parmi les nuits,

There vanish those titles of lords of the earth, of arbiters of peace, of thunderbolts of war. As they have lost their sceptres, they have lost their flatterers. And with them go down in a common fall all those whom their fortune once made their servants.

Elegy

You languish, my verses : since the icicles of absence extinguish your ardours at their source, your flanks no longer heave with sighs, or your arteries beat with vital spirits, or your veins with blood. So then, death grips you, and that ashen brow foreshows the tombs to which you will go down ? If you could see once again in the heavens that light which is hidden from the beams of your eyes, you would live, you say, but its ravished brightness has ravished at the same time the light of your life. You could not spend your days

Ni faire beau visage en ces affreux ennuis.
Ce contraire est trop grand: vivre auprès de ma belle
Et n'approcher la mort quand on s'éloigne d'elle.
Il faut donques mourir et par nécessité
Qu'à la fin votre hiver succède à votre été.

Papillons bien-aimés, nourrissons de mon âme,
Puisque votre origine est prise de ma flamme
Et que ma flamme garde encore son ardeur,
D'où vous vient, d'où vous vient cette prompte froideur?
Ce beau feu, dont j'avais votre vie allumée,
Me l'avez-vous changé si soudain en fumée?
Vous me laissez, ingrats, et la déloyauté
Récompense l'amour que je vous ai porté.

Est-ce que vous craignez que votre tendre vue
Se rebouche si bien contre la pointe aiguë
Des rayons du soleil, qu'à l'épreuve du jour
On ne vous juge point de vrais enfants d'Amour?
Et que ces beaux esprits dont on fait tant de compte,
S'ils vous ont découverts, ne vous couvrent de honte?
Craindriez-vous point qu'encor votre difformité

among nights, or have pleasant looks in these fearful torments. This opposition is too great: to live near my beauty and not approach death when you go away from her. So you must die and, by necessity, in the end your winter must succeed your summer.

Well-loved butterflies, nurslings of my soul, since you had your origin in my flame, and my flame still retains its heat, whence comes, whence comes your sudden coldness? That proud fire with which I lit your life, have you so swiftly turned it into smoke? You leave me, thankless children, and your unfaithfulness rewards the love which I bore you.

Do you fear that your tender eyes will be so blunted against the sharp darts of the beams of the sun that, by the test of daylight, you will not be judged true children of Love? And that those clever wits who are held in such esteem would cover you with shame if they discovered you? Again, might you not fear that your deformity

Ne déplût d'aventure aux yeux de la beauté
Pour qui vous travaillez, et par trop de coutume
Qu'on sente vos douceurs changer en amertume?

   Hélas, ne mourez point et servez pour le moins
A ma fidélité de fidèles témoins!
Que si des Basilics l'œil malin vous offense
Marchant parmi ces fleurs, j'en prendrai la défense,
Et du miroir luisant de mon autorité
J'éteindrai tout soudain cette malignité.
Lorsqu'on vous poursuivra je serai votre asile,
Et quand les vents battraient votre nef si fragile,
Vous ne sauriez vous perdre au phare de mon feu …

Sonnet

Si j'avais comme vous, mignardes colombelles,
Des plumages si beaux sur mon corps attachés,
On aurait beau tenir mes esprits empêchés
De l'indomptable fer de cent chaînes nouvelles.

might perhaps be displeasing to the eyes of that beauty for whom
you labour, and that by too much familiarity your sweetness might
seem to change into bitterness?

   Ah, do not die, but serve at least as faithful witnesses to my
faithfulness. For if the malignant eye of the Basilisks offends you
as you walk among these flowers, I will come to your defence, and
with the shining mirror of my authority I will quickly snuff out
their baleful stare. When you are pursued I will be your refuge, and
were the winds to batter your frail vessel, you could not be lost to
the beacon of my fire.

Sonnet

PRETTY doves, if I had like you such fine plumage fastened to my
body, in vain would they try to shackle my spirit with the unbreak-
able iron of a hundred fresh chains.

Sur les ailes du vent je guiderais mes ailes,
J'irais jusqu'au séjour où mes biens sont cachés:
Ainsi, voyant de moi ces ennuis arrachés,
Je ne sentirais plus ces absences cruelles.

Colombelles, hélas! que j'ai bien souhaité
Que mon corps vous semblât autant d'agilité
Que mon âme d'amour à votre âme ressemble.

Mais quoi! je le souhaite, et me trompe d'autant.
Ferais-je bien voler un amour si constant
D'un monde tout rempli de vos ailes ensemble?

Stances de la mort

Mes yeux, ne lancez plus votre pointe éblouie
Sur les brillants rayons de la flammeuse vie;
Sillez-vous, couvrez-vous de ténèbres, mes yeux:
Non pas pour étouffer vos vigueurs coutumières,
Car je vous ferai voir de plus vives lumières,
Mais sortant de la nuit vous ne verrez que mieux.

I would slant my wings on the wings of the wind, I would go
to the abode where my treasure is hidden: so, seeing these sorrows
plucked from me, I would no longer feel this cruel absence.

Little doves, alas, how much have I longed that my body should
be as like you in its lightness as my soul resembles your soul in
love.

Alas, I long for it and deceive myself no less. Could I ever make
so constant a love take flight from a world filled full with all your
wings together?

Stanzas on Death

My eyes, no longer dart your dazzled looks upon the bright beams
of fiery life; close, cover yourselves with darkness, my eyes: not
in order to dim your normal keenness, for I will cause you to see
(yet) brighter lights, but because you will see all the better on
coming out of the dark.

Je m'ennuie de vivre et mes tendres années,
Gémissant sous le faix de bien peu de journées,
Me trouvent au milieu de ma course cassé:
Si n'est-ce pas du tout par défaut de courage,
Mais je prends, comme un port à la fin de l'orage,
Dédain de l'avenir pour l'horreur du passé.

... La chair, des vanités de ce monde pipée,
Veut être dans sa vie encor enveloppée,
Et l'esprit pour mieux vivre en souhaite la mort.
Ces partis m'ont réduit en un péril extrême:
Mais, mon Dieu, prends parti de ces partis toi-même,
Et je me rangerai du parti le plus fort.

Sans ton aide, mon Dieu, cette chair orgueilleuse
Rendra de ce combat l'issue périlleuse,
Car elle est en son règne et l'autre est étranger:
La chair sent le doux fruit des voluptés présentes,
L'esprit ne semble avoir qu'un espoir des absentes,
Et le fruit pour l'espoir ne se doit point changer.

I am weary of living and my tender years, groaning beneath the load of few enough days, find me broken in the middle of my journey. Yet it is in no way for lack of courage; but I have attained, like a port after the storm, contempt of the future through horror of the past.

The flesh, duped by the vanities of this world, desires still to be clothed with life, and the spirit, in order to live better, desires the death of the flesh. These factions have brought me into mortal danger. But, Lord, side with (one of) these factions yourself, and I will rally to the strongest side.

Without your aid, Lord, this proud flesh will make the outcome of this struggle uncertain, for the flesh is in its own kingdom and the other is alien here: the flesh tastes the sweet fruit of present delights, the spirit seems to have only a hope of absent ones – and the fruit must (surely) not be exchanged for the hope.

Et puis si c'est ta main qui façonna le monde,
Dont la riche beauté à ta beauté réponde,
La chair croit que le Tout pour elle fût parfait:
Tout fut parfait pour elle, et elle davantage
Se vante d'être, ô Dieu, de tes mains un ouvrage.
Hé! déferais-tu donc ce que tes mains ont fait?

Voilà comme l'effort de la charnelle ruse
De son bien pour son mal ouvertement abuse,
En danger que l'esprit ne ploie enfin sous lui.
Viens donc, et mets la main, mon Dieu, dedans ce trouble,
Et la force à l'esprit par ta force redouble:
Un bon droit a souvent besoin d'un bon appui.

Ne crains point, mon esprit, d'entrer en cette lice,
Car la chair ne combat ta puissante justice
Que d'un bouclier de verre et d'un bras de roseau:
Dieu t'armera de fer pour piler ce beau verre,
Pour casser ce roseau, et la fin de la guerre
Sera pour toi la vie, et pour elle un tombeau.

And then if it was your hand which fashioned the world, whose
rich beauty corresponds to your beauty, the flesh believes that the
Whole was made perfect for it. All was made perfect for it, and it,
moreover, prides itself on being, Lord, a work of your hands. Ah,
would You unmake what your hands have made?

That is how the onslaught of the cunning flesh openly abuses its
good to its detriment, with the risk that the spirit may yield at last
beneath it. Come then, O God, and intervene in this conflict, and
redouble the strength of the spirit with your strength: a good cause
often has need of good support.

Fear not, my spirit, to enter these lists, for the flesh only opposes
your righteous power with a shield of glass and a reed-like arm.
God will arm you with steel to shatter that fine glass, to break that
reed, and the end of the struggle will be life for you and a tomb
for it.

C'est assez enduré que de cette vermine
La superbe insolence à ta grandeur domine.
Tu lui dois commander, cependant tu lui sers :
Tu dois purger la chair, et cette chair te souille ;
Voire, de te garder un désir te chatouille,
Mais cuidant te garder, mon esprit, tu te perds.

... Je sais bien, mon esprit, que cet air et cette onde,
Cette terre, ce feu, ce ciel qui ceint le monde,
Enfle, abîme, retient, brûle, éteint tes désirs :
Tu vois je ne sais quoi de plaisant et d'aimable,
Mais le dessus du ciel est bien plus estimable,
Et de plaisants amours et d'aimables plaisirs.

Ces amours, ces plaisirs dont les troupes des anges
Caressent du grand Dieu les merveilles étranges
Aux accords rapportés de leurs diverses voix,
Sont bien d'autres plaisirs, amours d'autre nature :
Ce que tu vois ici n'en est pas la peinture,
Ne fût-ce rien sinon pour ce que tu le vois.

We have suffered the overbearing insolence of that vermin to dominate your greatness long enough. You should command it, yet you serve it. You should purge the flesh, and the flesh defiles you. Indeed, a desire to preserve yourself tempts you, but thinking to preserve yourself, my spirit, you destroy yourself.

I well know, my spirit, that this air and this ocean, this earth, this fire, this sky which girdles the world, swells up, engulfs, holds back, burns, extinguishes your desires: you see I know not what that is pleasant and lovable; but the height of heaven is far more to be prized, both for pleasant love and for lovable pleasure.

That love, that pleasure with which the bands of angels caress the strange marvels of mighty God, to the concerted harmonies of their various voices, is very different pleasure, love of another nature. What you see here below is not the portrait of it, if only because you do see it.

Invisibles beautés, délices invisibles,
Ravissez-moi du creux de ces manoirs horribles,
Fondez-moi cette chair et rompez-moi ces os:
Il faut passer vers vous à travers mon martyre,
Mon martyre en mourant, car hélas! je désire
Commencer au travail et finir au repos.

Mais dispose, mon Dieu, ma tremblante impuissance
A ces pesants fardeaux de ton obéissance;
Si tu veux que je vive encore, je le veux.
Eh quoi? m'envies-tu ton bien que je souhaite?
Car ce ne m'est que mal que la vie imparfaite
Qui languit sur la terre, et qui vivrait aux cieux.

Non, ce ne m'est que mal, mais mal plein d'espérance
Qu'après les durs ennuis de ma longue souffrance,
Tu m'étendras ta main, mon Dieu, pour me guérir.
Mais tandis que je couve une si belle envie,
Puisqu'un bien est le bout et le but de ma vie,
Apprends-moi de bien vivre, afin de bien mourir.

Invisible beauties, delights invisible, snatch me up from the
depths of these horrible dwellings, melt this flesh of mine and break
these my bones; I must go towards you through my own suffering,
the suffering of my death, for ah, I desire to begin in travail and
to end in rest.

But incline, my God, my trembling impotence to those heavy
burdens of your obedience; if you wish me to live still, I too wish
it. So then, do you grudge me your bliss, for which I long? For
there is only pain for me in this imperfect life which languishes on
earth, and would live in heaven.

Yes, it is only pain for me, but pain full of hope that after the
harsh tortures of my long suffering, you will stretch out your hand,
my God, to heal me. But while I cherish so sweet a longing, since
good is the end and the aim of my life, teach me to live well in
order to die well.

Sonnets de la mort

MAIS si faut-il mourir, et la vie orgueilleuse,
Qui brave de la mort, sentira ses fureurs,
Les soleils hâleront ces journalières fleurs
Et le temps crèvera cette ampoule venteuse;

Ce beau flambeau, qui lance une flamme fumeuse,
Sur le vert de la cire éteindra ses ardeurs,
L'huile de ce tableau ternira ses couleurs
Et ces flots se rompront à la rive écumeuse.

J'ai vu ces clairs éclairs passer devant mes yeux,
Et le tonnerre encor qui gronde dans les cieux,
Où d'une ou d'autre part éclatera l'orage.

J'ai vu fondre la neige et ses torrents tarir,
Ces lions rugissants je les ai vus sans rage:
Vivez, hommes, vivez, mais si faut-il mourir.

Sonnets on Death

AND yet we must die and proud life, which mocks at death, will feel its fury; the suns will wither these flowers of a day and time will burst this phial of wind.

This fine candle which flares with a smoking flame will burn out its ardour in the green of the wax, the oils of this picture will dim their colours and these waves will break on the foamy shore.

I have seen the bright lightning pass before my eyes, and the thunder also rumbling in the heavens, where from one quarter or another the storm will break.

I have seen the snows melt and their streams run dry, I have seen these roaring lions stripped of rage: Live, men, live, but yet you must die.

Qui sont, qui sont ceux-là dont le cœur idolâtre
Se jette aux pieds du monde et flatte ses honneurs,
Et qui sont ces valets, et qui sont ces seigneurs?
Et ces âmes d'ébène et ces faces d'albâtre?

Ces masques déguisés, dont la troupe folâtre
S'amuse à caresser je ne sais quels donneurs
De fumées de cour, et ces entrepreneurs
De vaincre encor le ciel qu'ils ne peuvent combattre?

Qui sont ces louvoyeurs qui s'éloignent du port,
Hommagers à la vie et félons à la mort,
Dont l'étoile est leur bien, le vent leur fantaisie?

Je vogue en même mer et craindrais de périr,
Si ce n'est que je sais que cette même vie
N'est rien que le fanal qui me guide au mourir.

WHO are these, who are these, whose idolatrous hearts fawn at the feet of the world and ogle its honours, and who are these lackeys and who are these lords? These ebon souls and these alabaster faces?

These disguised maskers, whose giddy band wastes its time in flattering some vague dispensers of courtly vanities, and these who again undertake to conquer that heaven which they are powerless to fight?

Who are these tacking schemers sailing ever further from port, fawners on life and traitors to death, whose pole-star is their profit, whose wind is their caprice?

I sail on the same sea and should fear to perish, did I not know that this same life is only the beacon which shows me the way to die.

Tout s'enfle contre moi, tout m'assaut, tout me tente,
Et le monde, et la chair, et l'ange révolté,
Dont l'onde, dont l'effort, dont le charme inventé
Et m'abîme, Seigneur, et m'ébranle, et m'enchante.

Quelle nef, quel appui, quelle oreille dormante,
Sans péril, sans tomber, et sans être enchanté,
Me donras-tu? Ton temple où vit ta sainteté,
Ton invincible main, et ta voix si constante?

Et quoi? Mon Dieu, je sens combattre maintesfois
Encor avec ton temple et ta main et ta voix
Cet ange révolté, cette chair, et ce monde.

Mais ton temple pourtant, ta main, ta voix sera
La nef, l'appui, l'oreille, où ce charme perdra,
Où mourra cet effort, où se rompra cette onde.

Everything swells up against me, everything assails me, everything tempts me: the world, the flesh, and the rebel angel, whose
wave, whose onslaught, whose deceitful spell engulfs me, Lord,
and weakens and enchants me.

What ship, what stay, what sleeping ear, will you give me
against danger, against falling, and against enchantment? Your
temple in which your holiness dwells, your invincible arm, and
your steadfast voice?

But what is this? My God, I feel many a time still warring against
your temple and your arm and your voice, this rebel angel, this
flesh and this world.

And yet your temple, your arm, and your voice will be the ship,
the stay, the ear, on which that spell will lose its power, that onslaught will die, that wave will break.

JEAN-BAPTISTE CHASSIGNET

Le Mépris de la vie et consolation contre la mort

ASSIEDS-TOI sur le bord d'une ondante rivière:
Tu la verras fluer d'un perpétuel cours,
Et flots sur flots roulant en mille et mille tours
Décharger par les prés son humide carrière.

Mais tu ne verras rien de cette onde première
Qui naguère coulait; l'eau change tous les jours,
Tous les jours elle passe, et la nommons toujours
Même fleuve, et même eau, d'une même manière.

Ainsi l'homme varie, et ne sera demain
Telle comme aujourd'hui du pauvre corps humain
La force que le temps abrévie et consomme:

Le nom sans varier nous suit jusqu'au trépas,
Et combien qu'aujourd'hui celui ne sois-je pas
Qui vivais hier passé, toujours même on me nomme.

SIT down on the bank of a rippling river; you will see it flowing in
a perpetual current, and, rolling wave after wave in a thousand twists
and turns, outpouring its watery course through the meadows.

But you will see nothing of that first wave which once flowed by.
The water changes every day, every day it passes and we still call it
the same river, and the same water, in the same way.

So does man vary, and tomorrow the strength of the poor
human body which time shortens and consumes will not be the
same as today:

The name follows us until death without changing and, although
today I am not the same man who was living yesterday, yet am I
still called the same.

Comme petits enfants d'une larve outrageuse,
D'un fantôme, ou d'un masque, ainsi nous avons peur,
Et redoutons la mort, la concevant au cœur
Telle comme on la fait, hâve, triste et affreuse.

Comme il plaît à la main ou loyale ou trompeuse
Du graveur, du tailleur, ou du peintre flatteur
La nous représenter sur un tableau menteur,
Nous l'imaginons telle, agréable ou hideuse.

Ces appréhensions, torturant nos cerveaux,
Nous chassent devant elle, ainsi comme bouveaux
Courent devant le loup, et n'avons pas l'espace

De la bien remarquer: ôtons le masque feint,
Lors nous la trouverons autre qu'on ne la peint,
Gracieuse à toucher, et plaisante de face.

La vie est du futur un souhait agréable
Et regret du passé, un désir indompté
De goûter et tâter ce qu'on n'a pas goûté,
De ce qu'on a goûté un dégoût incurable;

As little children of a grisly spectre, of a phantom, or of a mask, so are we afraid, and we fear death, imagining it in our hearts as it is represented, gaunt, sad, and terrible.

As it pleases the honest or deceitful hand of the engraver, the sculptor, or the flattering painter to depict it to us in a false picture, so we imagine it, pleasant or hideous.

These fears, torturing our brains, drive us before them like young steers fleeing before the wolf, and we have no space to observe it rightly: let us take off the false mask, then we shall find it other than it is painted, agreeable to touch and pleasant of face.

Life is a pleasant anticipation of the future and a regret for the past, an uncontrollable desire to taste and touch what has not been tasted, an incurable distaste for what has been tasted;

Un vain ressouvenir de l'état désirable
Des siècles jà passés, du futur souhaité
Un espoir incertain, frivolement jeté
Sur le vain fondement d'une attente muable;

Une horreur de soi-même, un souhait de sa mort,
Un mépris de sa vie, un gouffre de remords,
Un magasin de pleurs, une mer de tempête:

Où plus nous approchons du rivage lointain,
Plus nous nous regrettons et lamentons en vain
Que le vent ait si tôt notre course parfaite.

Donne l'enseigne au vent, étendant tes conquêtes
Du Midi jusqu'au Nord et, publiant tes lois
Au Ponant et Levant, fais trembler sous ta voix
Des potentats voisins les couronnes sujettes.

Tiens dans tes ports guerriers cent mille flottes prêtes
Pour écorner l'orgueil des arrogants Chinois,

a vain recalling of the desirable state of past ages, an uncertain
hope of a wished-for future, frivolously built up on the vain
foundation of shifting expectations;

a horror of oneself, a desire for death, a contempt of life, a pit of
remorse, a storehouse of tears, a storm-tossed sea:

in which the nearer we come to the distant shore, the more we
regret and vainly lament that the wind has ended our journey so
soon.

Unfurl your banner to the wind, extending your conquests from
the south to the north and, proclaiming your laws in the east and
the west, make the subject crowns of the neighbouring princes
tremble at the sound of your voice.

In your ports of war keep a hundred thousand ships ready to
whittle the pride of the arrogant Chinese and, fastening the yoke

Et, mettant sous le joug les félons Japonois,
Dépouille les trésors des terres plus secrètes.

Refrène le François, captive l'Allemand,
Supplante l'Espagnol, dompte le Musulman,
Et porte en Italie et la peste et la guerre :

Si mourras-tu, chétif, et ne posséderas
De tant de régions que tu délaisseras
Que le tour du tombeau : sept ou huit pieds de terre.

CINGLE depuis la France au royaume Turquesque,
De là va visiter les murs de Sun-Tien
Et des fiers Japonais le royaume ancien,
Puis fais tourner la voile à la côte Moresque.

Passe encore au-delà de la mer Arabesque,
Et si tu n'es content du noir Égyptien,
Va remarquer les ports de l'empire Indien
Furetant les trésors de la gent barbaresque.

Si tu treuve' un seul homme affranchi de la mort
Partout où tu courras, dis qu'elle te fait tort
D'aigrir contre toi seul sa vengeante rancune :

on the false Japanese, ransack the treasures of the remotest lands.
   Curb back the Frenchman, enchain the German, drive out the
Spaniard, subdue the Muslim, and carry to Italy plague and war:
   yet you will die, puny man, and of so many domains which you
will abandon you will possess only the length of the grave, seven or
eight feet of earth.

SAIL away from France to the realm of the Turks, from there go
and visit the walls of Tsungsin and the ancient realm of the fierce
Japanese, then set your course back to the Moorish coast.
   Pass again beyond the Arabian sea, and if the dark Egyptian does
not please you, go and see the ports of the empire of Ind, ran-
sacking the treasures of the Barbary folk.
   If you find a single man not subject to death wherever you go,
say that death wrongs you in venting its spite on you alone.

Mais si tout homme est né pour choir au monument,
Apprends à tout le moins à mourir constamment;
Moindre se fait le mal par la perte commune.

LES poissons écaillés aiment les moites eaux,
Les fleuves et les lacs; les animaux sauvages
Aiment les bois touffus, les creux et les bocages,
Et l'air doux et serein est aimé des oiseaux;

Les grillons babillards aiment l'émail des preaux,
S'égayant au printemps parmi le vert herbage,
Les lézards et serpents envenimés de rage
Aiment des murs rompus les humides caveaux.

Bref, naturellement chacun aime et désire
Le lieu originel d'où sa naissance il tire,
Auquel mêmes il doit résider longuement:

L'homme seul, dérivant comme plante divine
Du ciel spirituel sa féconde origine,
Préfère à sa patrie un long bannissement.

But if every man was born to go down to the tomb, then learn at least to die steadfastly. The evil becomes less when it is the common lot.

THE scaly fishes love the wet waters, the rivers, and the lakes; the wild beasts love the thick woods, the caves, and the copses, and the mild, clear sky is loved by the birds;

The chattering crickets love the bright hues of the meadows, making merry in spring among the green grass, the lizards and serpents envenomed with fury love the damp crannies in ruined walls.

In short, each naturally loves and desires the place of origin from which it draws its being, and which also it must inhabit for a long time:

Only man, like a divine plant deriving his fertile origin from the spiritual sky, prefers a long exile to his true home.

A beaucoup de danger est sujette la fleur :
Ou l'on la foule au pied ou les vents la ternissent,
Les rayons du soleil la brûlent et rôtissent,
La bête la dévore, et s'effeuille en verdeur.

Nos jours, entremêlés de regret et de pleur,
A la fleur comparés comme la fleur fleurissent,
Tombent comme la fleur, comme la fleur périssent,
Autant comme du froid tourmentés de l'ardeur.

Non de fer ni de plomb, mais d'odorantes pommes
Le vaisseau va chargé, ainsi les jours des hommes
Sont légers, non pesants, variables et vains,

Qui, laissant après eux d'un peu de renommée
L'odeur en moins de rien comme fruit consommée,
Passent légèrement hors du cœur des humains.

Retourne le miroir vers la voûte azurée,
Le ciel incontinent y sera figuré ;
Devers la terre soit le miroir reviré,
La terre au même instant y sera figurée.

To many a peril the flower is exposed: either it is trampled underfoot or the winds wither it, the beams of the sun burn and scorch it,
the animal devours it, and its leaves fall while they are still green.

Our days, intermingled with sorrow and tears, compared to the
flower like the flower blossom, fall like the flower, like the flower
perish, tormented by heat as much as by cold.

Not with iron or with lead but with sweet-smelling apples does
the vessel go laden: so the days of man are light, unsubstantial,
variable, and vain,

And, leaving after them the scent of a little fame, in less than an
instant consumed like fruit, pass lightly away out of human hearts.

Turn up the mirror towards the azure vault, the sky will immediately be reflected in it: let the mirror be turned back towards the
earth, at once the earth will be reflected there.

Telle est du feu d'amour la force immodérée,
Que le cœur, de sa flamme ardemment torturé,
Se transforme aussitôt au sujet désiré,
Étant en son désir l'âme démesurée.

Si tu aimes le ciel, céleste tu seras,
Si tu aimes la terre en terre tu cherras,
Et de terre vivant tu deviendras terrestre.

Nabuchodonosor, pour avoir trop aimé
Le monde terrien, fut ainsi transformé
L'espace de sept ans en animal champestre.

QUELQUEFOIS les chevaux vont caparaçonnés
De drap d'or et d'argent, richesse inestimable,
Toutefois arrivés en la fumante étable
On leur ôte l'habit duquel ils sont ornés,

Et ne leur reste rien sur les dos étonnés
Que lasseté, sueur, et plaie dommageable,
Dont l'éperon, la course et le faix les accable,
Défaillant sous les bonds en courbettes tournés.

Such is the overpowering strength of the fire of love, that the
heart, ardently tormented by its flame, transforms itself at once into
the desired object, since the soul knows no bounds in its desires.

If you love heaven, you will be celestial, if you love the earth,
you will fall to earth, and living by earth you will become earthly.

Thus Nebuchadnezzar, for having loved the earthly world too
well, was transformed for the space of seven years into a beast of
the fields.

SOMETIMES horses go caparisoned with cloth of gold and silver,
incalculable wealth, and yet when they reach the steaming stable,
the trappings which cover them are taken off,

And nothing remains on their bewildered backs but weariness,
sweat, and hurtful sore, which the spur, the ride, and the weight in-
flict on them, as they grow faint under the (strain of) prancing and
curvetting round.

Ainsi marche le prince accompagné sur terre,
Puis, quand le trait subit de la Parque l'enferre,
Tous ses honneurs lui sont incontinent ôtés,

Car de tant de ressorts et provinces sujettes
Les rois n'emportent rien sous les tombes muettes
Que les forfaits commis en leurs principautés.

J'AI voulu voyager, à la fin le voyage
M'a fait en ma maison mal content retirer.
En mon étude seul j'ai voulu demeurer,
Enfin la solitude a causé mon dommage.

J'ai voulu naviguer, enfin le navigage
Entre vie et trépas m'a fait désespérer.
J'ai voulu pour plaisir la terre labourer,
Enfin j'ai méprisé l'état du labourage.

J'ai voulu pratiquer la science et les arts,
Enfin je n'ai rien su; j'ai couru le hasard
Des combats carnassiers, la guerre ore m'offense.

So goes the prince arrayed on earth, then, when the sudden arrow of fate pierces him, all his honours are suddenly taken from him,

For of so many powers and subject provinces, kings carry nothing into the silent tombs but the evil deeds committed in their kingdoms.

I WANTED to travel, in the end travel caused me to retire dissatisfied to my house. I wanted to remain alone in my study, in the end solitude worked my harm.

I wanted to sail the seas, in the end seafaring made me despair between life and death. I wanted to till the earth for pleasure, in the end I despised the tiller's state.

I wanted to practise learning and the arts, in the end I learnt nothing; I ran the gauntlet of murderous battles, now war disgusts me.

O imbécilité de l'esprit curieux,
Qui, mécontent de tout, de tout est désireux,
Et, douteux, n'a de rien parfaite connaissance.

THÉOPHILE DE VIAU

Lettre à son frère

Mon frère, mon dernier appui,
Toi seul dont le secours me dure,
Et qui seul trouves aujourd'hui
Mon adversité longue et dure;
Ami ferme, ardent, généreux,
Que mon sort le plus malheureux
Pique davantage à le suivre,
Achève de me secourir:
Il faudra qu'on me laisse vivre
Après m'avoir fait tant mourir.

O imbecility of the inquisitive mind, which, dissatisfied with everything, is desirous of everything, and which, doubting, has perfect knowledge of nothing.

Letter to His Brother

(Written from prison to his brother Paul, a Huguenot captain. Boussères in the second stanza was their country home on the Garonne.)

My brother, my last support, who alone continue to help me and who alone today think my misfortune long and hard; staunch, eager, generous friend, whom the extreme misery of my lot prompts to sympathize with it all the more, make a last effort to save me. They will have to let me live after having made me die for so long.

... Quelque lac qui me soit tendu
Par de si subtils adversaires,
Encore n'ai-je point perdu
L'espérance de voir Boussères.
Encore un coup, le dieu du jour
Tout devant moi fera sa cour
Aux rives de notre héritage,
Et je verrai ses cheveux blonds
Du même or qui luit sur le Tage
Dorer l'argent de nos sablons.

Je verrai ces bois verdissants
Où nos îles et l'herbe fraîche
Servent aux troupeaux mugissants
Et de promenoir et de crèche.
L'aurore y trouve à son retour
L'herbe qu'ils ont mangée le jour.
Je verrai l'eau qui les abreuve,
Et j'oirai plaindre les graviers
Et repartir l'écho du fleuve
Aux injures des mariniers.

Whatever snare is laid for me by such subtle adversaries, I have still not lost hope of seeing Boussères. Once again the god of day will pay his court right before me on the banks of our estate, and I shall see his yellow locks gilding the silver of our sands with the same gold that gleams on the Tagus.

I shall see those green woods among which our islands and the fresh grass provide the lowing herds both with a place to walk in and a manger. The dawn finds at its return the same grass on which they grazed the day before. I shall see the water which slakes their thirst and I shall hear the gravel-banks murmuring and the river-echoes startled by the oaths of the boatmen.

... Je cueillerai ces abricots,
Ces fraises à couleur de flammes
Dont nos bergers font des écots
Qui seraient ici bons aux dames,
Et ces figues et ces melons
Dont la bouche des aquilons
N'a jamais su baiser l'écorce,
Et ces jaunes muscats si chers
Que jamais la grêle ne force
Dans l'asile de nos rochers.

Je verrai sur nos grenadiers
Leurs rouges pommes entr'ouvertes.
Où le ciel, comme à ses lauriers,
Garde toujours des feuilles vertes
Je verrai ce touffu jasmin
Qui fait ombre à tout le chemin
D'une assez spacieuse allée,
Et la parfume d'une fleur
Qui conserve dans la gelée
Son odorat et sa couleur.

I shall pick those apricots, those flame-coloured strawberries
from which our shepherds make snack meals which here would be
good enough for the ladies, and those figs and melons whose skin
the mouth of the cold winds has never been able to kiss, and those
precious yellow muscat grapes which the hail never violates in the
shelter of our rocks.

I shall see the red, half-opened fruit on our pomegranate-trees,
on which heaven, as with its own laurels, always keeps green leaves.
I shall see that leafy jasmine which shades the whole length of quite
a broad garden-walk and scents it with a flower which keeps its
fragrance and its colour through the frosts.

Je reverrai fleurir nos prés,
Je leur verrai couper les herbes;
Je verrai quelque temps après
Le paysan couché sur les gerbes;
Et, comme ce climat divin
Nous est très libéral de vin,
Après avoir rempli la grange
Je verrai du matin au soir
Comme les flots de la vendange
Écumeront dans le pressoir.

Là, d'un esprit laborieux,
L'infatigable Bellegarde
De la voix, des mains et des yeux
A tout le revenu prend garde.
Il connaît d'un exacte soin
Ce que les prés rendent de foin,
Ce que nos troupeaux ont de laine,
Et sait mieux que les vieux paysans
Ce que la montagne et la plaine
Nous peuvent donner tous les ans.

I shall see our meadows flower again; I shall see their grass being cut; some time later I shall see the peasant lying on the corn-sheaves; and as that divine climate gives us wine in abundance, after the barn has been filled I shall see the floods of the grape-harvest foaming from morning till evening in the wine-press.

There, industriously inclined, the tireless Bellegarde supervises the whole yield of the estate with voice, hands, and eyes. He knows exactly how much hay the meadows give, how much wool our flocks have, and can tell better than the old peasants what the mountain and the plain can give us each year.

... Si je passais dans ce loisir
Encore autant que j'ai de vie,
Le comble d'un si cher plaisir
Bornerait toute mon envie.
Il faut qu'un jour ma liberté
Se lâche en cette volupté.
Je n'ai plus de regret au Louvre,
Ayant vécu dans ces douceurs.
Que la même terre me couvre
Qui couvre mes prédécesseurs.

Ode

Un corbeau devant moi croasse,
Une ombre offusque mes regards;
Deux belettes et deux renards
Traversent l'endroit où je passe;
Les pieds faillent à mon cheval,
Mon laquais tombe du haut mal;
J'entends craqueter le tonnerre;
Un esprit se présente à moi;
J'ois Charon qui m'appelle à soi,
Je vois le centre de la terre.

If I were to spend all the life that is left me in that calm spot, the satisfaction of so dear a pleasure would be the limit of my desire. One day I must surely be set free among those delights. Having lived that sweet life, I have no more regrets for the Louvre. Let the same earth cover me which covers my ancestors.

Ode

A RAVEN croaks in front of me, a shadow startles my eyes; two weasels and two foxes cross the path down which I pass; my horse's feet slip, my servant falls in a fit; I hear the thunder crackling; a spectre appears before me; I hear Charon calling me to him, I see the centre of the earth.

Ce ruisseau remonte à sa source;
Un bœuf gravit sur un clocher;
Le sang coule de ce rocher;
Un aspic s'accouple d'une ourse;
Sur le haut d'une vieille tour
Un serpent déchire un vautour;
Le feu brûle dedans la glace;
Le soleil est devenu noir;
Je vois la lune qui va choir;
Cet arbre est sorti de sa place.

Le Matin

L'AURORE sur le front du jour
Sème l'azur, l'or et l'ivoire,
Et le soleil, lassé de boire,
Commence son oblique tour.

Ses chevaux au sortir de l'onde,
De flamme et de clarté couverts,
La bouche et les naseaux ouverts,
Ronflent la lumière du monde.

That stream is flowing backwards; an ox climbs a belfry; blood flows from that rock; an asp couples with a she-bear; at the top of an old tower a snake is tearing up a vulture; fire burns in the ice; the sun has turned black; I see the moon about to fall; that tree has moved from its place.

The Morning

OVER the face of the day the dawn sows azure, gold, and ivory, and the sun, weary of drinking (in the sea), begins its slanting course.

Its horses, coming out of the waves, covered with flame and brightness, with open mouths and nostrils snort out the light of the world.

La lune fuit devant nos yeux,
La nuit a retiré ses voiles,
Peu à peu le front des étoiles
S'unit à la couleur des cieux.

Déjà la diligente avette
Boit la marjolaine et le thym,
Et revient riche du butin
Qu'elle a pris sur le mont Hymette.

Je vois le généreux lion
Qui sort de sa demeure creuse,
Hérissant sa perruque affreuse
Qui fait fuir Endymion.

Sa dame, entrant dans les bocages,
Compte les sangliers qu'elle a pris,
Ou dévale chez les esprits
Errants aux sombres marécages.

The moon flees before our eyes, night has withdrawn her veils,
slowly the face of the stars merges into the colour of the skies.
Already the industrious bee drinks of the marjoram and thyme
and comes back rich with the loot which it has taken on Mount
Hymettus.
I see the noble lion coming out of his hollow cave, bristling his
frightful mane which makes Endymion flee.
His lady,* retreating into the woods, counts the wild boars she
has taken, or goes down among the spirits which wander in the
dark marshes.

* Endymion's lady, the Moon – that is, Diana, huntress and goddess of the underworld.

Je vois les agneaux bondissants
Sur les blés qui ne font que naître :
Cloris, chantant, les mène paître
Parmi ces coteaux verdissants.

Les oiseaux d'un joyeux ramage
En chantant semblent adorer
La lumière qui vient dorer
Leur cabinet et leur plumage.

La charrue écorche la plaine,
Le bouvier qui suit les sillons
Presse de voix et d'aiguillons
Le couple de bœufs qui l'entraîne.

Alix apprête son fuseau ;
Sa mère, qui lui fait la tâche,
Presse le chanvre qu'elle attache
A sa quenouille de roseau.

Une confuse violence
Trouble le calme de la nuit,
Et la lumière avec le bruit
Dissipent l'ombre et le silence.

I see the lambs leaping over the young corn; Chloris, singing, leads them out to graze among those green slopes.

With joyous twitterings the birds seem, as they sing, to worship the light which gilds their little houses and their plumage.

The plough galls the plain; the ploughman, walking along the furrows, urges on with voice and goad the pair of oxen which draw it.

Alix gets her spindle ready; her mother, preparing her work for her, presses the hemp which she attaches to her distaff made of reed.

Confused activity disturbs the calm of the night, and light and noise drive away darkness and silence.

Alidor cherche à son réveil
L'ombre d'Iris qu'il a baisée,
Et pleure en son âme abusée
La fuite d'un si doux sommeil.

Les bêtes sont dans leur tanière
Qui tremblent de voir le soleil;
L'homme, remis par le sommeil,
Reprend son œuvre coutumière.

Le forgeron est au fourneau:
Ois comme le charbon s'allume!
Le fer rouge dessus l'enclume
Étincelle sous le marteau.

Cette chandelle semble morte:
Le jour la fait évanouir;
Le soleil vient nous éblouir:
Vois qu'il passe au travers la porte.

Il est jour, levons-nous, Philis:
Allons à notre jardinage
Voir s'il est, comme ton visage,
Semé de roses et de lis.

Alidor, awakening, looks for the ghost of Iris which he kissed, and weeps in his deluded heart to find that so sweet a dream has fled.

The beasts are in their lairs, trembling to see the sun; man, refreshed by sleep, takes up his usual tasks.

The blacksmith is at the forge; hear the coal roaring into flame! The red-hot iron on the anvil sparks beneath the hammer.

This candle seems dead: the daylight makes it fade; the sun comes to dazzle us: see him coming through the door!

It is day; let us get up, Phyllis: let us go to our garden and see if, like your face, it is sprinkled with roses and lilies.

Les Nautoniers

Les Amours plus mignards à nos rames se lient,
Les Tritons à l'envie nous viennent caresser,
Les vents sont modérés, les vagues s'humilient
Par tous les lieux de l'onde où nous voulons passer.

Avec notre destin va le cours des étoiles,
L'orage ne fait point blêmir nos matelots,
Et jamais Alcyon sans regarder nos voiles
Ne commit sa nichée à la merci des flots.

Notre océan est doux comme les eaux d'Euphrate,
Le Pactole et le Tage sont moins riches que lui,
Ici jamais nocher ne craignit le pirate,
Ni d'un calme trop long ne ressentit l'ennui.

Sous un climat heureux, loin du bruit du tonnerre,
Nous passons à loisir nos jours délicieux,
Et là jamais notre œil ne désira la terre,
Ni sans quelque dédain ne regarda les cieux.

The Mariners

The daintiest Loves cling to our oars, the Tritons come jostling to caress us, the winds are calmed, the waves humble themselves in every part of the ocean where we wish to go.

The course of the stars accompanies our destiny, the storm never makes our seamen blench, and never did Alcyone, without (first) looking at our sails, entrust her nestlings to the mercy of the waves.

Our ocean is as smooth as the waters of Euphrates, the Pactolus and the Tagus are less rich than it, here never did sailor fear the pirate, nor suffer the tedium of too long a calm.

Under a happy clime, far from the sound of thunder, we pass at leisure our delightful days, and here our eyes have never longed for the land, or looked at the skies without some disdain.

Agréables beautés pour qui l'âme soupire,
Éprouvez avec nous un si joyeux destin,
Et nous dirons partout qu'un si rare navire
Ne fut jamais chargé d'un si rare butin.

Épigramme

CETTE femme a fait comme Troie:
De braves gens sans aucun fruit
Furent dix ans à cette proie,
Un cheval n'y fut qu'une nuit.

ANTOINE-GIRARD DE SAINT-AMANT

La Solitude

OH, QUE j'aime la solitude!
Que ces lieux sacrés à la nuit,
Éloignés du monde et du bruit,
Plaisent à mon inquiétude!
Mon Dieu! que mes yeux sont contents
De voir ces bois, qui se trouvèrent

Agreeable beauties for whom the heart sighs, come and taste with us such a joyful lot, and we will tell the whole world that so rare a ship has never been laden with so rare a prize.

Epigram

THIS woman behaved like Troy: gallant men without success spent ten years besieging her; a horse succeeded in one night.

Solitude

OH, how I love solitude! How much these places, sacred to night, far removed from men and noise, please my unquiet mind. God, how contented are my eyes to see these woods, which were there

A la nativité du temps,
Et que tous les siècles révèrent,
Être encore aussi beaux et verts,
Qu'aux premiers jours de l'univers!

Un gai zéphire les caresse
D'un mouvement doux et flatteur.
Rien que leur extrême hauteur
Ne fait remarquer leur vieillesse.
Jadis Pan et ses demi-dieux
Y vinrent chercher du refuge
Quand Jupiter ouvrit les cieux
Pour nous envoyer le déluge,
Et, se sauvant sur leurs rameaux,
A peine virent-ils les eaux.

Que sur cette épine fleurie,
Dont le printemps est amoureux,
Philomèle, au chant langoureux,
Entretient bien ma rêverie!
Que je prends de plaisir à voir
Ces monts pendant en précipices,

at the birth of time and which all the ages respect, still as lovely and
as green as in the first days of creation.

A gay zephyr fondles them softly and caressingly. Only their
great height shows their age. In days of old, Pan and his demi-
gods came to seek shelter in them, when Jupiter opened the
heavens to send us down the Flood, and – escaping on to their
branches – they hardly saw the waters.

How well on this flowery thorn-bush, with which the spring is
in love, does Philomel with languorous song maintain my reverie.
What pleasure I find in seeing these mountains hanging in preci-

Qui, pour les coups du désespoir,
Sont aux malheureux si propices,
Quand la cruauté de leur sort
Les force à rechercher la mort!

Que je trouve doux le ravage
De ces fiers torrents vagabonds
Qui se précipitent par bonds
Dans ce vallon vert et sauvage!
Puis, glissant sous les arbrisseaux,
Ainsi que des serpents sur l'herbe,
Se changent en plaisants ruisseaux,
Où quelque naïade superbe
Règne comme en son lit natal
Dessus un trône de cristal!

Que j'aime ce marais paisible!
Il est tout bordé d'alisiers,
D'aulnes, de saules et d'osiers,
A qui le fer n'est point nuisible.
Les nymphes, y cherchant le frais,
S'y viennent fournir de quenouilles,
De pipeaux, de joncs et de glais,
Où l'on voit sauter les grenouilles

pices which, for despairing acts, are so suitable for poor wretches, when the cruelty of their lot forces them to seek out death.

How sweet I find the savage force of these fierce roving torrents which rush leaping down into this green and wild valley, then, gliding beneath the bushes, like snakes over the grass, are changed into delightful streams, in which some haughty naiad reigns as though on her native bed upon a crystal throne.

How I love this peaceful pond! It is fringed with rowan-trees, alders, willows, and osiers, which the axe never harms. The nymphs, seeking some cool place, come here to provide themselves with bulrushes, reed-pipes, reeds, and irises, among which you see

ANTOINE-GIRARD DE SAINT-AMANT

Qui de frayeur s'y vont cacher
Sitôt qu'on veut s'en approcher.

Là, cent mille oiseaux aquatiques
Vivent, sans craindre, en leur repos,
Le giboyeur fin et dispos,
Avec ses mortelles pratiques.
L'un, tout joyeux d'un si beau jour,
S'amuse à becqueter sa plume;
L'autre alentit le feu d'amour
Qui dans l'eau même se consume,
Et prennent tous innocemment
Leur plaisir en cet élément.

Jamais l'été ni la froidure
N'ont vu passer dessus cette eau
Nulle charrette ni bateau,
Depuis que l'un et l'autre dure;
Jamais voyageur altéré
N'y fit servir sa main de tasse;
Jamais chevreuil désespéré
N'y finit sa vie à la chasse;
Et jamais le traître hameçon
N'en fit sortir aucun poisson.

the frogs jumping and hiding themselves in panic as soon as you try to approach.

There, a myriad water-fowl live peacefully with no fear of the cunning, watchful fowler with his deadly practices. One, delighting in such a lovely day, passes the time preening its feathers. Another abates the fire of love, which is consumed in the water itself, and all of them innocently take their pleasure in that element.

Never have summer or winter's cold seen cart or boat pass over this water since either (winter or summer) endures. Never has thirsty traveller cupped his hand in it. Never has desperate roe-buck ended his life there in the hunt; and never did the treacherous hook bring any fish from out of it.

Que j'aime à voir la décadence
De ces vieux châteaux ruinés,
Contre qui les ans mutinés
Ont déployé leur insolence!
Les sorciers y font leur sabat;
Les démons follets s'y retirent,
Qui d'un malicieux ébat
Trompent nos sens et nous martirent;
Là se nichent en mille trous
Les couleuvres et les hiboux.

L'orfraie, avec ses cris funèbres,
Mortels augures des destins,
Fait rire et danser les lutins
Dans ces lieux remplis de ténèbres.
Sous un chevron de bois maudit
Y branle le squelette horrible
D'un pauvre amant qui se pendit
Pour une bergère insensible,
Qui d'un seul regard de pitié
Ne daigna voir son amitié.

Aussi le Ciel, juge équitable,
Qui maintient les lois en vigueur,

How I love to see the decay of these old ruined castles, against which the rebellious years have flaunted their insolence! The wizards hold their sabbath there, in there lurk the elfish goblins, who delude our senses and plague us with their mischievous sport; there in countless holes adders and owls nest.

The screech-owl, with its baleful cries, deadly harbingers of doom, makes the goblins laugh and dance in these haunts filled with darkness. Under a beam of wood accursed jigs the fearful skeleton of a poor lover who hanged himself for a stony-hearted shepherd-ess, who did not deign to favour his love with a single pitying glance.

And so heaven, the impartial judge who enforces the laws,

Prononça contre sa rigueur
Une sentence épouvantable:
Autour de ces vieux ossements
Son ombre, aux peines condamnée,
Lamente en longs gémissements
Sa malheureuse destinée,
Ayant, pour croître son effroi,
Toujours son crime devant soi.

Là se trouvent sur quelques marbres
Des devises du temps passé;
Ici l'âge a presque effacé
Des chiffres taillés sur les arbres;
Le plancher du lieu le plus haut
Est tombé jusque dans la cave
Que la limace et le crapaud
Souillent de venin et de bave;
Le lierre y croît au foyer,
A l'ombrage d'un grand noyer ...

Le Printemps des environs de Paris

ZÉPHIRE a bien raison d'être amoureux de Flore;
C'est le plus bel objet dont il puisse jouir;

pronounced a dreadful sentence upon her cruelty: around these ancient bones, her ghost, condemned to torments, laments its unhappy fate with long-drawn moans – having, to increase its horror, its crime always present before it.

There are seen on marble slabs emblems of times gone by; here, the years have almost effaced initials carved on the trees; the floor of the topmost room has fallen right through to the cellar, which the slug and the toad foul with poison and with slime; there, the ivy grows on the hearth in the shade of a great walnut-tree.

Spring on the outskirts of Paris

ZEPHYR has good reason to be in love with Flora; she is the

On voit à son éclat les soins s'évanouir,
Comme les libertés devant l'œil que j'adore.

Qui ne serait ravi d'entendre sous l'aurore
Les miracles volants qu'au bois je viens d'ouir!
J'en sens avec les fleurs mon cœur s'épanouir,
Et mon luth négligé leur veut répondre encore.

L'herbe sourit à l'air d'un air voluptueux;
J'aperçois de ce bord fertile et tortueux
Le doux feu du soleil flatter le sein de l'onde.

Le soir et le matin la Nuit baise le Jour;
Tout aime, tout s'embrase, et je crois que le monde
Ne renaît au printemps que pour mourir d'amour.

L'Hiver des Alpes

CES atomes de feu qui sur la neige brillent,
Ces étincelles d'or, d'azur et de cristal
Dont l'hiver, au soleil, d'un lustre oriental
Pare ses cheveux blancs que les vents éparpillent;

loveliest sight which he can enjoy. Before her radiance all cares are seen to vanish, as men's freedoms do before the eyes which I adore.

Who would not be ravished to hear at dawn the flying miracles which I have just heard in the wood! Thanks to them I feel my heart blossoming with the flowers, and my neglected lute longs once again to answer them.

With a voluptuous air the grass smiles at the air; from this fertile and winding bank I see the gentle fire of the sun caressing the bosom of the water.

At evening and morning, night kisses day; all things love, all grow hot, and I believe that the world is reborn in spring only to die of love.

Winter in the Alps

THESE fiery atoms glittering on the snow, these sparks of gold, of azure, and of crystal with which Winter, in sunshine, with oriental splendour adorns its white hair tossed by the winds;

Ce beau coton du ciel de quoi les monts s'habillent,
Ce pavé transparent fait du second métal,
Et cet air net et sain, propre à l'esprit vital,
Sont si doux à mes yeux que d'aise ils en pétillent.

Cette saison me plaît, j'en aime la froideur;
Sa robe d'innocence et de pure candeur
Couvre en quelque façon les crimes de la terre.

Aussi l'Olympien la voit d'un front humain;
Sa colère l'épargne, et jamais le tonnerre
Pour désoler ses jours ne partit de sa main.

Plainte sur la mort de Sylvie

Ruisseau qui cours après toi-même
Et qui te fuis toi-même aussi,
Arrête un peu ton onde ici
Pour écouter mon deuil extrême.
Puis, quand tu l'auras su, va-t'en dire à la mer
Qu'elle n'a rien de plus amer.

That fine skiey cotton with which the mountains clothe themselves, that transparent pavement made of the second metal [silver], and this clean, healthy air, favourable to the vital spirit, are so sweet to my eyes that they sparkle with delight.

This season pleases me, I like its cold. Its mantle of innocence and of candid purity in some sort covers the crimes of the earth.

And so Olympian Jove turns a kindly face upon it. His anger spares it and never was the thunder loosed from his hand to sadden its days.

Dirge for the Death of Silvia

Stream who hasten after yourself, and flee from yourself also, halt your waters here for a moment and give ear to my heavy grief. Then, when you have heard it, go and tell the sea that it has nothing more bitter than this.

Raconte-lui comme Sylvie,
Qui seule gouverne mon sort,
A reçu le coup de la mort
Au plus bel âge de la vie,
Et que cet accident triomphe en même jour
De toutes les forces d'Amour.

Las! je n'en puis dire autre chose,
Mes soupirs tranchent mon discours.
Adieu, ruisseau, reprends ton cours
Qui, non plus que moi, se repose;
Que si, par mes regrets, j'ai bien pu t'arrêter,
Voici des pleurs pour te hâter.

Le Melon

... C'EN est fait, le voilà coupé,
Et mon espoir n'est point trompé.
O dieux! que l'éclat qu'il me lance
M'en confirme bien l'excellence!
Qui vit jamais un si beau teint!
D'un jaune sanguin il se peint;
Il est massif jusques au centre,
Il a peu de grains dans le ventre,

Tell it how Silvia, sole mistress of my fate, has suffered death's blow in the flower of life, and that this disaster has discomfited in one day all the forces of love.

Alas, I can say no more. My sighs cut short my words. Farewell stream, flow on your course, which knows repose no more than I. And if my lamentations have been able to halt you, here are tears to hasten you on.

The Melon

WELL, that's it. Now it is cut, and my hopes are not disappointed. O gods, the radiance that it casts leaves no doubt of its excellence! Who ever saw such a lovely hue! It is tinted a reddish yellow; it is firm right to the centre, it has few pips in its belly, and those few,

Et ce peu-là, je pense encor
Que ce soient autant de grains d'or;
Il est sec, son écorce est mince;
Bref, c'est un vrai manger de prince;
Mais, bien que je ne le sois pas,
J'en ferai pourtant un repas.
    Ha! soutenez-moi, je me pâme!
Ce morceau me chatouille l'âme.
Il rend une douce liqueur
Qui me va confire le cœur;
Mon appétit se rassasie
De pure et nouvelle ambroisie,
Et mes sens, par le goût séduits,
Au nombre d'un sont tous réduits.

    Non, le coco, fruit délectable,
Qui lui tout seul fournit la table
De tous les mets que le désir
Puisse imaginer et choisir,
Ni les baisers d'une maîtresse,
Quand elle-même nous caresse,
Ni ce qu'on tire des roseaux
Que Crète nourrit dans ses eaux,
Ni le cher abricot, que j'aime,
Ni la fraise avecque la crème,

I really believe, are so many grains of gold. It is not watery, its rind is thin: in short, a feast for a king. But, although I am not one, yet will I make a meal of it.

Ha! Hold me up, I swoon! This delicious morsel tickles my very soul. It oozes a sweet juice which will steep my heart in ecstasy. My appetite is sated with a new and pure ambrosia, and all my senses, captivated by taste, are concentrated into one.

No, neither the coconut, that delectable fruit which by itself provides the table with all the dishes which desire can imagine and choose, nor the kisses of a mistress when she herself caresses us, nor what is drawn from the [sugar] canes which Crete grows in its waters, nor the dear apricot which I love, nor the strawberry with

Ni la manne qui vient du ciel,
Ni le pur aliment du miel,
Ni la poire de Tours sacrée,
Ni la verte figue sucrée,
Ni la prune au jus délicat,
Ni même le raisin muscat
(Parole pour moi bien étrange),
Ne sont qu'amertume et que fange
Au prix de ce MELON divin,
Honneur du climat angevin.

... O manger précieux! délices de la bouche!
O doux reptile herbu, rampant sur une couche!
O beaucoup mieux que l'or, chef-d'œuvre d'Apollon!
O fleur de tous les fruits! O ravissant MELON!
Les hommes de la cour seront gens de parole,
Les bordels de Rouen seront francs de vérole,
Sans vermine et sans gale on verra les pédants,
Les preneurs de petun auront de belles dents,
Les femmes des badauds ne seront plus coquettes,
Les corps pleins de santé se plairont aux cliquettes,
Les amoureux transis ne seront plus jaloux,
Les paisibles bourgeois hanteront les filous,

cream, nor the manna which falls from heaven, nor the sacred pear of Tours, nor the green and sugared fig, nor the plum with delicate juice, nor even the muscat grape (strange indeed that *I* should say so), are more than gall and mud compared to this divine MELON, the glory of the Angevin clime.

O precious food, delight of the palate! O sweet grassy reptile, crawling on your green couch! O better far than gold, O Sun God's masterpiece! O flower of all the fruits, ravishing MELON! The men of the Court will be men of their word, the brothels of Rouen will be free of the pox, de-loused and clear-skinned will pedants be seen, tobacco-users will have white teeth, fools will no longer have flighty wives, healthy bodies will delight in lepers' rattles, moonstruck lovers will cease to be jealous, peaceful citizens will consort with thieves, the best inns will become deserted, the

Les meilleurs cabarets deviendront solitaires,
Les chantres du Pont-Neuf diront de hauts mystères,
Les pauvres Quinze-Vingts vaudront trois cents argus,
Les esprits doux du temps paraîtront fort aigus,
Maillet fera des vers aussi bien que Malherbe,
Je haïrai Faret, qui se rendra superbe,
Pour amasser des biens avare je serai,
Pour devenir plus grand mon cœur j'abaisserai,
Bref, O MELON sucrin, pour t'accabler de gloire,
Des faveurs de Margot je perdrai la mémoire
Avant que je t'oublie et que ton goût charmant
Soit biffé des cahiers du bon gros SAINT-AMANT.

L'Enamouré

PARBIEU! j'en tiens, c'est tout de bon,
Ma libre humeur en a dans l'aile,
Puisque je préfère au jambon
Le visage d'une donzelle.
Je suis pris dans le doux lien
De l'archerot idalien.

ballad-singers of the Pont Neuf will speak high mysteries, the poor Fifteen-Score (an institution for the blind) will be as good as three hundred Arguses, the simple-minded of this age will seem very acute, Maillet will write verses as good as Malherbe's, I shall take to hating Faret, who will grow pompous, I shall be greedy to amass riches; to become greater I will demean my heart, in short, O sugary MELON, to heap you with glory, I will lose the memory of Margot's favours before I forget you and your delightful taste is crossed off the books of good fat SAINT-AMANT.

The Lovesick Swain

OD'S LIFE! I've caught it, properly. My roving fancy has been winged, since I prefer the face of a damsel to ham. I am caught in the sweet snare of the Idalian archer-boy. The godlet son of the

Ce dieutelet, fils de Cyprine,
Avecques son arc mi-courbé,
A féru ma rude poitrine
Et m'a fait venir à jubé.

Mon esprit a changé d'habit:
Il n'est plus vêtu de revêche;
Il se raffine et se fourbit
Aux yeux de ma belle chevêche.
Plus aigu, plus clair et plus net
Qu'une dague de cabinet,
Il estocade la tristesse,
Et, la chassant d'autour de soi,
Se vante que la politesse
Ne marche plus qu'avecques moi.

Je me fais friser tous les jours,
On me relève la moustache;
Je n'entrecoupe mes discours
Que de rots d'ambre et de pistache;
J'ai fait banqueroute au petun;
L'excès du vin m'est importun;
Dix pintes par jour me suffisent:

Cyprian with his curving bow has pierced my rugged breast and made me come to heel.

My wit has changed its garb: it is no longer clad in homespun. It grows refined and polished before the eyes of my pretty owl. Sharper, brighter, and more sparkling than some toy dagger, it thrusts and cuts at melancholy and, driving it from all around, boasts that true refinement walks only now with me.

I have my beard curled every day, the ends of my moustache are twirled up. I only punctuate my conversation with belches of pistachio and amber. I have driven the tobacconists bankrupt. Excess of wine is distasteful to me. Ten pints a day suffice me *; and

* More accurately, about 16 pints. The *pinte* is a larger measure than the English pint.

Encore, ô falotte beauté
Dont les regards me déconfisent,
Est-ce pour boire à ta santé!

Le Paresseux

Accablé de paresse et de mélancolie,
Je rêve dans un lit où je suis fagoté
Comme un lièvre sans os qui dort dans un pâté,
Ou comme un Don Quichotte en sa morne folie.

Là, sans me soucier des guerres d'Italie,
Du Comte Palatin ni de sa royauté,
Je consacre un bel hymne à cette oisiveté
Où mon âme en langueur est comme ensevelie.

Je trouve ce plaisir si doux et si charmant
Que je crois que les biens me viendront en dormant,
Puisque je vois déjà s'en enfler ma bedaine.

then, O pallid beauty, whose looks undo me utterly, it is to drink
to your health.

The Idler

Weighed down with sloth and melancholy, I dream in a bed in
which I lie bundled like a filleted hare sleeping in a pie, or like a
Don Quixote in his gloomy madness.

There, without troubling about the wars in Italy, or the Count
Palatine and his titles of royalty, I devote a fine hymn to this idleness in which my languid soul is as good as buried.

I find this pleasure so sweet and delightful that I think that good
things will come to me while sleeping, since already I see my belly
swelling with them.

And so much do I hate work that, with my eyes half-closed and
one hand outside the sheets, dear Baudoin, I could only just bring
myself to write you these verses.

Et hais tant le travail que, les yeux entr'ouverts,
Une main hors des draps, cher Baudoin, à peine
Ai-je pu me résoudre à t'écrire ces vers.

[*Sonnet inachevé*]

FAGOTÉ plaisamment comme un vrai Simonnet,
Pied chaussé, l'autre nu, main au nez, l'autre en poche,
J'arpente un vieux grenier, portant sur ma caboche
Un coffin de Hollande en guise de bonnet.

Là, faisant quelquefois le saut du sansonnet
Et dandinant du cul comme un sonneur de cloche,
Je m'égueule de rire, écrivant d'une broche
En mots de Pathelin ce grotesque sonnet.

Mes esprits, à cheval sur des coquecigrues,
Ainsi que papillons s'envolent dans les nues,
Y cherchant quelque fin qu'on ne puisse trouver.
Nargue! C'est trop rêver, c'est trop ronger ses ongles:
Si quelqu'un sait la rime, il peut bien l'achever.

Unfinished Sonnet

WEIRDLY got-up like a real guy, one foot shod, the other bare,
one hand to my nose, the other in my pocket, I pace round an old
garret, wearing on my noodle a Dutch basket to serve as a night-
cap.
There, sometimes hopping like a dickey-bird and waggling my
bottom like a bell-ringer, I split my sides with laughing as I write
this grotesque sonnet in comic words with a roasting-spit.
My spirits, riding on never-never fancies, soar up like butterflies
into the clouds, in search of some ending which can't be found.
Hell, that's enough brooding, enough gnawing of nails. If anyone knows the rhyme, he can finish it.

CLAUDE DE MALLEVILLE

La Belle Matineuse

Le silence régnait sur la terre et sur l'onde,
L'air devenait serein et l'Olympe vermeil,
Et l'amoureux Zéphyre, affranchi du sommeil,
Ressuscitait les fleurs d'une haleine féconde.

L'Aurore déployait l'or de sa tresse blonde
Et semait de rubis le chemin du Soleil:
Enfin ce dieu venait en plus grand appareil
Qu'il soit jamais venu pour éclairer le monde,

Quand la jeune Philis, au visage riant,
Sortant de son palais plus clair que l'orient,
Fit voir une lumière et plus vive et plus belle.

Sacré flambeau du jour, n'en soyez point jaloux,
Vous parûtes alors aussi peu devant elle
Que les feux de la nuit avaient fait devant vous.

The Fair Nymph of Dawn

Silence reigned over earth and water, the sky was growing clear and Olympus rosy, and the amorous Zephyr, released from sleep, was reviving the flowers with his life-giving breath.

The Dawn was displaying the gold of her yellow locks and strewing the path of the Sun with rubies: in short, that god was coming in greater pomp than he has ever come to light the world,

when young Phyllis, with smiling face, coming out from her palace brighter than the Orient, showed us a more brilliant and lovelier light.

Sacred lamp of day, be not jealous, but you then appeared of as little account before her as the stars of the night had done before you.

VINCENT VOITURE

La Belle Matineuse

DES portes du matin l'amante de Céphale
Ses roses épandait dans le milieu des airs,
Et jetait sur les cieux nouvellement ouverts
Ces traits d'or et d'azur qu'en naissant elle étale,

Quand la nymphe divine, à mon repos fatale,
Apparut, et brilla de tant d'attraits divers
Qu'il semblait qu'elle seule éclairait l'univers
Et remplissait de feux la rive orientale.

Le Soleil, se hâtant pour la gloire des cieux,
Vint opposer sa flamme à l'éclat de ses yeux
Et prit tous les rayons dont l'Olympe se dore.

L'onde, la terre et l'air s'allumaient à l'entour;
Mais auprès de Philis on le prit pour l'aurore,
Et l'on crut que Philis était l'astre du jour.

The Fair Nymph of Dawn

FROM the gates of the morning the mistress of Cephalus (the Dawn) was scattering her roses through the air, and was casting on the newly opened skies those shafts of gold and azure which she displays at her birth,

When that heavenly nymph, fatal to my peace, appeared and shone with so many varied charms that it seemed that she alone gave light to the world and filled the eastern shore with fire.

The Sun, hastening on for the honour of the heavens, came to parry the brightness of her eyes with his flame, and took all the beams with which Olympus is gilded.

The sea, the earth, and the air grew bright all around; but beside Phyllis he was taken for the dawn, and they thought that Phyllis was the star of day (the sun himself).

Sur sa maîtresse rencontrée en habit de garçon,
un soir de carnaval

... Un soir que j'attendais la belle
Qui depuis deux ans m'ensorcelle,
Je vis comme tombé des cieux
Ce Narcisse, objet de ma flamme,
Et dès qu'il fut devant mes yeux,
Je le sentis dedans mon âme.

Sa face riante et naïve
Jetait une flamme si vive
Et tant de rayons alentour,
Qu'à l'éclat de cette lumière
Je doutai que ce fût l'Amour
Avecque les yeux de sa mère.

Mille fleurs fraîchement écloses,
Les lis, les œillets et les roses
Couvraient la neige de son teint.

On His Mistress Encountered in Boy's Clothes,
One Evening in Carnival Time

One evening, when I was waiting for the lovely girl who has bewitched me for the past two years, I saw, as though fallen from the
skies, this Narcissus, the object of my passion, and no sooner was
he before my eyes than I felt him in my heart.

His laughing and open face cast so bright a flame and so many
beams around him, that by the splendour of that light, I almost believed that he was Love, with the eyes of his mother Venus.

A thousand newly blossoming flowers, lilies, carnations, and
roses, covered the snow of his complexion. But beneath those

Mais dessous ces fleurs entassées
Le serpent dont je fus atteint
Avait ses embûches dressées.

Sur un front blanc comme l'ivoire
Deux petits arcs de couleur noire
Étaient mignardement voûtés;
D'où ce dieu qui me fait la guerre,
Foulant aux pieds mes libertés,
Triomphe sur toute la terre.

Ses yeux, le paradis des âmes,
Pleins de ris, d'attraits et de flammes,
Faisaient de la nuit un beau jour:
Astres de divines puissances,
De qui l'empire de l'amour
Prend ses meilleures influences.

Surtout il avait une grâce,
Un je ne sais quoi qui surpasse
De l'Amour les plus doux appas,
Un ris qui ne se peut décrire,
Un air que les autres n'ont pas,
Que l'on voit, et qu'on ne peut dire ...

heaped-up flowers the serpent whose fangs I had felt had his ambush ready.

On a brow as white as ivory, two little dark bows were daintily curved; with which that god who harasses me, trampling my freedom underfoot, triumphs over the whole world.

His eyes, the paradise of hearts, full of laughter, charms, and fire, turned the night into day: stars of divine power, from which the rule of love derives its strongest influence.

He had, above all, a grace, a certain quality which goes beyond the sweetest charms of Love, a smile which cannot be described, a look which others lack, which is seen and cannot be told in words.

L'Année est bonne

LES demoiselles de ce temps
Ont, depuis peu, beaucoup d'amants.
On dit qu'il n'en manque à personne:
    L'année est bonne.

Nous avons vu, les ans passés,
Que les galants étaient glacés.
Mais maintenant, tout en foisonne:
    L'année est bonne.

Le temps n'est pas bien loin encor
Qu'ils se vendaient au poids de l'or,
Et, pour le présent, on les donne:
    L'année est bonne.

Le soleil, de nous rapproché,
Rend le monde plus échauffé.
L'amour règne, le sang bouillonne:
    L'année est bonne ...

It's a good year

THE young ladies of this time have had many lovers lately. They
say that no one goes without. It's a good year.

We have seen, in previous years, that the gallants were nipped by
frost. But now the place abounds with them. It's a good year.

The time is not so distant yet when they were sold for their
weight in gold, but just now they are given away. It's a good year.

The sun, drawing closer to us, makes the world warmer. Love
reigns, blood grows hot. It's a good year.

A une demoiselle qui avait les manches de sa
chemise retroussées et sales

Vous, qui tenez incessamment
Cent amants dedans votre manche,
Tenez-les au moins proprement,
Et faites qu'elle soit plus blanche.

Vous pouvez bien avec raison,
Usant des droits de la victoire,
Mettre vos galants en prison,
Mais qu'elle ne soit pas si noire.

Mon cœur, qui vous est si dévot,
Et que vous réduisez en cendre,
Vous le tenez dans un cachot
Comme un prisonnier qu'on va pendre.

Est-ce que, brûlant nuit et jour,
Je remplis ce lieu de fumée,
Et que le feu de mon amour
En a fait une cheminée?

To a Young Lady Who Wore the Sleeves of her Shift
Rolled Up and Dirty

You, who constantly keep a hundred lovers up your sleeve, at least
keep them cleanly and see that your sleeve is whiter.

You may quite legitimately, exercising a conqueror's rights, put
your suitors in prison, but don't let it be such a dark one.

My heart, which is so devoted to you, and which you reduce to
ashes – you keep it in a dungeon, like a prisoner waiting to be
hanged.

Can it be that, burning night and day, I fill this place with smoke
and that the fire of my love has made a chimney of it?

Rondeau

Vous l'entendez mieux que je ne pensois.
Si quelque amant bien-disant et matois
Vous croit payer en vous nommant son âme,
C'est du latin qui passe votre gamme;
Vous n'entendez des termes si courtois.

Mais s'il en vient qui dise à haute voix
Qu'il veut prouver, fût-il Turc ou Anglois,
Par beaux effets la grandeur de sa flamme,
　　　Vous l'entendez.

Je donnerai telle somme par mois:
Outre cela, joyaux, perles de choix,
Satin, velours à souhait, à madame.
Cet entretien vous charme et vous enflamme;
C'est dire d'or et parler bon françois.
　　　Vous l'entendez.

Rondeau

You understand better than I thought. If some smooth-tongued and crafty lover thinks to pay you by speaking of his heart, that is Greek and quite beyond you; you do not understand such courtly terms.

But if one comes proclaiming loudly that he will prove, be he Turk or Englishman, the strength of his passion with goods and cash, you understand him.

I will give such-and-such a sum per month; in addition jewels, choice pearls, satin, velvet as required, to Madam. This declaration delights and inflames you. 'Tis golden speech and good plain French. You understand.

Rondeau

Six rois prièrent l'autre jour
Tyrcis de leur faire la cour;
Mais il soufflait un vent de bise
Qui perçait jusqu'à la chemise.
Cela le fit demeurer court.

Il a le ventre d'un tambour,
Ce qui le rend tant soit peu lourd
Et fait que parfois il méprise
        Six rois.

Il ne fait point cas de l'amour.
Quand on l'appelle il fait le sourd;
Mais pour prêter son entremise
En quelque fâcheuse entreprise,
Il ne le ferait jamais pour
        Six rois.

Rondeau *

Six kings begged Tircis to pay court to them the other day; but
an icy wind was blowing which cut right through to your shirt.
That pulled him up short

He has a belly like a drum, which makes him just a little sluggish
and causes him occasionally to despise six kings.

He doesn't think much of love. When you call him he pretends
not to hear. But as for lending his services for any dubious enter-
prise, he would never do it for six kings.

---

* Written for a certain François Coquet, renowned for his fat-
ness, who once remarked: 'I would not go for six kings.'

Chanson sur l'air des Lanturlu

L E roi notre sire
Pour bonnes raisons
Que l'on n'ose dire
Et que nous taisons,
Nous a fait défense
De plus chanter *lanturlu*,
Lanturlu, lanturlu, lanturlu, lanturlu.

La reine sa mère
Reviendra bientôt,
Et Monsieur son frère
Ne dira plus mot.
Il sera paisible
Pourvu qu'on ne chante plus
Lanturlu, lanturlu, lanturlu, lanturlu.

De la Grand'Bretagne
Les ambassadeurs,
Ceux du roi d'Espagne
Et des Électeurs,
Se sont venus plaindre
D'avoir partout entendu
Lanturlu, lanturlu, lanturlu, lanturlu.

Song to the tune of Lanturlu *

O U R sire the King, for good reasons, which one dare not disclose and which we do not reveal, has forbidden us to go on singing *taradiddle, taradiddle, taradiddle, taradiddle, taradiddle.*

The Queen his mother will soon return, and his brother *Monsieur* will say no more. He will be quiet, provided there is no more singing of *taradiddle, etc.*

The ambassadors of Great Britain, of the King of Spain, and of the Electors came to complain of always hearing *taradiddle, etc.*

---

* *Lanturlu* was the refrain of a popular mocking song in Richelieu's time.

Ils ont fait leur plainte
Fort éloquemment,
Et parlé sans crainte
Du gouvernement.
Pour les satisfaire,
Le roi leur a répondu:
Lanturlu, lanturlu, lanturlu, lanturlu.

Dans cette querelle
Le bon cardinal,
Dont l'âme fidèle
Ne pense à nul mal,
A promis merveilles
Et puis a dit à Bautru:
Lanturlu, lanturlu, lanturlu, lanturlu.

Dessus cette affaire
Le nonce parla,
Et notre Saint-Père,
Entendant cela,
Au milieu de Rome
S'écria comme un pendu:
Lanturlu, lanturlu, lanturlu, lanturlu.

They made their complaint most eloquently, and spoke very frankly about the Government. To satisfy them, the King replied: *Taradiddle, etc.*

In this dispute the good Cardinal, whose loyal heart thinks no evil, promised the moon and then said to Bautru: *Taradiddle, etc.*

The nuncio spoke about this matter, and our Holy Father, hearing of it, screamed out like a hanged man in the middle of Rome: *Taradiddle, etc.*

Pour bannir de France
Ces troubles nouveaux,
Avec grand'prudence
Le Garde des Sceaux
A scellé des lettres
Dont voici le contenu:
Lanturlu, lanturlu, lanturlu, lanturlu.

Étrenne d'une tortue

POUR vous venir baiser la main
Je partis, au mois de septembre,
Du bout du faubourg Saint-Germain;
Et nuit et jour faisant chemin,
J'arrivai hier céans à la fin de décembre.
Quelquefois Salladin va plus diligemment,
Mais il n'est rien de tel que d'aller sûrement.
Voulant doncque vous étrenner,
Pour vous faire heureusement vivre
Je n'ai rien de meilleur que je puisse donner
Si ce n'est mon exemple à suivre.

To banish from France these new disturbances, the Lord Privy
Seal, with great discretion, sealed dispatches of which this was the
content: *Taradiddle, taradiddle, taradiddle, taradiddle.*

On the New-Year Gift of a Tortoise *

To come and kiss your hand, I set out in September from the end
of the Faubourg Saint-Germain; and travelling night and day, I
arrived in this house yesterday at the end of December. Sometimes
Salladin † goes more speedily, but there is nothing like going
surely.

So wishing to bring you a New Year gift, to help you to live
happily I have nothing better to offer you than my own example.

* Sent by a lady with three other animals to a certain Monsieur
Esprit.   † Richelieu's courier.

Vous autres beaux esprits battez trop de pays.
    Croyez-moi, suivez mon avis.
Soit que vous poursuiviez évêché, femme ou fille,
Faites tout comme moi, hâtez-vous lentement;
Ne formez qu'un dessein, suivez-le constamment.
Mais c'est trop discourir, je rentre en ma coquille.

Pour Madame d'Aiguillon

"La terre brillante de fleurs
    Fait éclater mille couleurs
    D'aujourd'hui seulement connues.
    L'astre du jour, en souriant,
    Jette sur la face des nues
L'or et l'azur dont il peint l'orient.

"Le ciel est couvert de saphirs,
    Les doux et gracieux zéphirs
    Soupirent mieux que de coutume;
    L'aurore a le teint plus vermeil,
    Et semble que le jour s'allume
D'un plus beau feu que celui du soleil.

You brilliant minds race about too much. Believe me, follow my advice. Whether you are after a bishopric, a woman, or a girl, do everything as I do, make haste slowly. Form a single plan and follow it through steadily. But that's quite enough talk, I'm going back into my shell.

For Madame d'Aiguillon

'The earth, gleaming with flowers, blazes out in a thousand colours, unknown until today. The day-star smilingly casts upon the face of the clouds the gold and azure with which he paints the east.

'The sky is covered with sapphires, the soft and gracious zephyrs sigh more sweetly than usual; the dawn has a rosier hue, and it seems that the day is lit with a lovelier light than that of the sun.

«Les oiseaux aux charmantes voix
Mieux que jamais dedans ce bois
Se font une amoureuse guerre.
Sans doute la troupe des dieux
A quitté le ciel pour la terre,
Ou la divine Oronte est dans ces lieux.

«Oronte, dont les yeux vainqueurs
Ont assujetti mille cœurs,
Dont elle refuse l'hommage;
Qui naissant a reçu des cieux
Toutes les grâces en partage
Et les faveurs des hommes et des dieux.

«Par la force de ses attraits,
Ces vieux troncs, ces noires forêts
Ressentent l'amoureuse flamme.
Tout cède à des charmes si chers,
Et ses yeux qui nous ôtent l'âme
D'un seul regard la donnent aux rochers.»

'The sweet-voiced birds wage their amorous war more tunefully than ever in this wood. No doubt the troop of the gods has left heaven for earth, or divine Oronte is in this place.

'Oronte, whose conquering eyes have subdued a thousand hearts, whose homage she refuses; who at her birth received from heaven all the graces as her gift, and the favours of men and of gods.

'By the power of her attractions, these ancient trunks, these dark forests, feel the flame of love. All things yield before such precious charms, and her eyes, which steal away our hearts, with a single glance give a heart to the rocks.'

Ainsi, sortant de Fontenay
Dedans le chemin de Gournay,
Faisant des vers à l'aventure
Suivant l'humeur qui l'emportait,
L'insensible et le froid Voiture
Parlait d'amour, comme s'il en sentait.

Les nymphes des eaux et des bois,
Écoutant sa dolente voix,
Ne purent s'empêcher de rire.
Mais un faune qui l'entendit
Aux dryades se prit à dire:
«Possible est-il plus vrai qu'il ne le dit.»

CHARLES VION DE DALIBRAY

Sonnet bachique

Je ne vais point aux coups exposer ma bedaine,
Moi qui ne suis connu ni d'Armand ni du Roi;
Je veux savoir combien un poltron comme moi
Peut vivre n'étant point soldat ni capitaine.

So, coming out from Fontenay along the Gournay road, idly composing verse as the mood inspired him, the cold, unfeeling Voiture spoke of love as though he felt it.

The nymphs of the woods and waters, hearing his doleful voice, could not restrain their laughter. But a faun who heard him turned and said to the dryads: 'Perhaps he is more sincere than he sounds.'

Drinking Sonnet

I am not going to expose my paunch to blows, I who am unknown both to Armand (Richelieu) and the King; I want to find out how long a coward like myself can live without being a soldier or captain.

Je mourrais, s'il fallait qu'au milieu d'une plaine
Je fusse estropié de ce bras dont je bois;
Ne me conte donc plus qu'on meurt autant chez soi
A table, entre les pots, qu'où ta valeur te mène.

Ne me conte donc plus qu'en l'ardeur des combats
On se rend immortel par un noble trépas,
Cela ne fera point que j'aille à l'escarmouche.

Je veux mourir entier, et sans gloire et sans nom,
Et crois-moi, cher Clindor, si je meurs par la bouche,
Que ce ne sera pas par celle du canon.

Sur une horloge de sable

CETTE poussière que tu vois
Qui tes heures compasse
Et va recourant tant de fois
Par un petit espace:

Jadis Damon je m'appelois,
Que la divine grâce
De Philis pour qui je brûlois
A mis en cette place.

I should die, if in the middle of some plain I were to lose this
arm that I drink with; so stop telling me that one is as likely
to die in one's home, at table, among the pots, as where your valour
leads you.

Stop telling me that in the heat of battle one becomes immortal
through a noble death; that won't get me to go out soldiering.

I want to die in one piece, unfamed and unsung, and believe me,
dear Clindor, if I die by the mouth, it will not be by the mouth of
the cannon.

On an Hourglass

THIS dust which you see, which marks out your hours, and so
often goes running through a narrow space:

Damon I was once called, whom the divine grace of Phyllis for
whom I burned put in this place.

Le feu secret qui me rongea
En cette poudre me changea
Qui jamais ne repose:

Apprends, amant, que par le sort
L'espérance t'est close
De reposer même en ta mort.

TRISTAN L'HERMITE

[*Les Fleurs et la grotte*]

··· JE vous pourrais montrer si vous veniez un jour
En un parc qu'ici près depuis peu j'ai fait clore,
Mille amants transformés, qui des lois de l'Amour
      Sont passés sous celles de Flore;
Ils ont pour aliment les larmes de l'aurore.
      Dieux! que ne suis-je entre ces fleurs
Si vous devez un jour m'arroser de vos pleurs?

Vous y verriez Clytie, aux sentiments jaloux,
Qui n'a pu jusqu'ici guérir de la jaunisse;

The hidden fire which gnawed me changed me into this powder which is never at rest.

Learn, lover, that by fate you are sealed off from hope of resting even in death.

[*The Flowers and the Grotto*]

IF you came one day to a garden which I have lately had enclosed near here, I could show you a thousand transformed lovers, who have passed from the rule of Love under the laws of Flora. They have the tears of the dawn for food. O gods! why am I not among those flowers, if you are to water me one day with your tears?

There you would see Clytie, the jealous-natured thing, who so far has not been able to recover from jaundice; and the flower of

Et la fleur de ce Grec dont le bouillant courroux
      Ne peut souffrir une injustice;
Vous y verriez encore Adonis et Narcisse,
      Dont l'un fut aimé de Cypris,
L'autre fut de son ombre aveuglément épris.

Je vous ferais savoir tout ce que l'on en dit,
Vous contant leurs vertus et leurs métamorphoses:
Quelle fleur vint du lait que Junon répandit,
      Et quel sang fit rougir les roses
Qui grossissent d'orgueil dès qu'elles sont écloses,
      Voyant leur portrait si bien peint
Dans la vive blancheur des lis de votre teint.

Piqué secrètement de leur éclat vermeil,
Un folâtre Zéphire à l'entour se promène,
Et, pour les garantir de l'ardeur du soleil,
      Les évente de son haleine;
Mais lorsqu'il les émeut, il irrite ma peine,
      Car aimant en un plus haut point,
Je vois que mes soupirs ne vous émeuvent point.

that Greek * whose boiling rage cannot stomach an injustice; you would also see Adonis and Narcissus, of which the one was loved by Cypris and the other was blindly infatuated by his own shadow.

I would teach you all that is told of them, relating their virtues and their metamorphoses: which flower came from the milk which Juno shed, and which blood reddened the roses which swell with pride as soon as they bloom, seeing their portrait so well painted amid the gleaming whiteness of the lilies of your complexion.

Secretly spurred by their rosy beauty, a playful zephyr roams around, and, to protect them from the heat of the sun, fans them with his breath; but when he stirs them he exasperates my pain, for, loving on a higher level, I see that my sighs stir you not at all.

---

* Ajax, who killed himself in fury when the arms of Achilles were awarded to Odysseus instead of to himself. A kind of hyacinth sprang from his blood. See Garnier's *Elégie sur la mort de Ronsard.*

Là, mille arbres chargés des plus riches présents
Dont la terre à son gré les mortels favorise,
Et sur qui d'un poinçon je grave tous les ans
      Votre chiffre et votre devise,
Font en mille bouquets éclater la cerise,
      La prune au jus raffraîchissant,
Et le jaune abricot au goût si ravissant.

Là, parmi des jasmins dressés confusément,
Et dont le doux esprit à toute heure s'exhale,
Cependant que partout le chaud est véhément,
      On se peut garantir du hâle,
Et se perdre aisément dans ce plaisant dédale,
      Comme entre mille aimables nœuds
Mon âme se perdit parmi vos beaux cheveux.

Une grotte superbe et des rochers de prix,
Que des pins orgueilleux couronnent de feuillage,
Y garde la fraîcheur sous ses riches lambris,
      Qui sont d'un rare coquillage.
Mille secrets tuyaux cachés sur son passage
      Mouillent soudain les imprudents
Qui sans discrétion veulent entrer dedans.

There, a thousand trees loaded with the richest gifts with which the earth liberally favours mortal men, and on which I engrave your emblem and your motto with an etching-tool every year, burst into countless clusters of cherries, plums with refreshing juice, and the yellow apricot with its delicious taste.

There, among jasmines planted at hazard, whose sweet essence is breathed out night and day, while everywhere the heat is intense one can find protection from sunburn and easily lose oneself in that agreeable maze – as among countless pleasant curls my heart lost itself in your lovely hair.

A magnificent grotto and rocks of rare stone, which proud pines crown with foliage, preserves the cool inside its rich walls, which are made of costly sea-shells. Numberless secret pipes hidden along the entrance suddenly drench incautious intruders who indiscreetly venture in there.

D'un côté l'on y voit une petite mer
Que traverse en nageant un amoureux Léandre;
De rage autour de lui l'onde vient écumer,
            Et lui tâche de s'en défendre,
Apercevant Héro qui veille pour l'attendre
            Et d'impatience et d'amour
Brûle avec son flambeau sur le haut d'une tour.

Aux niches de rocher qui sont aux environs
On voit toujours mouvoir de petits personnages :
Ici des charpentiers et là des forgerons,
            Qui travaillent à leurs ouvrages;
Et force moulinets, faits à divers usages,
            Qui tournent bien diligemment
A la faveur de l'eau qui coule incessamment.

Une table de marbre, où je vais me mirer
Alors que je n'ai pas le visage si blême,
Pourrait bien de beau linge et de fleurs se parer
            Quand la chaleur serait extrême,
Si vous vouliez venir y manger de la crême
            Et des fraises, que chèrement
Je ne fais conserver que pour vous seulement.

On one side is to be seen a little sea, which an amorous Leander
is swimming across; the water foams in fury around him and he
tries to breast it, catching sight of Hero who sits up waiting for him
and, with impatience and love, burns with her torch at the top of a
tower.

In recesses in the rock nearby, one sees little figures continually
moving; carpenters here and blacksmiths there, working at their
tasks; and many little wheels, for various purposes, turning busily
by means of the water which flows continuously.

A marble table, in which I go to look at my reflection when my
face is not so pallid as now, might well be embellished with fine
linen and flowers on some day of excessive heat, if you cared to
come and eat strawberries and cream which I keep lovingly for you
alone.

Vous n'y trouveriez pas de superbes apprêts
Comme ceux que mérite une beauté divine,
Mais vous pourriez à l'ombre au moins y boire frais
    En des vases de cornaline,
Et vos yeux, en vingt plats de porcelaine fine
    Pourraient confronter à souhait
La blancheur de vos mains avec celle du lait ...

GEORGES DE SCUDÉRY

Sonnet

AIMEZ ou n'aimez pas, changez, soyez fidèle,
Tout cela pour Philis est fort indifférent;
Comme votre conquête a peu touché la belle,
Elle perd votre cœur ainsi qu'elle le prend.

L'on ne peut la nommer ni douce ni cruelle,
Son insensible esprit ne combat ni se rend;
Elle entend les soupirs que l'on pousse pour elle,
Mais ce cœur de rocher ne sait ce qu'il entend.

You would not find any of the luxurious preparations which a divine beauty deserves, but you could at least have cool drinks in the shade from vases of cornelian, and your eyes, in twenty dishes of delicate porcelain, could compare as long as they pleased the whiteness of your hands with that of the milk.

Sonnet

LOVE or do not love, change, be constant, all that is quite indifferent to Phyllis; as her conquest of you has left the fair lady unmoved, she loses your heart just as (heedlessly) as she wins it.

    She cannot be called either tender or cruel, her unfeeling spirit neither resists nor surrenders; she hears the sighs which are uttered for her, but that stony heart does not know what it hears.

L'Amour, tout dieu qu'il est, avec toute sa flamme,
Ne dissoudra jamais les glaçons de son âme,
Et cette souche enfin n'aimera jamais rien.

O malheureux amant! O penser qui me tue!
Quel bizarre destin se rencontre le mien!
Comme Pygmalion j'adore ma statue.

PIERRE LE MOYNE

[Au cœur des pyramides]

… Sous le pied de ces monts taillés et suspendus
Il s'étend des pays ténébreux et perdus,
De spacieux déserts, des solitudes sombres
Faites pour le séjour des morts et de leurs ombres.
Là sont les corps des Rois et les corps des Sultans,
Diversement rangés selon l'ordre du temps.
Les uns sont enchâssés dans les creuses images
A qui l'art a donné leur taille et leurs visages,
Et dans ces vains portraits, fastueux monuments,
Leur orgueil se conserve avec leurs ossements.
Les autres, embaumés, sont posés en des niches
Où leurs ombres, encore éclatantes et riches,

Love, divine though he is, with all his fire, will never melt the
ice of her heart, and that block in short will never love anything.
O unhappy lover! O thought which kills me! What a strange
destiny crosses mine! Like Pygmalion I adore my statue.

[In the Heart of the Pyramids]

Beneath the foot of these hewn and hanging mountains there
stretch dark and lost regions, wide deserts, sombre solitudes, made
to be inhabited by the dead and their ghosts. There are the bodies of
the kings and the sultans, variously ranked in the order of the ages.
Some are enshrined in hollow images, to which the artist has given
their shape and their faces, and in those vain likenesses, pompous
memorials, their pride is preserved together with their bones.
Others, embalmed, are laid in niches, where their shades, still

Semblent perpétuer, malgré les lois du sort,
La pompe de leur vie en celle de leur mort.
    De ce muet sénat, de cette cour terrible,
Le silence épouvante et l'aspect est horrible.
Là sont les devanciers joints à leurs descendants;
Tous les règnes y sont, on y voit tous les temps;
Et cette Antiquité, ces siècles dont l'histoire
N'a pu sauver qu'à peine une obscure mémoire,
Réunis par la mort en cette sombre nuit,
Y sont sans mouvement, sans lumière et sans bruit...

Judith

HOLOPHERNE est couché, le flambeau qui sommeille
A mêlé sa lumière avec l'obscurité,
Et Judith fait de l'ombre un voile à sa beauté
De peur qu'à son éclat le Barbare s'éveille.

Le fer que tient en main cette chaste merveille
Ajoute à son visage une fière clarté,
Et pour la confirmer en cette extrêmité
Son bon ange lui fait ce discours à l'oreille:

splendid and rich, seem to perpetuate – in defiance of the laws of
destiny – the pomp of their life in the pomp of their death.
    Of this mute senate, of this terrible court, the silence horrifies
and the sight is dreadful. There are the ancestors together with their
descendants. All the reigns are there, all the ages are seen. And that
Antiquity, those centuries of which history has been able to preserve only a dim memory, assembled by death in that gloomy darkness, are there without movement, without light and without
sound.

Judith

HOLOPHERNES is lying down, the slumbering torch has merged
its light into the darkness, and Judith makes a veil for her beauty
with the shadow, for fear that the Barbarian should be awakened by
its splendour.
    The blade which that chaste marvel holds in her hand adds a
savage gleam to her face, and to strengthen her in this supreme
moment, her good angel whispers these words in her ear:

« Assure-toi, Judith, tu vas tuer un mort;
Le sommeil et le vin par un commun effort
Ont déjà commencé son meurtre et ta conquête;

«Ton captif ne doit pas te donner de la peur,
Et ton bras sans danger pourra couper la tête
D'un homme à qui tes yeux ont arraché le cœur.»

La Madeleine

Ici, d'un repentir célèbre et glorieux,
Madeleine, à soi-même indulgente et cruelle,
Guérit de son péché la blessure mortelle
Et par ses larmes tire un nouveau feu des cieux.

Son luxe converti devient religieux.
L'esprit de ses parfums se fait dévot comme elle.
Ces rubis sont ardents de sa flamme nouvelle
Et ces perles en pleurs se changent à ses yeux.

Beaux yeux, sacrés canaux d'un précieux déluge,
Innocents corrupteurs de votre amoureux juge,
Ne serez-vous jamais sans flammes et sans dards?

'Fear nothing, Judith, you are about to kill a dead man; sleep
and wine by a mutual onslaught have already begun his slaying
and your triumph;
'Your captive ought not to inspire you with fear, and your arm
can safely cut off the head of a man whose heart your eyes have
torn out.'

The Magdalen

Here (in this picture), by a famous and glorious repentance, the
Magdalen, indulgent and cruel to herself, heals the mortal wound
of her sin and draws a new fire from heaven with her tears.
Her luxury, converted, becomes religious. The essence of her
perfumes becomes pious like her. Those rubies are glowing with
her new fire, and those pearls change into tears in her eyes.
Sweet eyes, sacred channels of a precious flood, innocent cor-
ruptors of your loving judge, will you never be without flames and
arrows?

PIERRE LE MOYNE

Au moins pour le moment faites cesser vos charmes:
La terre fume encor du feu de vos regards,
Et déjà vous brûlez le ciel avec vos larmes.

DU BOIS HUS

La Nuit des nuits

Le jour, ce beau fils du soleil
Dont le visage nonpareil
Donne le teint aux belles choses,
Prêt d'entrer en la mer, enlumine son bord
De ses dernières roses,
Et ses premiers rayons vont lui marquer le port.

Ce doux créateur des beautés,
Roi des glorieuses clartés
Qui dessus nous sont répandues,
Nous donnant le bonsoir se cache dans les eaux,
Et les ombres tendues
Avertissent le ciel d'allumer ses flambeaux.

At least for a time discontinue your charms: the earth still
smokes with the fire of your glances, and already you are burning
heaven with your tears.

The Night of Nights *

The day, that fair son of the sun whose peerless face gives radiance
to all fair things, ready to plunge into the sea, flushes its shore with
its last roses, and its first beams (tomorrow) will show it its haven.

That gentle creator of beauties, king of the glorious lights which
are scattered above us, bidding us good-night, hides in the waters,
and the spreading shadows warn the sky to kindle its torches.

* Christmas Eve.

Les bois ne paraissent plus verts,
La nuit entrant dans l'univers
Couvre le sommet des montagnes,
Déjà l'air orphelin arrose de ses pleurs
La face des campagnes,
Et les larmes du soir tombent dessus les fleurs.

Le monde change de couleur:
Une générale paleur
Efface la beauté des plaines,
Et les oiseaux surpris sur le bord des marais,
Courtisans des fontaines,
Se vont mettre à couvert dans le sein des forêts.

Quelques brins d'écarlate et d'or
Paraissent attachés encor
A quelque pièce de nuage:
Des restes de rayon peignant tout à l'entour
Le fond du paysage,
Font un troisième temps qui n'est ni nuit ni jour.

Les rougeurs qu'on voit dans les airs
Jeter ces languissants éclairs

The woods no longer appear green; the night, coming into the universe, covers the tops of the mountains; already the orphaned air waters the face of the countryside with its tears and the sobs of the evening fall upon the flowers.

The world changes colour: a general pallor effaces the beauty of the plains, and the birds, surprised on the edge of the water-meadows – courtiers of the pools – go to find shelter in the heart of the forests.

A few streaks of scarlet and gold can still be seen hanging to some fragment of cloud; lingering gleams of sun, painting the distant landscape all around, make a third time which is neither night nor day.

That red flush, which is to be seen in the sky giving out those

Qui meurent dans les plis de l'onde,
Sont les hontes du jour fuyant le successeur
Qui le chasse du monde,
L'astre des belles nuits que gouverne sa sœur.

Le silence vêtu de noir,
Retournant faire son devoir,
Vole sur la mer et la terre,
Et l'océan, joyeux de sa tranquillité,
Est un liquide verre
Où la face du ciel imprime sa beauté.

Le visage du firmament
Descendu dans cet élément
Y fait voir sa figure peinte;
Les feux du ciel sans peur nagent dedans la mer
Et les poissons sans crainte
Glissent parmi ces feux qui semblent les aimer.

Dans le fond de ce grand miroir
La Nature se plaît à voir
L'onde et la flamme si voisines,

languishing beams which die in the folds of the waves, is the blushes
of the day fleeing from the successor who drives it from the world,
the luminary of the fair nights which are ruled by its sister (the
day's sister, the moon).

Black-clad silence, returning to its task, glides over earth and sea,
and the ocean, rejoicing in its own quiet, is a liquid glass on which
the face of the sky imprints its beauty.

The face of the firmament, come down into this (liquid) element,
shows its features painted there; the lights of heaven swim unafraid
in the sea, and the fish glide fearlessly among those lights which
seem to love them.

In the depths of that great mirror Nature rejoices to see water

Et les astres tombés en ces pays nouveaux,
     Salamandres marines,
Se baignent à plaisir dans le giron des eaux.

     L'illustre déesse des mois,
     Quittant son arc et son carquois,
     Descend avec eux dedans l'onde;
Son croissant est sa barque, où, l'hameçon en main
     Fait de sa tresse blonde,
Elle pêche à loisir les perles du Jourdain.

     Le ciel en ce soir bienheureux,
     S'habillant de ses plus beaux feux,
     Éclate plus qu'à l'ordinaire,
Et la nuit infidèle à son obscurité
     A sur notre hémisphère
Beaucoup moins de noirceur qu'elle n'a de clarté.

     Soleil, quitte-lui ta maison;
     Celle qui vient sur l'horizon
     Est grosse du Dieu que j'adore;
Les torches qu'elle allume en la place du jour,

and fire so close, and the stars, fallen into this new region – sala-
manders of the sea – bathe to their hearts' content in the bosom of
the waters.

The honoured goddess of the months, putting aside her bow
and her quiver, goes down with them into the water. Her crescent
is her boat, from which, holding the hook made from her blond
tresses, she fishes at her ease for the pearls of the Jordan.

The sky on this blessed evening, clothing itself with its loveliest
lights, shines more brightly than usual, and the night, abandoning
its gloom, has above our hemisphere much less darkness than she
has light.

Sun, yield your house to her; she who comes over the horizon is
big with the God I adore; the torches which she kindles in place of

Plus belles que l'aurore,
Lui couronnent le front de lumières d'amour.

... Riche et miraculeuse Nuit
Qui sans bouche et sans aucun bruit
Enfantes pourtant la PAROLE,
Sois toujours révérée en ce vaste univers,
Et que ta gloire vole
De l'un à l'autre bout sur l'aile de mes vers ...

MARTIAL DE BRIVES

Paraphrase du Cantique des Trois Enfants

ÊTRES qui n'avez rien que l'être,
Êtres qui croissez seulement,
Êtres bornés au sentiment,
Êtres capables de connaître,   *Benedicite*
                                     omnia opera
Venez par des transports sacrés   *Domini*
Franchir les différents degrés,   *Domino*
Soit du genre, soit de l'espèce,
Et prenez soin de vous unir

the day – lovelier than the dawn – crown her brow with beams of love.

Rich and miraculous Night, which without mouth and with no sound yet bring forth THE WORD, be for ever revered in this vast universe, and may your glory fly from end to end of it on the wing of my verse.

Paraphrase of the Song of the Three Young Men *

All the works of the Lord, bless the Lord

BEINGS who have only being, beings who are only growing, beings limited to feeling, beings capable of knowledge, come by holy ecstasies to transcend the various degrees, either of genus or of species, and take heed to come together to bless the Lord without ceasing, since without ceasing He takes heed to bless you.

* The original Latin 'Song of the Three Young Men' (in the fiery furnace) is an apocryphal addition to the Book of Daniel.

A bénir le Seigneur sans cesse,
Puisque sans cesse il prend le soin de vous bénir.

Anges, substances immortelles,
Dépendantes divinités,
Du flambeau des éternités   *Benedicite*
Intelligentes étincelles,   *Angeli*
Esprits en qui sans mouvement   *Domini*
Pendant un éternel moment   *Domino*
Dieu prend plaisir de se répandre,
Bénissez les saintes beautés
Que vous ne pouvez pas comprendre,
Et portez vos ardeurs plus loin que vos clartés.

... Vertus qu'en faveur de l'espèce
Dieu loge dans l'individu,
Afin que, l'un étant perdu,   *Benedicite*
L'autre lui succède sans cesse,   *omnes*
Propriétés qui déclarez   *virtutes*
Dans les Êtres confédérés   *Domini*
Les titres de leurs alliances,   *Domino*
Traits d'un même être en divers corps,
Unions dans les différences,
Bénissez le Seigneur de ces rares accords.

Angels of the Lord, bless the Lord

Angels, immortal substances, dependent divine beings, sparks endowed with mind from the torch of the eternities, spirits in whom God, unmoving, delights to diffuse Himself during an eternal moment, bless the holy loveliness which you cannot understand, and let (the fire of) your ardour outrun the light of your understanding.

All virtues of the Lord, bless the Lord

Virtues which, in the interest of the species, God lodges in the individual, so that, when one is lost, another succeeds it continually, properties which proclaim their titles of alliance in the confederate Essences, features of the same being in various bodies, unions in differences, bless the Lord for these rare harmonies.

... Paillettes d'or, claires étoiles
Dont la nuit fait ses ornements,
Et que comme des diamants   *Benedicite*
Elle sème dessus ses voiles,   *stellae caeli*
Fleurs des parterres azurés,   *Domino*
Points de lumière, clous dorés
Que le ciel porte sur sa roue,
De vous soit à jamais béni
L'Esprit souverain qui se joue
A compter sans erreur votre nombre infini.

... Ondes subtilement tracées
D'un azur si sombre et si clair,
Qu'on prend dans les plaines de l'air   *Et nubes*
Pour des collines entassées,   *Domino*
Longs ordres de riches bouillons,
Plis de l'air, célestes sillons,
Belles rides, pompeux nuages,
Bénissez le Maître des Cieux,
Et que vos couleurs soient langages
Pour parler hautement de sa gloire à nos yeux.

Stars of heaven, bless the Lord
  Golden spangles, bright stars which the night wears as its ornaments and which it strews like diamonds upon its veils, flowers of
the azure borders, points of light, gilded studs which heaven bears
on its wheel, be praised by you for ever the Sovereign Spirit which
makes light of counting your infinite numbers unerringly.

And the clouds, bless the Lord
  Waves cunningly traced in so dark and so clear a blue, which
look like hills piled up in the plains of the sky, long chains of rich
foam, airy folds, skiey furrows, lovely ripples, splendid clouds,
bless the Master of the Heavens, and let your colours be languages
to speak loudly of his glory to our eyes.

Simples précieux et vulgaires,
Herbes de toutes les saisons,
D'où coulent les mortels poisons
Ou les remèdes salutaires,
Lignes peintes, filets mouvants
Qu'on voit flotter au gré des vents
Comme une verte chevelure,
Vif émail qui vivez si peu,
Froides languettes de verdure,
A bénir le Seigneur soyez langues de feu.

Benedicite
universa
germinantia
in terra
Domino

... Vaste océan, monde liquide,
Lice des carrosses ailés
Que les quatre vents attelés
Traînent où la fureur les guide,
Monstre qu'on voit toujours caché
Et dans votre lit attaché
Comme un frénétique incurable,
Baisez d'un flot humilié
Vos augustes chaînes de sable
Et bénissez la main qui vous en a lié.

Benedicite
maria

All things growing upon earth, bless the Lord
Rare and common simples, herbs of all the seasons, from which
come mortal poisons or health-giving remedies, coloured lines,
moving nets which we see swaying at the will of the winds like
green hair, bright hues which live so short a time, cold little
tongues of verdure, to bless the Lord be tongues of fire.

Bless Him, you seas
Vast ocean, liquid world, arena of the winged coaches which the
four harnessed winds drag wherever their wild course takes them,
monster always seeming hidden and fastened to your bed like a
raving madman, kiss with humbled waves your noble chains of
sand, and bless the hand which bound you with them.

... Vous dont les nochers se retirent
S'ils veulent sauver leurs vaisseaux,
Baleines qu'on voit sur les eaux   *Benedicite*
Comme des îles qui respirent,   *cete et omnia*
Et vous, tout petits habitants   *quae*
De ces palais creux et flottants   *moventur*
Que forme le marbre de l'onde,   *in aquis*
Bénissez Dieu, muets poissons,   *Domino*
Puisque sa conduite profonde
A mis votre silence au rang de nos chansons.

Oiseaux qui par vos beaux plumages
Tenez l'œil de l'homme ravi,
Et qui ravissez à l'ennui   *Benedicite*
Son oreille par vos ramages,   *omnes*
Voix visibles, sons emplumés,   *volucres*
Orgues de chair, luths animés,   *caeli*
Chantres qui sur la tablature   *Domino*
Que vous lisez en votre cœur
Chantez avec art par nature,
Invitez la nature à bénir son Auteur.

Whales and all things which move in the waters, bless the Lord
You from whom the sailors draw away if they wish to save their
vessels, whales appearing on the waters like breathing islands, and
you, tiny inhabitants of those hollow floating palaces formed by the
marble of the sea, praise God, mute fishes, since his mysterious
ways have made your silence equal to our songs.

All fowls of the air, bless the Lord
Birds which delight the eye of man with your fine plumage and
distract his ear from care with your songs, visible voices, feathered
sounds, organs of flesh, living lutes, singers who, from the score
which you read in your hearts, sing with art by nature's light, bid
nature to bless her Author.

Esprits de chair, âmes de boue,
Bêtes esclaves de vos sens,
Ouvrages bas et languissants   *Benedicite*
De la nature qui se joue,   *omnes bestiae*
Cerfs et lions, brebis et loups,   *et pecora*
Animaux farouches et doux,   *Domino*
Ne soyez plus incompatibles,
Adorez Dieu paisiblement,
Et puisqu'il vous a fait sensibles,
Bénissez son saint nom avecque sentiment.

Homme, en qui ces diverses choses
Dont ce vaste monde est rempli,
Comme en un monde recueilli   *Benedicite*
Sont délicatement encloses,   *filii*
Pierre et plante conjointement   *hominum*
Par l'être, et par l'accroissement,   *Domino*
Bête en la chair, en l'esprit ange,
Puisque tous êtres sont en vous,
Honorez Dieu d'une louange
Qui·seule ait la vertu de le bénir pour tous.

All beasts and cattle, bless the Lord
    Spirits of flesh, souls of clay, beasts enslaved by your senses, low and dull-brained works of frolicsome Nature, stags and lions, sheep and wolves, fierce and gentle animals, be no longer incompatible, worship God in peace, and, since He has given you feeling, with feeling bless his holy name.

Sons of man, bless the Lord
    Man, in whom these various things with which this great world is filled are contained in miniature as though in a contracted world – stone and plant conjointly in essence and through growth, beast in the flesh, angel in the spirit – since all beings are in you, glorify God with praises which alone have the virtue to bless Him in the name of all.

228

JULES PILET DE LA MESNARDIÈRE

Le Soleil couchant

LE grand astre va lentement
Vers les saphirs de l'onde amère,
Et Vénus, dans l'autre hémisphère,
Donne ordre à leur appartement.

… Ces grands rideaux à fond vermeil,
Dont l'or pétille dans la nue,
Sont d'une étoffe peu connue
Aux pays où va le soleil …

… La pourpre qui luit sous ses pas
En l'air s'écarte en mille pointes
Où, parfois, deux couleurs sont jointes,
Et parfois ne se joignent pas.

Dieux! la merveilleuse clarté!
Alceste, admirez la nuance
De ce jaune clair qui s'avance
Sous cet incarnat velouté.

The Setting Sun

THE great star goes slowly towards the sapphires of the salt wave, and Venus in the other hemisphere puts their apartment in order.

Those great curtains with rosy ground, whose gold sparkles in the clouds, are of a stuff hardly known in the countries where the sun is going.

The crimson which gleams beneath his feet breaks up in the air into a thousand streaks, in which two colours sometimes join and sometimes remain apart.

O gods, what a marvellous light! Alceste, admire the delicate tone of that light yellow moving forward beneath that velvety pink.

229

L'œillet d'Inde serait ainsi
Dans sa douce et sombre dorure,
Si sur les pans de sa bordure
La rose tranchait le souci.

Mais voilà cet éclat changé
En un mélange plus modeste.
Voyez ce rocher bleu-céleste
Où déborde un pâle orangé.

Voyez ces rayons gracieux
Qui, là-bas, forçant le passage,
De fils d'or percent le nuage,
Aussi loin que portent nos yeux.

Que ces flocons blancs ont d'appas!
Vous diriez que c'est de la neige
Qu'un doux soleil, qui la protège,
Perce, illumine et ne fond pas.

Alceste l'égale en ce point.
Pour nous ses feux elle tempère
Et sa lueur brillante et claire
Enflamme et ne consume point.

The African marigold would be like that in its soft, dull gilding, if on the outer faces of its petals the rose encountered the pansy.

But now that splendour has changed into a more modest blending. Look at that sky-blue rock, from which a pale-orange brims over.

Look at those graceful beams over there which, forcing their way through, pierce the clouds with threads of gold as far as our eyes can see.

How attractive those white flakes are! One would think that it was snow, which a mild sun, preserving it, shines through, lights up, and does not melt.

Alceste resembles it on that score. She tempers her fires for us and her bright, clear glow inflames but does not consume.

Des plus bizarres papillons
Aimez-vous bien les bigarrures?
Et les différentes parures
Des mieux émaillés oisillons?

Voyez ce lustre variant
De mille couleurs entassées
Qu'un trait de lumière a tracées
Sur ce fond brun, vers l'orient.

Voyez ces tirades de feu
Dont le ciel vers le nord éclate;
Et, dans ces plaines d'écarlate,
Ce bois d'amarante et de bleu.

Que les flots crêpés d'un zéphyr
Sont bien peints dans ces pommelures,
De qui l'ordre et les mouchetures
Semblent figurés à plaisir!

Quoique l'on vante son berceau,
L'Auteur fécond de la lumière
Dessus le seuil de la carrière
N'est point si pompeux ni si beau.

Do you like the motley tints of the most exotic butterflies? And the variegated markings of the most brilliantly coloured birds?

Look at that changing lustre of a thousand accumulated colours which a shaft of light has traced on that dun background towards the east.

Look at those bursts of fire in which the sky breaks out towards the north; and, in those plains of scarlet, that wood of amaranth and blue.

How well the curly waves of a zephyr are depicted in those dapplings, whose arrangement and flecked markings seem deliberately designed!

Although his birthplace is admired, the fruitful Author of Light is not so splendid or so beautiful on the threshold of his course.

Les opales du point du jour
Et ses jacinthes sombre-claires
Sont bien des objets plus vulgaires
Que les rubis de son retour.

Jamais eut-il rien d'approchant
Sur le bord des climats du Gange?
Java perdrait-il pas au change
De cette Inde avec son couchant?

... Sa rondeur croît en descendant.
Telle est la sphère de notre âme:
Le cercle infini de sa flamme
S'augmente par son occident

...Après nous avoir divertis
De mille adorables figures,
Le peintre et ses rares peintures
Dans les eaux vont être engloutis.

Dans l'air il laisse les couleurs
Qui font les jasmins et les roses,
Et toutes ses métamorphoses
Sont les germes d'autant de fleurs. ...

The opals of daybreak and its cloudy-clear jacinths are much commoner objects than the rubies of his decline.

Was there ever anything to approach them on the shores of Ganges' clime? Would not Java lose to be compared to this India with its sunset?

His globe grows bigger as it sinks. Such is the sphere of our soul: the infinite circle of its flame is swollen by its westering.

After having entertained us with a thousand delectable designs, the painter and his rare paintings are about to be swallowed up in the waters.

In the air he leaves the colours which make the jasmines and the roses, and all his metamorphoses are the germs of as many flowers.

JACQUES DE CAILLY

Les Sots

En mon cœur la haine abonde.
J'en regorge à tout propos :
Depuis que je hais les sots,
Je hais presque tout le monde.

Sur les mauvais médecins

Votre précieuse personne
A quatre médecins aujourd'hui s'abandonne
Et suit aveuglément leur traitement vénal.
Gillet, mon amitié veut que je vous le die,
  Quatre médecins sont un mal
  Plus grand que votre maladie.

Sur le reproche qu'on lui a fait de copier l'antiquité

Dis-je quelque chose assez belle,
L'Antiquité toute en cervelle

On Fools

In my heart hate abounds. I seethe with it on every occasion. Since I've taken to hating fools, I hate almost everybody.

On Bad Doctors

Your precious person is handed over today to four doctors, and follows their mercenary treatment blindly. Gillet, my friendship for you obliges me to tell you that four doctors are a greater affliction than your illness.

On being reproached for copying antiquity

If I say something rather good, Antiquity gets in a fearful state and

233

Me dit: «Je l'ai dit avant toi.»
C'est une plaisante donzelle;
Que ne venait-elle après moi?
J'aurais dit la chose avant elle.

Les Dérivations

ALFANA vient d'*equus* sans doute,
Mais il faut avouer aussi
Qu'en venant de là jusqu'ici
Il a bien changé sur la route.

PAUL SCARRON

Paris

UN amas confus de maisons,
Des crottes dans toutes les rues,
Ponts, églises, palais, prisons,
Boutiques bien ou mal pourvues,

says: 'I said that before you.' She's a funny wench. Why didn't she come after me? Then I should have said the thing first.

Derivations

ALFANA comes from *equus* of course, but it must also be admitted that, in coming from there to here, it has changed a lot on the way.

(*Alfana* is a Spanish word for *horse*. The reference is probably to Gilles Ménage's *Origines de la langue française* (1650), which suggested a number of such derivations.)

Paris

A JUMBLED mass of houses, filth in all the streets, bridges, churches, palaces, prisons, well or poorly stocked shops,

Force gens noirs, blancs, roux, grisons,
Des prudes, des filles perdues,
Des meurtres et des trahisons,
Des gens de plume aux mains crochues,

Maint poudré qui n'a point d'argent,
Maint homme qui craint le sergent,
Maint fanfaron qui toujours tremble,

Pages, laquais, voleurs de nuit,
Carrosses, chevaux, et grand bruit,
C'est là Paris: que vous en semble?

SUPERBES monuments de l'orgueil des humains,
Pyramides, tombeaux dont la vaine structure
A témoigné que l'art, par l'adresse des mains
Et l'assidu travail, peut vaincre la nature:

Vieux palais ruinés, chefs-d'œuvre des Romains
Et les derniers efforts de leur architecture,
Colisée, où souvent ces peuples inhumains
De s'entr'assassiner se donnaient tablature:

Many people, dark, fair, red-haired, grey-haired, prudes, aban-
doned girls, murders and betrayals, greedy-fingered lawyers,
Many a man with powdered head and no money, many a man
who fears the police, many a braggart who trembles continually,
Pages, lackeys, footpads, coaches, horses, and constant din, that's
Paris: how do you like it?

LOFTY monuments to mortal pride, pyramids, tombs whose proud
structure has proved that art, with skilful hands and assiduous
labour, can surpass nature:
Old ruined palaces, masterpieces of the Romans and the supreme
achievement of their architecture, Coliseum, in which that inhuman populace often gave itself the spectacle of mutual slaughters:

Par l'injure des ans vous êtes abolis,
Ou du moins, la plupart, vous êtes démolis;
Il n'est point de ciment que le temps ne dissoude.

Si vos marbres si durs ont senti son pouvoir,
Dois-je trouver mauvais qu'un méchant pourpoint noir,
Qui m'a duré deux ans, soit percé par le coude?

Épitaphe

CELUI qui ci maintenant dort
Fit plus de pitié que d'envie,
Et souffrit mille fois la mort
Avant que de perdre la vie.

Passant, ne fais ici de bruit,
Prends garde qu'aucun ne l'éveille;
Car voici la première nuit
Que le pauvre Scarron sommeille.

You have been wiped out by the ravages of time, or at least you are largely destroyed: there is no cement which time does not loosen.

If your hard marbles have felt its power, ought I to find it wrong that a cheap black doublet, which has lasted me for two years, should be out at the elbow?

Epitaph

HE who sleeps here now aroused more pity than envy. He suffered death a thousand times before he lost his life.

Traveller, make no noise here, take care that none should wake him; for this is the first night that poor Scarron has slept.

GEORGES DE BRÉBEUF

Épigramme

OLINDE n'a rien que de rare
Et qui ne vient que des cantons
Que mainte région sépare
De celui que nous habitons.
Sa simarre brillante et fine
Vient du royaume de la Chine,
L'Inde a fourni son bracelet,
Sa glace fut faite à Venise,
Gênes a vendu son collet
Et la Hollande sa chemise.
Rome a fait les gants qu'elle porte,
Dont l'odeur agréable et forte
Garde le nez de mauvais vents;
Londres son habit de campagne;
Le Gange a vu naître ses dents,
Et son teint brillant vient d'Espagne.

Epigram

OLINDA has only rare things, which come only from countries
which many a land divides from the one which we inhabit. Her
gorgeous and fine-spun dress comes from the kingdom of China,
India supplied her bracelet, her mirror was made in Venice, Genoa
provided her collar, and Holland her chemise. Rome made the
gloves she wears, whose strong and pleasant perfume preserves the
nose from foul airs; London made her country clothes; the Ganges
saw the birth of her teeth, and her brilliant complexion comes from
Spain.

JEAN DE LA FONTAINE

Invocation

O DOUCE Volupté, sans qui, dès notre enfance,
Le vivre et le mourir nous deviendraient égaux;
Aimant universel de tous les animaux,
Que tu sais attirer avecque violence!
    Par toi tout se meut ici-bas,
    C'est pour toi, c'est pour tes appas,
    Que nous courons après la peine:
    Il n'est soldat, ni capitaine,
Ni ministre d'État, ni prince, ni sujet,
    Qui ne t'ait pour unique objet.
Nous autres nourrissons, si, pour fruit de nos veilles,
Un bruit délicieux ne charmait nos oreilles,
Si nous ne nous sentions chatouillés de ce son,
    Ferions-nous un mot de chanson?
Ce qu'on appelle gloire en termes magnifiques,
Ce qui servait de prix dans les jeux olympiques,
N'est que toi proprement, divine Volupté,
Et le plaisir des sens n'est-il de rien compté?

Invocation

O SENSUOUS Delight, without whom, from our childhood, life
and death would seem the same to us; universal magnet of all living
things, how violently you are able to attract! Everything here below takes its motion from you, it is for you, for your charms, that
we court hardship: there is no soldier, nor captain, nor minister of
state, nor prince, nor subject, who does not have you for his sole
object. We nurslings of the Muses – if, to reward our vigils, a delightful sound did not charm our ears, if we did not feel pleasurably
moved by that sound, should we trouble to compose a word of
song? What is called 'glory' in lofty style, what constituted the
prize at the Olympic games, is really only you, divine Delight – and
is the pleasure of the senses counted as nothing? What is the purpose of Flora's gifts, the setting sun and the dawn, Pomona and her

Pour quoi sont faits les dons de Flore,
Le soleil couchant et l'aurore,
Pomone et ses mets délicats,
Bacchus, l'âme des bons repas,
Les forêts, les eaux, les prairies,
Mères des douces rêveries?
Pour quoi tant de beaux arts, qui tous sont tes enfants?
Mais pour quoi les Chloris aux appas triomphants
Que pour maintenir ton commerce?
J'entends innocemment: sur son propre désir
Quelque rigueur que l'on exerce,
Encor y prend-on du plaisir.

Volupté, Volupté, qui fus jadis maîtresse
Du plus bel esprit de la Grèce,
Ne me dédaigne pas, viens-t'en loger chez moi;
Tu n'y seras pas sans emploi:
J'aime le jeu, l'amour, les livres, la musique,
La ville et la campagne, enfin tout; il n'est rien
Qui ne me soit souverain bien,
Jusqu'au sombre plaisir d'un cœur mélancolique.
Viens donc; et de ce bien, ô douce Volupté,

delicate foods, Bacchus – the soul of good meals – the forests, the waters, the meadows, mothers of sweet musings? For what are so many fine arts, all of them your children? And for what the Chlorises with their conquering charms, if not to maintain our intercourse with you? I mean, innocently: for, whatever discipline one exercises over one's own desires, one still finds pleasure in them.

Delight, Delight who once were mistress of the finest mind in Greece, do not disdain me, come and dwell with me; you will not be idle here. I like gaming and cards, love, books, music, town and country, in short everything; there is nothing which is not supremely enjoyable to me, even to the sombre pleasure of a melancholy heart. Come, then; and of that enjoyment, O sweet Delight,

Veux-tu savoir au vrai la mesure certaine?
Il m'en faut tout au moins un siècle bien compté;
Car trente ans, ce n'est pas la peine.

Adonis

[*Vénus et Adonis*]

... TOUT ce qui naît de doux en l'amoureux empire,
Quand d'une égale ardeur l'un pour l'autre on soupire,
Et que, de la contrainte ayant banni les lois,
On se peut assurer au silence des bois:
Jours devenus moments, moments filés de soie,
Agréables soupirs, pleurs enfants de la joie,
Vœux, serments et regards, transports, ravissements,
Mélange dont se fait le bonheur des amants,
Tout par ce couple heureux fut lors mis en usage.
   Tantôt ils choisissaient l'épaisseur d'un ombrage.
Là, sous des chênes vieux où leurs chiffres gravés
Se sont avec les troncs accrus et conservés,
Mollement étendus ils consumaient les heures,
Sans avoir pour témoins, en ces sombres demeures,
Que les chantres des bois, pour confidents qu'Amour,

would you know truly the exact extent? I need at the very least a full century of it; for thirty years is not worth while.

[*Venus and Adonis*]

ALL that springs sweet from the empire of love when with equal ardour each sighs for the other, and when, having banished the laws of constraint, one can entrust oneself to the silence of the woods: days turned into moments, moments spun with silk, pleasant sighs, tears born of joy, vows, pledges and glances, ecstasies, delight – a blend which makes up the happiness of lovers – all this was then practised by that fortunate pair.

Sometimes they sought out a shady bower. There, under ancient oaks on which their carved emblems have grown and endured with the trunks, softly pillowed they whiled away the hours, observed in those twilit haunts by none but the woodland songsters, counselled

Qui seul guidait leurs pas en cet heureux séjour.
  Tantôt sur des tapis d'herbe tendre et sacrée
Adonis s'endormait auprès de Cythérée,
Dont les yeux, enivrés par des charmes puissants,
Attachaient au héros leurs regards languissants.
Bien souvent ils chantaient les douceurs de leurs peines;
Et quelquefois assis sur le bord des fontaines,
Tandis que cent cailloux, luttant à chaque bond,
Suivaient les longs replis du cristal vagabond,
«Voyez, disait Vénus, ces ruisseaux et leur course;
Ainsi jamais le temps ne remonte à sa source.
Vainement pour les dieux il fuit d'un pas léger;
Mais vous autres mortels le devez ménager,
Consacrant à l'Amour la saison la plus belle.»
    Souvent, pour divertir leur ardeur mutuelle,
Ils dansaient aux chansons, de nymphes entourés.
Combien de fois la lune a leurs pas éclairés,
Et, couvrant de ses rais l'émail d'une prairie,
Les a vus à l'envi fouler l'herbe fleurie!
Combien de fois le jour a vu les antres creux
Complices des larcins de ce couple amoureux. ...

by none but Love, who alone guided their steps in that happy place.
  Sometimes, on carpets of soft and sacred grass, Adonis fell asleep
at the side of Cytherea, whose eyes, bewitched by powerful spells,
fixed their languishing looks on the hero. Often they sang of the
sweetness of their sufferings; and sometimes as they sat on the edge
of a brook, while a myriad pebbles, rolled down by the bounding
water, followed the long coils of the wandering crystal: 'See,' said
Venus, 'these streams and their course. So Time never returns to
its source. For the gods it passes light-footed and unheeded. But
you mortals should be sparing of it, dedicating your springtime
to love.'
  Often, to beguile their mutual fire, they danced to songs, by
nymphs surrounded. How often the moon lit their steps and,
flooding with its beams some bright-hued meadow, saw them tread
together the flowery grass. How often did daylight see the hollow
caves abetting the stolen pleasures of that amorous pair!

Le Songe de Vaux

Discours d'Hortésie

"J'IGNORE l'art de bien parler,
Et n'emploierai pour tout langage
Que ces moments qu'on voit couler
Parmi des fleurs et de l'ombrage.
Là luit un soleil tout nouveau;
L'air est plus pur, le jour plus beau;
Les nuits sont douces et tranquilles;
Et ces agréables séjours
Chassent le soin, hôte des villes,
Et la crainte, hôtesse des cours.

«Mes appas sont les alcyons
Par qui l'on voit cesser l'orage
Que le souffle des passions
A fait naître dans un courage.
Seule, j'arrête ses transports;
La raison fait de vains efforts
Pour en calmer la violence,

The Dream of Vaux *

I AM unskilled in fine speech, and shall use as my sole language those moments which slip by among flowers and shade. There a wholly new sun shines; the air is purer, the day more fair; the nights are soft and calm; and these pleasant places drive out care, which dwells in towns, and fear, which dwells in courts.

My charms are the halcyons by whom is stilled the storm which the blast of the passions has stirred up in a heart. I alone halt its fury; reason makes vain efforts to calm its violence, and, if any-

* Before an assembly of demi-gods and other judges the four 'fairies' of Architecture, Painting, Gardening, and Poetry are putting forward their claims to pre-eminence. Hortesia, representing landscape-gardening, is speaking here.

Et, si rien s'oppose à leur cours,
C'est la douceur de mon silence,
Plus que la force du discours.

... « J'embellis les fruits et les fleurs:
Je sais parer Pomone et Flore;
C'est pour moi que coulent les pleurs
Qu'en se levant verse l'aurore.
Les vergers, les parcs, les jardins,
De mon savoir et de mes mains
Tiennent leurs grâces non pareilles;
Là j'ai des prés, là j'ai des bois;
Et j'ai partout tant de merveilles
Que l'on s'égare dans leur choix.

«Je donne au liquide cristal
Plus de cent formes différentes,
Et le mets tantôt en canal,
Tantôt en beautés jaillissantes;
On le voit souvent par degrés
Tomber à flots précipités;
Sur des glacis je fais qu'il roule,
Et qu'il bouillonne en d'autres lieux;

thing resists its course, it is the quietness of my silence rather than the force of words.

I give beauty to the fruits and flowers, I can adorn Pomona and Flora; it is for me that the tears flow which the dawn sheds when it rises. The orchards, the parks, the gardens, derive their peerless graces from my skill and from my hands; there I have meadows, and there woods; and everywhere I have so many marvels that it is bewildering to choose among them.

I give the liquid crystal a hundred different forms, and make it sometimes into a canal, sometimes into beautiful spurting shapes; often it is seen tumbling in rushing waves down step-like falls; I

Parfois il dort, parfois il coule,
Et toujours il charme les yeux.

«Je ne finirais de longtemps
Si j'exprimais toutes ces choses:
On aurait plus tôt au printemps
Compté les œillets et les roses.
Sans m'écarter loin de ces bois,
Souvenez-vous combien de fois
Vous avez cherché leurs ombrages:
Pourriez-vous bien m'ôter le prix,
Après avoir par mes ouvrages
Si souvent charmé vos esprits?» ...

Traduction paraphrasée de la prose Dies Iræ

DIEU détruira le siècle au jour de sa fureur.
Un vaste embrasement sera l'avant-coureur,
Des suites du péché long et juste salaire.
Le feu ravagera l'univers à son tour;
Terre et cieux passeront; et ce temps de colère
Pour la dernière fois fera naître le jour.

make it roll down smooth slopes, and seethe in other places; sometimes it sleeps, sometimes it flows, and always it delights the eye.

I should never finish if I described all these things: it would be
quicker to count the carnations and the roses in spring. Without
going far from these woods, remember how many times you have
sought out their shade: can you refuse me the prize after having so
often had your spirits soothed by the works of my hands?

Paraphrase of the Hymn Dies Iræ

GOD will destroy all earthly things in the day of his fury. A vast
conflagration will be the warning sign, the long-merited chastise-
ment of the consequences of sin. The fire will ravage the universe in
its turn; heaven and earth will pass away and this hour of wrath will
bring forth the day for the last time.

Cette dernière aurore éveillera les morts.
L'ange rassemblera les débris de nos corps;
Il les ira citer au fond de leur asile.
Au bruit de la trompette, en tous lieux dispersé,
Toute gent accourra. David et la Sibylle
Ont prévu ce grand jour et nous l'ont annoncé.

De quel frémissement nous nous verrons saisis!
Qui se croira pour lors du nombre des choisis?
Le registre des cœurs, une exacte balance,
Paraîtront aux côtés d'un Juge rigoureux.
Les tombeaux s'ouvriront, et leur triste silence
Aura bientôt fait place aux cris des malheureux.

La nature et la mort, pleines d'étonnement,
Verront avec effroi sortir du monument
Ceux que dès son berceau le monde aura vu vivre.
Les morts de tous les temps demeureront surpris
En lisant leurs secrets aux annales d'un livre
Où même les pensers se trouveront écrits.

That final dawn will awaken the dead. The angel will bring together the fragments of our bodies; he will summon them from the depths of their hiding-places. At the sound of the trumpet, though dispersed in all places, all the peoples will flock up. David and the Sibyl foresaw that great day and announced it to us.

With what fear and trembling shall we be seized! Who will then believe that he is among the chosen? The record-book of souls, an exact pair of scales, will appear at the side of the stern Judge. The graves will open, and their sad silence will soon give way to cries of misery.

Nature and Death, filled with amazement, will see with terror coming out from the grave those whom the earth has borne since its beginning. The dead of all ages will be plunged in astonishment to read their secrets in the records of a book in which even thoughts will be found written.

Tout sera révélé par ce livre fatal;
Rien d'impuni. Le Juge, assis au tribunal,
Marquera sur son front sa volonté suprême.
Qui prierai-je en ce jour d'être mon défenseur?
Sera-ce quelque juste? Il craindra pour lui-même,
Et cherchera l'appui de quelque intercesseur.

Roi, qui fais tout trembler devant ta majesté,
Qui sauves les élus par ta seule bonté,
Source d'actes bénins et remplis de clémence,
Souviens-toi que pour moi tu descendis des cieux;
Pour moi, te dépouillant de ton pouvoir immense,
Comme un simple mortel tu parus à nos yeux.

J'eus part à ton passage: en perdras-tu le fruit?
Veux-tu me condamner à l'éternelle nuit,
Moi, pour qui ta bonté fit cet effort insigne?
Tu ne t'es reposé que las de me chercher;
Tu n'as souffert la croix que pour me rendre digne
D'un bonheur qui me puisse à toi-même attacher.

Everything will be revealed by that fateful book; nothing will go unpunished. The Judge, sitting in his court, will show his final will in his face. To whom shall I pray on that day to defend me? Some righteous man? He will be fearing for himself, and seeking the support of some mediator.

O King who make all things tremble before your majesty, who save the chosen by your bounty alone, source of kindly and merciful acts, remember that for me You came down from heaven; for me, stripping off your immense power, You appeared to our eyes as a mortal man.

I had my share in your coming: will You waste the fruit of it? Will You condemn me to eternal night, I for whom your bounty made that signal effort? You did not rest until You were weary of seeking me; You endured the cross only to make me worthy of a joy which might bind me to You.

Tu pourrais aisément me perdre et te venger.
Ne le fais point, Seigneur; viens plutôt soulager
Le faix sous qui je sens que mon âme succombe.
Assure mon salut dès ce monde incertain;
Empêche malgré moi que mon cœur ne retombe
Et ne te force enfin de retirer ta main.

Avant le jour du compte efface entier le mien.
L'illustre pécheresse, en présentant le sien,
Se fit remettre tout par son amour extrême;
Le larron, te priant, fut écouté de toi:
La prière et l'amour ont un charme suprême;
Tu m'as fait espérer même grâce pour moi.

Je rougis, il est vrai, de cet espoir flatteur;
La honte de me voir infidèle et menteur,
Ainsi que mon péché, se lit sur mon visage.
J'insiste toutefois, et n'aurai point cessé
Que ta bonté, mettant toute chose en usage,
N'éclate en ma faveur et ne m'ait exaucé.

You could easily destroy me and avenge Yourself. Do not do so,
Lord; come rather and lighten the burden under which I feel my
soul fainting. Secure my salvation in this uncertain world; prevent
my heart from relapsing in spite of me, and from forcing You at
the last to withdraw your hand.

Before the day of reckoning, wipe out mine completely. That
famous sinner (the Magdalen), in presenting hers, had everything remitted because of her boundless love; the thief, when he
prayed to You, was heeded; prayer and love exercise a supreme
spell; You have given me hope of the same pardon for myself.

It is true that I blush at this flattering hope; the shame of seeing
myself faithless and deceitful can be read in my face, as can my sin.
Yet I persist and I will not cease until your mercy, invoking every
means, is shown openly towards me and grants my prayer.

Fais qu'on me place à droite, au nombre des brebis;
Sépare-moi des boucs réprouvés et maudits.
Tu vois mon cœur contrit et mon humble prière;
Fais-moi persévérer dans ce juste remords.
Je te laisse le soin de mon heure dernière:
Ne m'abandonne pas quand j'irai chez les morts.

Épitaphe de Molière

Sous ce tombeau gisent Plaute et Térence,
Et cependant le seul Molière y gît.
Il les faisait revivre en son esprit,
Par leur bel art réjouissant la France.
Ils sont partis! et j'ai peu d'espérance
De les revoir malgré tous nos efforts.
Pour un long temps, selon toute apparence,
Térence et Plaute et Molière sont morts.

Let me be placed on your right hand, among your sheep; separate me from the goats, rejected and damned. You see my contrite heart and my humble prayer. Make me persevere in this righteous repentance. I leave the care of my last hour in your hand: do not abandon me when I go among the dead.

Epitaph on Molière

UNDER this tombstone lie Plautus and Terence, yet Molière alone lies there. He made them live again in his mind, delighting France with their excellent art. They have gone, and I have little hope of seeing them again for all that we may do. For a long time, to all appearances, Terence and Plautus and Molière are dead.

Épitaphe d'un paresseux

JEAN s'en alla comme il était venu,
Mangea le fonds avec le revenu,
Tint les trésors chose peu nécessaire.
Quant à son temps, bien le sut dispenser:
Deux parts en fit, dont il soulait passer
L'une à dormir et l'autre à ne rien faire.

Fables

La Cigale et la fourmi

LA cigale, ayant chanté
    Tout l'été,
Se trouva fort dépourvue
Quand la bise fut venue:
Pas un seul petit morceau
De mouche ou de vermisseau:
Elle alla crier famine
Chez la fourmi sa voisine,
La priant de lui prêter
Quelque grain pour subsister
Jusqu'à la saison nouvelle:

Epitaph on an Idle Fellow

JOHN left just as he had come (naked), used up the capital with the income, considered wealth as a thing of small importance. As for his time, he made good use of it. He divided it into two parts, of which he used to spend one sleeping and the other doing nothing.

The Cicada and the Ant

THE cicada, having sung all summer, found herself quite destitute when the winter winds came. Not a single little morsel of fly or of grub. She went to cry her hunger to her neighbour the ant, begging her to lend her a grain or two to live on until the next spring season.

Je vous paîrai, lui dit-elle,
Avant l'août, foi d'animal,
Intérêt et principal.
La fourmi n'est pas prêteuse;
C'est là son moindre défaut:
Que faisiez-vous au temps chaud?
Dit-elle à cette emprunteuse.
— Nuit et jour à tout venant
Je chantais, ne vous déplaise.
— Vous chantiez! j'en suis fort aise.
Eh bien, dansez maintenant.

Le Corbeau et le renard

Maître Corbeau, sur un arbre perché,
    Tenait en son bec un fromage.
Maître Renard, par l'odeur alléché,
    Lui tint à peu près ce langage:
    Hé! bon jour, Monsieur du Corbeau!
Que vous êtes joli! que vous me semblez beau!
    Sans mentir, si votre ramage
    Se rapporte à votre plumage,
Vous êtes le phénix des hôtes de ces bois.

'I will pay you back,' she told her, 'both interest and principal before August, on my word as an animal.'

The ant does not lend readily: that is the least of her weaknesses. 'What did you do in the hot weather?' she said to this borrower. 'May it please you, I sang day and night to all who passed by.' 'You sang! I'm delighted to hear it. Well, now dance.'

The Crow and the Fox

Master Crow, perched upon a tree, held a cheese in his beak. Master Fox, attracted by the smell, addressed him more or less in these words: 'Ah, good day, Mr Fitz-Crow, how fine you are, how handsome you look! If your song is anything like your plumage, you are the paragon of the dwellers in these woods.'

A ces mots le corbeau ne se sent pas de joie;
    Et, pour montrer sa belle voix,
Il ouvre un large bec, laisse tomber sa proie.
Le renard s'en saisit, et dit: Mon bon monsieur,
    Apprenez que tout flatteur
  Vit aux dépens de celui qui l'écoute.
Cette leçon vaut bien un fromage, sans doute.
    Le corbeau, honteux et confus,
Jura, mais un peu tard, qu'on ne l'y prendrait plus.

Le Renard et les raisins

CERTAIN renard gascon, d'autres disent normand,
Mourant presque de faim, vit au haut d'une treille
    Des raisins, mûrs apparemment,
    Et couverts d'une peau vermeille.
Le galant en eût fait volontiers un repas.
    Mais comme il n'y pouvait atteindre,
Ils sont trop verts, dit-il, et bons pour des goujats.

    Fit-il pas mieux que de se plaindre?

At these words the crow was beside himself with joy and, to show his fine voice, he opened a vast beak and dropped his loot. The fox snapped it up and said: 'My dear sir, learn that all flatterers live at the cost of those who listen to them. This lesson is certainly worth a cheese.'

The crow, shamefaced and abashed, swore – but rather late – that he would not be caught again in that way.

The Fox and the Grapes

A CERTAIN Gascon fox – others say Norman – was almost dying of hunger when he saw, high up on a vine, some grapes, plainly ripe and with rosy skins. The rascal would gladly have made a meal of them, but since he could not reach them: 'They are too green,' he said, 'and only good for bumpkins.'

Now wasn't that better than sitting down to cry?

Le rat qui s'est retiré du monde

LES Levantins en leur légende
Disent qu'un certain rat, las des soins d'ici-bas,
Dans un fromage de Hollande
Se retira loin du tracas.
La solitude était profonde,
S'étendant partout à la ronde.
Notre ermite nouveau subsistait là-dedans.
Il fit tant, de pieds et de dents,
Qu'en peu de jours il eut au fond de l'ermitage
Le vivre et le couvert: que faut-il davantage?
Il devint gros et gras: Dieu prodigue ses biens
A ceux qui font vœu d'être siens.
Un jour, au dévot personnage
Des députés du peuple rat
S'en vinrent demander quelque aumône légère:
Ils allaient en terre étrangère
Chercher quelque secours contre le peuple chat.
Ratopolis était bloquée:
On les avait contraints de partir sans argent,
Attendu l'état indigent
De la république attaquée.

The rat who withdrew from the world

THE oriental legend tells how a certain rat, weary of this world's
cares, withdrew far from the noisy din into a Dutch cheese. The
solitude was profound, extending all around him. Our new-made
hermit settled down to live in it. He worked so hard, with claws and
teeth, that in a few days he had food and shelter deep in the hermi-
tage: what more is needed? He grew fat and sleek: God showers his
benefits on those who vow to serve him.

One day, some emissaries from Ratland came to this pious person to ask for some small charity. They were on their way abroad
to seek help against the nation of the cats. Ratopolis was blockaded;
they had been obliged to set out without money, because of the im-
poverished state of the invaded country. They asked very little,

Ils demandaient fort peu, certains que le secours
    Serait prêt dans quatre ou cinq jours.
    Mes amis, dit le solitaire,
Les choses d'ici-bas ne me regardent plus.
    En quoi peut un pauvre reclus
    Vous assister? que peut-il faire,
Que de prier le ciel qu'il vous aide en ceci?
J'espère qu'il aura de vous quelque souci.
    Ayant parlé de cette sorte,
    Le nouveau saint ferma sa porte.

    Qui désigné-je, à votre avis,
    Par ce rat si peu secourable?
    Un moine? Non, mais un dervis:
Je suppose qu'un moine est toujours charitable.

Le Coche et la mouche

DANS un chemin montant, sablonneux, malaisé,
Et de tous les côtés au soleil exposé,
    Six forts chevaux tiraient un coche.

being certain that aid would be forthcoming within four or five days.

    'My friends,' said the hermit, 'the things of this world no longer concern me: in what way can a poor recluse assist you? What can he do except pray heaven to help you in this matter? I hope that it will pay some heed to you.' So saying, the new saint shut his door.

    Who, in your opinion, do I mean by this most unhelpful rat? A monk? No, no, a dervish. I assume that a monk is always charitable.

The Stage-Coach and the Fly

UP a hilly road, sandy and rough, with no shade anywhere from the sun, six strong horses were pulling a stage-coach. The women, the

Femmes, moine, vieillards, tout était descendu:
L'attelage suait, soufflait, était rendu.
Une mouche survient et des chevaux s'approche,
Prétend les animer par son bourdonnement,
Pique l'un, pique l'autre, et pense à tout moment
    Qu'elle fait aller la machine,
S'assied sur le timon, sur le nez du cocher.
    Aussitôt que le char chemine
    Et qu'elle voit les gens marcher,
Elle s'en attribue uniquement la gloire,
Va, vient, fait l'empressée: il semble que ce soit
Un sergent de bataille allant en chaque endroit
Faire avancer ses gens et hâter la victoire.
    La mouche, en ce commun besoin,
Se plaint qu'elle agit seule, et qu'elle a tout le soin:
Qu'aucun n'aide aux chevaux à se tirer d'affaire.
    Le moine disait son bréviaire:
Il prenait bien son temps! Une femme chantait:
C'était bien de chansons qu'alors il s'agissait!
Dame mouche s'en va chanter à leurs oreilles,
    Et fait cent sottises pareilles.

monk, the old men, had all got off. The team were sweating and blowing, exhausted. A fly comes along, approaches the horses, attempts to urge them on with her buzzing, stings one, stings another, and believes all the time that it is she who is making the thing move; she settles on the shaft, on the coachman's nose. As soon as the vehicle is moving and she sees the passengers walking on, she gives herself the whole credit and dashes to and fro, fussing around. She might be a battle-commander moving from place to place to urge on his men and hasten the victory. In this general emergency, the fly complains that she alone is active, that the whole of the anxiety is hers: no one helps the horses to get over their difficulties. The monk is reciting his breviary: he is in no hurry! A woman is singing – what a moment to sing songs! Lady Fly goes and sings in their ears and does a hundred equally silly things. After great efforts,

Après bien du travail, le coche arrive au haut.
Respirons maintenant! dit la mouche aussitôt:
J'ai tant fait que nos gens sont enfin dans la plaine.
Çà, messieurs les chevaux, payez-moi de ma peine.

Ainsi certaines gens, faisant les empressés,
    S'introduisent dans les affaires:
    Ils font partout les nécessaires,
Et, partout importuns, devraient être chassés.

L'Éducation

LARIDON et César, frères dont l'origine
Venait de chiens fameux, beaux, bien faits et hardis,
A deux maîtres divers échus au temps jadis,
Hantaient, l'un les forêts, et l'autre la cuisine.
Ils avaient eu d'abord chacun un autre nom:
    Mais la diverse nourriture
Fortifiant en l'un cette heureuse nature,
En l'autre l'altérant, un certain marmiton
    Nomma celui-ci Laridon.

the coach reaches the top of the hill. 'Now we can breathe!' exclaims the fly. 'At last I've managed to get these folk on to the level. Now, sir horses, pay me for my trouble.'

So certain people, fanning busily about, push their way into other people's business. They pretend to be indispensable everywhere – and, everywhere a nuisance, ought to be shooed away.

Education

PINCHER and Caesar, brothers whose pedigree sprang from famous dogs, good-looking, well-shaped, and bold, falling to two different masters in times gone by, frequented, one the forests, the other the kitchen. At first each had had another name, but their different upbringing having strengthened their natural qualities in one and debased them in the other, a certain kitchen-boy named the second Pincher.

Son frère ayant couru mainte haute aventure,
Mis maint cerf aux abois, maint sanglier abattu,
Fut le premier César que la gent chienne ait eu.
On eut soin d'empêcher qu'une indigne maîtresse
Ne fît en ses enfants dégénérer son sang.
Laridon négligé témoignait sa tendresse
   A l'objet le premier passant.
   Il peupla tout de son engeance:
Tourne-broches par lui rendus communs en France
Y font un corps à part, gens fuyant les hasards,
   Peuple antipode des Césars.

On ne suit pas toujours ses aïeux ni son père:
Le peu de soin, le temps, tout fait qu'on dégénère.
Faute de cultiver la nature et ses dons,
Oh! combien de Césars deviendront Laridons!

L'Huître et les plaideurs

UN jour deux pèlerins sur le sable rencontrent
Une huître, que le flot y venait d'apporter.
Ils l'avalent des yeux, du doigt ils se la montrent;

His brother, having accomplished many a noble deed, bayed the death of many a stag, brought down many a boar, was the first Caesar that the doggy race has had. Care was taken to ensure that no unworthy mistress should allow his line to degenerate in his children. Pincher, neglected, gave proof of his affection to any fair object who passed by. He peopled the whole place with his progeny. Turnspits, having grown common in France thanks to him, form a body apart, danger-avoiding, a tribe antipodal to the Caesars.

We do not always follow our forbears or our father. Neglect, time, everything causes us to degenerate. For want of cultivating nature and her gifts, oh! how many Caesars will become Pinchers.

The Oyster and the Litigants

ONE day on the shore two travellers came across an oyster, which the sea had just washed up. They devoured it with their eyes,

A l'égard de la dent il fallut contester.
L'un se baissait déjà pour ramasser la proie;
L'autre le pousse, et dit: Il est bon de savoir
    Qui de nous en aura la joie.
Celui qui le premier a pu l'apercevoir
En sera le gobeur; l'autre le verra faire.
    – Si par là l'on juge l'affaire,
Reprit son compagnon, j'ai l'œil bon, Dieu merci.
    – Je ne l'ai pas mauvais aussi,
Dit l'autre, et je l'ai vue avant vous, sur ma vie.
– Eh bien, vous l'avez vue; et moi je l'ai sentie.
    Pendant tout ce bel incident,
Perrin Dandin arrive: ils le prennent pour juge.
Perrin, fort gravement, ouvre l'huître et la gruge,
    Nos deux messieurs le regardant.
Ce repas fait, il dit, d'un ton de président:
Tenez, la cour vous donne à chacun une écaille,
Sans dépens; et qu'en paix chacun chez soi s'en aille.

pointed it out to each other with their fingers; toothplay remained
to be debated. The first was already stooping to pick up the prize;
the second pushed him and said: 'It still has to be seen which of us
will enjoy it. The one who saw it first will be the swallower; the
other will watch him.'

'If that is how the matter is decided,' replied his companion, 'I
have good eyesight, God be thanked.'

'Mine isn't bad either,' said the other, 'and I'll stake my life I
saw it before you.'

'All right, you saw it; but I touched it.'

In the middle of this fine scene, Perrin Dandin comes up; they
ask him to act as judge. Perrin very solemnly opens the oyster and
gulps it down while our two gentlemen watch. Having made this
meal, he says in judicial tones: 'Well, the court awards a shell to
each of you, without costs. Let each now return peaceably to his
home.'

Mettez ce qu'il en coûte à plaider aujourd'hui;
Comptez ce qu'il en reste à beaucoup de familles:
Vous verrez que Perrin tire l'argent à lui,
Et ne laisse aux plaideurs que le sac et les quilles.

NICOLAS BOILEAU

Les Folies humaines

... CHAPELAIN veut rimer, et c'est là sa folie.
Mais bien que ses durs vers, d'épithètes enflés,
Soient des moindres grimauds chez Ménage sifflés,
Lui-même il s'applaudit, et d'un esprit tranquille,
Prend le pas au Parnasse au-dessus de Virgile.
Que ferait-il, hélas, si quelque audacieux
Allait pour son malheur lui dessiller les yeux,
Lui faisant voir ses vers et sans force et sans grâces
Montés sur deux grands mots comme sur deux échasses,
Ses termes sans raison l'un de l'autre écartés,
Et ses froids ornements à la ligne plantés?
Qu'il maudirait le jour où son âme insensée
Perdit l'heureuse erreur qui charmait sa pensée!

Reckon what it costs to go to law today; count up how much is left to so many families: you will find that Perrin absorbs the money and leaves the litigants only the bag and the skittles.*

On Human Follies

CHAPELAIN wants to write verse, and that is *his* form of madness. But although his stiff lines, swollen with epithets, are hissed at Ménage's by the tiniest scribes, he applauds himself and calmly sets himself above Virgil upon Parnassus. Alas, what would he do if some rash person did him the disservice of opening his eyes, made him really see his nerveless and graceless lines, mounted on two big words as though on two stilts, his terms pointlessly from each other separated, and his frigid 'ornaments' planted in line? How he would curse the day when his insensate spirit lost the pleasant illusion which lulled his mind!

* I.e. nothing of value – the paraphernalia of the game, but not the winnings.

Jadis certain bigot, d'ailleurs homme sensé,
D'un mal assez bizarre eut le cerveau blessé,
S'imaginant sans cesse, en sa douce manie,
Des esprits bienheureux entendre l'harmonie.
Enfin, un médecin fort expert en son art
Le guérit par adresse, ou plutôt par hasard.
Mais, voulant de ses soins exiger le salaire :
«Moi, vous payer! lui dit le bigot en colère,
Vous, dont l'art infernal, par des secrets maudits
En me tirant d'erreur m'ôte du paradis?»

J'approuve son courroux, car, puisqu'il faut le dire,
Souvent de tous nos maux la raison est le pire.
C'est elle qui, farouche, au milieu des plaisirs,
D'un remords importun vient brider nos désirs.
La fâcheuse a pour nous des rigueurs sans pareilles,
C'est un pédant qu'on a sans cesse à ses oreilles,
Qui toujours nous gourmande et, loin de nous toucher,
Souvent, comme Joli, perd son temps à prêcher.
En vain certains rêveurs nous l'habillent en reine,
Veulent sur tous nos sens la rendre souveraine,

Once a certain bigot, in other respects a sensible man, was afflicted in the brain with an odd failing, imagining continually, in his harmless delusion, that he heard the harmony of the blessed spirits. At last a very clever doctor cured him by skill, or rather by chance. But when he came to demand payment for his treatment, 'I! pay you!' said the bigot angrily, 'you, whose infernal art has disabused me by unhallowed secrets only to exclude me from paradise!'

I approve his indignation, for, since it must be said, reason is often the worst of all our afflictions. It is she who comes grimly, in the midst of our pleasures, to curb our desires with irksome remorse. The tiresome creature treats us with excessive severity, she is a pedant continually harping in our ears, who always scolds and, far from moving us, often, like Joli, wastes her time preaching. In vain do certain dreamers dress her up as a queen, try to make her sovereign over all our senses and, making a goddess of her on

Et, s'en formant en terre une divinité,
Pensent aller par elle à la félicité.
C'est elle, disent-ils, qui nous montre à bien vivre.
Ces discours, il est vrai, sont fort beaux dans un livre,
Je les estime fort: mais je trouve en effet
Que le plus fou souvent est le plus satisfait.

A Mon Jardinier

... ANTOINE, de nous deux, tu crois donc, je le vois,
Que le plus occupé dans ce jardin c'est toi?
Oh! que tu changerais d'avis et de langage,
Si deux jours seulement, libre du jardinage,
Tout à coup devenu poète et bel esprit,
Tu t'allais engager à polir un écrit
Qui dît, sans s'avilir, les plus petites choses,
Fît des plus secs chardons des œillets et des roses,
Et sût même aux discours de la rusticité
Donner de l'élégance et de la dignité.
... Bientôt de ce travail revenu sec et pâle,
Et le teint plus jauni que de vingt ans de hâle,

earth, think that they will go to bliss by means of her. It is she, they say, who shows us how to live rightly. Such sentiments, it is true, are very fine in a book, and I respect them highly. But I find that in reality the maddest man is often the most contented.

To My Gardener

So, Antoine, you think, I am sure, that the busier of us two in this garden is yourself. Oh, how differently you would think and speak if only for two days, freed from gardening, having suddenly become a poet and wit, you undertook to polish a piece of writing which would express the most trivial things without demeaning itself, would turn the thorniest thistles into carnations and roses, and would even succeed in giving elegance and dignity to rustic speech.

Soon, emerging from this work fevered and pale, with your face more yellowed than by twenty years of sunburn, you would say, as

Tu dirais, reprenant ta pelle et ton râteau:
«J'aime mieux mettre encor cent arpents au niveau,
Que d'aller follement, égaré dans les nues,
Me lasser à chercher des visions cornues,
Et, pour lier des mots si mal s'entr'accordants,
Prendre dans ce jardin la lune avec les dents.»
    Approche donc, et viens; qu'un paresseux t'apprenne,
Antoine, ce que c'est que fatigue et que peine.
L'homme ici-bas, toujours inquiet et gêné,
Est, dans le repos même, au travail condamné.
La fatigue l'y suit. C'est en vain qu'aux poètes
Les neuf trompeuses Sœurs dans leurs douces retraites
Promettent du repos sous leurs ombrages frais.
Dans ces tranquilles bois, pour eux plantés exprès,
La cadence aussitôt, la rime, la césure,
La riche expression, la nombreuse mesure,
Sorcières dont l'amour sait d'abord les charmer,
De fatigue sans fin viennent les consumer.
Sans cesse poursuivant ces fugitives fées,
On voit sous les lauriers haleter les Orphées.
Leur esprit toutefois se plaît dans son tourment,
Et se fait de sa peine un noble amusement.

you took up your spade and rake again: 'I would rather level a hundred more acres than crazily, lost in the clouds, exhaust myself pursuing phantom shapes, and – in order to put together such refractory words – stand in this garden reaching for the moon.'
    Draw near, then, come. Let an idle man show you, Antoine, what weariness and labour are. Man here below, always anxious and tormented, is condemned to work even when at rest. Fatigue pursues him. In vain do the nine deceitful Sisters (the Muses) in their quiet retreats promise rest to poets under their cool shade. In those peaceful woods planted specially for them, cadence, rhyme, caesura, richness of expression, rhythmic harmony – sorceresses whose love can at first enchant them – quickly come to consume them with endless weariness. Ceaselessly pursuing those elusive fairies, the Orpheuses are seen panting beneath their laurels. And yet their minds find pleasure in their torment and make a noble distraction of their

Mais je ne trouve point de fatigue si rude
Que l'ennuyeux loisir d'un mortel sans étude,
Qui, jamais ne sortant de sa stupidité,
Soutient, dans les langueurs de son oisiveté,
D'une lâche indolence esclave volontaire,
Le pénible fardeau de n'avoir rien à faire.
... Je te vais sur cela prouver deux vérités:
L'une, que le travail, aux hommes nécessaire,
Fait leur félicité plutôt que leur misère;
Et l'autre, qu'il n'est point de coupable en repos.
C'est ce qu'il faut ici montrer en peut de mots.
Suis-moi donc ... Mais je vois, sur ce début de prône,
Que ta bouche déjà s'ouvre large d'une aune,
Et que, les yeux fermés, tu baisses le menton.
Ma foi, le plus sûr est de finir ce sermon.
Aussi bien j'aperçois ces melons qui t'attendent,
Et ces fleurs qui là-bas entre elles se demandent
S'il est fête au village, et pour quel saint nouveau
On les laisse aujourd'hui si longtemps manquer d'eau.

suffering. But I find no weariness so great as the dull leisure of a man with no studious interests, who, never emerging from his stupidity, bears in the tedium of his idleness (the willing slave of a slothful indolence) the heavy burden of having nothing to do.

Whereupon I will prove two truths to you: The first, that work, necessary to men, brings them happiness rather than misery. And the other, that no guilty man enjoys peace. That is what I must now demonstrate briefly. So try to follow me. ... But I see, as I begin my homily, that your mouth is already opening a foot wide and that, your eyes having shut, your chin drops. Well, well, the best thing is to end this sermon. I also notice those melons waiting for you, and those flowers over there which are asking each other if it is a holiday in the village, and for what new saint they are left so long without water today.

JEAN-BAPTISTE ROUSSEAU

Pour une personne convalescente

Paraphrase du Cantique d'Ézéchias

J'AI vu mes tristes journées
Décliner vers leur penchant;
Au midi de mes années
Je touchais à mon couchant.
La Mort, déployant ses ailes,
Couvrait d'ombres éternelles
La clarté dont je jouis;
Et, dans cette nuit funeste,
Je cherchais en vain le reste
De mes jours évanouis.

Grand Dieu, votre main réclame
Les dons que j'en ai reçus;
Elle vient couper la trame
Des jours qu'elle m'a tissus;
Mon dernier soleil se lève,
Et votre souffle m'enlève

For a person recovering from illness

Paraphrase of the Song of Hezekiah *

I HAVE seen my sad days descending towards their decline; in the noon of my years I was near to my setting. Death, spreading wide its wings, covered with eternal shadows the light which I enjoyed; and in that funereal night I sought in vain for the rest of my vanished days.

Great God, your hand claims back the gifts which I received from it; it comes to cut the web of the days which it wove for me; my last sun rises and your breath sweeps me up from the land of

---

* See Isaiah 38.

De la terre des vivants,
Comme la feuille séchée,
Qui, de sa tige arrachée,
Devient le jouet des vents.

Comme un lion plein de rage,
Le mal a brisé mes os;
Le tombeau m'ouvre un passage
Dans ses lugubres cachots.
Victime faible et tremblante,
A cette image sanglante
Je soupire nuit et jour;
Et, dans ma crainte mortelle,
Je suis comme l'hirondelle
Sous les griffes du vautour.

Ainsi de cris et d'alarmes
Mon mal semblait se nourrir,
Et mes yeux, noyés de larmes,
Étaient lassés de s'ouvrir.
Je disais à la nuit sombre:
«O nuit, tu vas dans ton ombre
M'ensevelir pour toujours!»
Je redisais à l'aurore:
«Le jour que tu fais éclore
Est le dernier de mes jours!»

the living, like the withered leaf torn from the bough which becomes the sport of the winds.

Sickness has broken my bones like a raging lion; the grave opens a way for me into its gloomy dungeons. A weak and trembling victim, I sigh night and day before this grisly image, and in my mortal terror I am like the swallow under the vulture's claws.

So my sickness seemed to feed on groans and terrors, and my eyes, dimmed with tears, were weary of opening. I said to the dark night: 'O night, you are about to swallow me up for ever in your shadow!' I said again to the dawn: 'The day which you are bringing forth is the last of my days!'

Mon âme est dans les ténèbres,
Mes sens sont glacés d'effroi.
Écoutez mes cris funèbres,
Dieu juste, répondez-moi.
Mais enfin sa main propice
A comblé le précipice
Qui s'entr'ouvrait sous mes pas.
Son secours me fortifie,
Et me fait trouver la vie
Dans les horreurs du trépas.

Seigneur, il faut que la terre
Connaisse en moi vos bienfaits;
Vous ne m'avez fait la guerre
Que pour me donner la paix.
Heureux l'homme à qui la grâce
Départ ce don efficace
Puisé dans ses saints trésors,
Et qui, rallumant sa flamme,
Trouve la santé de l'âme
Dans les souffrances du corps!

My soul is in the shadows, my senses are numbed with fear.
Hear my dismal cries, just God, answer me. But at last his kindly
hand closed up the precipice which was opening at my feet. His
help strengthens me and makes me find life in the horrors of death.
    Lord, it is right that the earth should see your mercies manifested
in me. You have warred against me only to give me peace. Happy
the man to whom grace imparts this efficacious gift taken from
among its holy treasures, and who, rekindling his flame, finds the
health of the soul in the sufferings of the body.

C'est pour sauver la mémoire
De vos immortels secours,
C'est pour vous, pour votre gloire,
Que vous prolongez nos jours.
Non, non, vos bontés sacrées
Ne seront point célébrées
Dans l'horreur des monuments;
La Mort, aveugle et muette,
Ne sera point l'interprète
De vos saints commandements.

Mais ceux qui de sa menace,
Comme moi, sont rachetés,
Annonceront à leur race
Vos célestes vérités.
J'irai, Seigneur, dans vos temples,
Réchauffer par mes exemples
Les mortels les plus glacés,
Et, vous offrant mon hommage,
Leur montrer l'unique usage
Des jours que vous leur laissez.

It is to preserve the memory of your eternal mercies, it is for
Yourself, for your glory, that You prolong our days. No, no, your
divine loving-kindness shall not be celebrated in the horror of the
tombs; blind and voiceless death shall not be the interpreter of your
holy commandments.

But those who, like myself, are ransomed from its threat, shall
proclaim your heavenly truths to their people. I will go into your
temples, Lord, to give new warmth by my example to (even) the
most frigid of mortal men and, offering You my homage, will show
them the sole way to use the days which You leave them.

VOLTAIRE

Le Mondain

REGRETTERA qui veut le bon vieux temps,
Et l'âge d'or, et le règne d'Astrée,
Et les beaux jours de Saturne et de Rhée,
Et le jardin de nos premiers parents;
Moi je rends grâce à la nature sage
Qui, pour mon bien, m'a fait naître en cet âge
Tant décrié par nos tristes frondeurs:
Ce temps profane est tout fait pour mes mœurs.
J'aime le luxe, et même la mollesse,
Tous les plaisirs, les arts de toute espèce,
La propreté, le goût, les ornements:
Tou honnête homme a de tels sentiments.
Il est bien doux, pour mon cœur très immonde,
De voir ici l'abondance à la ronde,
Mère des arts et des heureux travaux,
Nous apporter, de sa source féconde,
Et des besoins et des plaisirs nouveaux.
    L'or de la terre et les trésors de l'onde,
Leurs habitants et les peuples de l'air,

The Civilized Man

LET him who will regret the good old days and the Golden Age
and the reign of Astraea, and the glorious days of Saturn and Rhea
and the garden of our first parents; but I give thanks to wise nature
which, for my good, let me be born in this age so decried by our sad
grumblers. This unholy time is just right for my way of life. I like
luxury and even deep comfort, all the pleasures, all the arts, cleanliness, taste, ornament; all civilized people have such feelings. It is
very sweet, for my most vile mind, to see this general prosperity –
the mother of the arts and of well-executed work – bringing us
from its copious store both new needs and new pleasures.

    The gold of the earth and the treasures of the deep, their deni-
zens and the peoples of the air, everything contributes to luxury, to

Tout sert au luxe, aux plaisirs de ce monde.
O le bon temps que ce siècle de fer!
Le superflu, chose très nécessaire,
A réuni l'un et l'autre hémisphère.
Voyez-vous pas ces agiles vaisseaux
Qui du Texel, de Londres, de Bordeaux,
S'en vont chercher, par un heureux échange,
Ces nouveaux biens, nés aux sources du Gange,
Tandis qu'au loin, vainqueurs des musulmans,
Nos vins de France enivrent les sultans!

Quand la nature était dans son enfance,
Nos bons aïeux vivaient dans l'ignorance,
Ne connaissant ni *le tien* ni *le mien*.
Qu'auraient-ils pu connaître? ils n'avaient rien,
Ils étaient nus; et c'est chose très claire
Que qui n'a rien n'a nul partage à faire.
Sobres étaient. Ah! je le crois encor:
Martialo n'est point du siècle d'or;
D'un bon vin frais ou la mousse ou la sève
Ne gratta point le triste gosier d'Ève;
La soie et l'or ne brillaient point chez eux.

the pleasures of this world. What a good time this iron age is! The superfluous, a most necessary thing, has brought the two hemispheres together. Do you not see those swift ships which, from Texel, London, Bordeaux, go out to seek, by a happy exchange, these new luxuries from the source of the Ganges – while far from here, conquering the Moslems, our French wines make sultans drunk!

When nature was in its infancy, our good forefathers lived in ignorance, knowing nothing of 'yours' and 'mine'. What could they have known? They had nothing, they were naked, and it is very plain that he who has nothing has nothing to share. They were frugal and sober – I can well believe it! Martialo * does not belong to the Golden Age; the foam and savour of a good cool wine never tickled the sad gullet of Eve. No silk and gold gleamed in

* A gastronomic expert.

Admirez-vous pour cela nos aïeux?
Il leur manquait l'industrie et l'aisance:
Est-ce vertu? c'était pure ignorance.
Quel idiot, s'il avait eu pour lors
Quelque bon lit, aurait couché dehors?
 Mon cher Adam, mon gourmand, mon bon père,
Que faisais-tu dans les jardins d'Éden?
Travaillais-tu pour ce sot genre humain?
Caressais-tu madame Ève, ma mère?
Avouez-moi que vous aviez tous deux
Les ongles longs, un peu noirs et crasseux,
La chevelure assez mal ordonnée,
Le teint bruni, la peau bise et tannée.
Sans propreté, l'amour le plus heureux
N'est plus amour, c'est un besoin honteux.
Bientôt lassés de leur belle aventure,
Dessous un chêne ils soupent galamment
Avec de l'eau, du millet et du gland;
Le repas fait, ils dorment sur la dure:
Voilà l'état de la pure nature ...

their homes. Do you admire our ancestors for that? They were without industries and comfort: is that a virtue? It was pure ignorance. What idiot would have slept out-of-doors if he had had a good bed then?

My dear Adam, my glutton, my good father, what did you do in the Garden of Eden? Did you work for this silly human race? Did you caress Madam Eve, my mother? Admit that both of you had long nails, rather black and grubby, unkempt hair, sunburnt faces, skins brownish and tanned. Without cleanliness, the happiest love is love no longer, it is a shameful need. Soon tiring of their fine affair, they sup romantically beneath an oak on water, birdseed and acorns. The meal done, they sleep on the bare ground. Such was the state of pure nature.

Les Vous *et les* Tu

PHILIS, qu'est devenu ce temps
Où, dans un fiacre promenée,
Sans laquais, sans ajustements,
De tes grâces seules ornée,
Contente d'un mauvais souper
Que tu changeais en ambroisie,
Tu te livrais, dans ta folie,
A l'amant heureux et trompé
Qui t'avait consacré sa vie?
Le ciel ne te donnait alors,
Pour tout rang et pour tous trésors,
Que les agréments de ton âge,
Un cœur tendre, un esprit volage,
Un sein d'albâtre et de beaux yeux.
Avec tant d'attraits précieux,
Hélas! qui n'eût été friponne?
Tu le fus, objet gracieux!
Et (que l'Amour me le pardonne!)
Tu sais que je t'en aimais mieux.

'You' formal and intimate

PHYLLIS, what has become of those days when, taken out in a
hackney-coach, with no footmen, no frills, adorned with just your
own charms, satisfied with a cheap supper which you changed into
food for the gods, you gave yourself in your careless way to your
lover, the lucky cuckold, who had sworn to be yours for life?
Heaven only gave you then, as your sole prestige and sole wealth,
the youthful attractions of your age, a tender heart, a flighty mind,
a lily-white breast, and sparkling eyes. With so many precious
charms, ah me, who would not have been a little rogue? You were,
you charming thing! And — may Love forgive me! — you know I
only loved you better for it, dear.

Ah, madame! que votre vie,
D'honneurs aujourd'hui si remplie,
Diffère de ces doux instants!
Ce large suisse à cheveux blancs,
Qui ment sans cesse à votre porte,
Philis, est l'image du Temps:
On dirait qu'il chasse l'escorte
Des tendres Amours et des Ris;
Sous vos magnifiques lambris
Ces enfants tremblent de paraître.
Hélas! je les ai vus jadis
Entrer chez toi par la fenêtre,
Et se jouer dans ton taudis.

Non, madame, tous ces tapis
Qu'a tissus la Savonnerie,
Ceux que les Persans ont ourdis,
Et toute votre orfèvrerie,
Et ces plats si chers que Germain
A gravés de sa main divine,
Et ces cabinets où Martin
A surpassé l'art de la Chine;

Ah Madam, how your life, so filled with distinction today, differs
from those sweet moments! That wide white wigged porter who
tells lies continually at your door is, Phyllis, the image of Time: he
seems to be driving away your escort of tender Cupids and smiles;
those children tremble to appear beneath your magnificent roof.
Ah me, I have seen them in other days climbing in through the
window and sporting round in your threadbare lodging.

No, Madam, all those carpets woven at the Savonnerie, the ones
woven in Persia and all your gold plate, and those precious dishes
engraved by Germain's divine hand, and those cabinets in which
Martin has excelled the art of China, your white Japanese vases – all

Vos vases japonais et blancs,
Toutes ces fragiles merveilles;
Ces deux lustres de diamants
Qui pendent à vos deux oreilles;
Ces riches carcans, ces colliers,
Et cette pompe enchanteresse,
Ne valent pas un des baisers
Que tu donnais dans ta jeunesse.

Épigramme sur l'Abbé de Saint-Pierre

N'A pas longtemps, de l'abbé de Saint-Pierre
On me montrait le buste tant parfait
Qu'onc ne sus voir si c'était chair ou pierre,
Tant le sculpteur l'avait pris trait pour trait.
Adonc restai perplexe et stupéfait,
Craignant en moi de tomber en méprise,
Puis dis soudain: «Ce n'est là qu'un portrait;
L'original dirait quelque sottise.»

those fragile marvels – those two clusters of diamonds which hang
from your ears, those rich chokers, those necklaces, and all that
fabulous luxury, are not worth one of the kisses which you gave,
honey, when you were young.

Epigram
On the Abbé de Saint-Pierre

NOT long ago I was shown a bust of the Abbé de Saint-Pierre
which was so perfect that I really could not decide if it was flesh
or stone, so faithfully had the sculptor rendered every feature. So I
stood there perplexed and bewildered, fearful of committing a
blunder. Then I said with sudden conviction: 'It is only a likeness;
the original would be making some stupid remark.'

JEAN-FRANÇOIS DE SAINT-LAMBERT

L'Été

O TOI dont l'Éternel a tracé la carrière,
Toi, qui fais végéter et sentir la matière,
Qui mesures le temps et dispenses le jour,
Roi des mondes errants qui composent ta cour,
Du Dieu qui te conduit noble et brillante image:
Les saisons, leurs présents, nos biens, sont ton ouvrage.

Tu disposas la terre à la fécondité
Quand tu la revêtis de grâce et de beauté;
Tu t'élevas bientôt sur la céleste voûte,
Et des traits plus ardents répandus sur ta route
De l'équateur au pôle ont pénétré les airs,
Le centre de la terre et l'abîme des mers.

A des êtres sans nombre ils donnent la naissance,
Tout se meut, s'organise, et sent son existence.
Le sable et le limon se sont-ils animés?
Dans les bois, dans les eaux, sur les monts enflammés,
Les germes de oiseaux, des poissons, des reptiles
S'élancent à la fois de leurs prisons fragiles.

Summer

YOU * whose course the Eternal Spirit has marked out, you who give growth and feeling to matter, who measure out time and mete out the day, king of the wandering worlds who compose your court, bright and noble image of the God who guides you: the seasons, their gifts, our riches, are your work.

You prepared the earth to be fertile when you clothed it with grace and beauty; soon you mounted to the height of the heavenly vault and hotter beams, shed about your path, penetrated the atmosphere, the depths of the earth and of the seas from the equator to the pole.

They give birth to innumerable beings, everything stirs, organizes itself, and is conscious of existence. Are the sand and the mud filled with life? In the woods, in the waters, on the burning mountains, the germs of birds, fish, reptiles, burst out all at once from their

* The sun.

Ici, le faon léger se joue avec l'agneau;
Là, le jeune coursier bondit près du chevreau;
Sur les bords opposés de ces feuilles légères
Résident des tribus l'une à l'autre étrangères;
Les calices des fleurs, les fruits, sont habités;
Dans les humbles gazons s'élèvent des cités;
Et des eaux de la nue une goutte insensible
Renferme un peuple atome, une foule invisible.

Comme un flot disparaît sous le flot qui le suit,
Un être est remplacé par l'être qu'il produit.
Ils naissent, Dieu puissant, lorsque ta voix féconde
Les appelle à leur tour sur la scène du monde.
Dévorés l'un par l'autre, ou détruits par le temps,
Ils ont à tes desseins servi quelques instants. . . .

L'Hiver

... L'HIVER en ce moment s'y livre à ses fureurs.
Il subjugue Neptune, il couvre de ses chaînes
Cette mer ténébreuse où les vastes baleines
Présentaient dans l'automne aux yeux des matelots
De mobiles écueils s'agitant sur les flots.

fragile prisons. Here, the nimble fawn plays with the lamb; there, the young steed bounds near the kid; on the opposite edges of those light leaves, tribes dwell which are foreign to one another; the calyxes of the flowers, the fruits, are inhabited; in humble clods of turf, cities spring up; and an inanimate drop of rain-water contains an atomy people, an invisible multitude.

As a wave disappears beneath the following wave, a being is replaced by the being it produces. They are born, O mighty God, when your life-giving voice calls them in their turn on to the stage of the world. Devoured by each other, or destroyed by time, they have served your purpose for a few moments.

Winter

WINTER now gives rein to its fury. It subdues Neptune, it covers with its chains that dark sea on which the huge whales appeared in autumn to the eyes of sailors like moving reefs stirring beneath the

Il envoie au midi la peur et les orages,
La famine et les vents, la mort et les ravages.
D'un froid âpre et funeste il pénètre nos sens.
Le soleil lance au loin quelques traits impuissants;
La nuit revient d'abord augmenter la froidure;
Des chaînes de cristal ont chargé la nature.

　　Je n'entends plus, le soir, la course des ruisseaux,
La cascade muette a suspendu ses eaux,
Et souvent le berger, au lever de l'aurore,
L'observe en l'écoutant, et croit l'entendre encore.
Les glaçons réunis sur les vastes étangs
Renferment sous un mur leurs tristes habitants.
Ce fleuve est enchaîné dans sa course rapide;
Il voudrait s'élancer de sa voûte solide,
Sous le cristal vainqueur il roule emprisonné.

　　De givre, de glaçons, ce bois est couronné;
Ils brillent suspendus à la branche flétrie,
Et d'un voile d'argent ils couvrent la prairie.
Mais de nouveaux frimas rassemblés dans les airs
Pèsent sans mouvement sur les coteaux déserts;
Et la voûte des cieux, qui semble être abaissée,
Dépose avec lenteur la vapeur condensée.

waves. It brings terror and storms to the south, famine and winds, death and destruction. It strikes our senses with a bitter and deadly cold. The distant sun throws out a few powerless beams, night soon returns to increase the cold. Nature is loaded with crystal chains.

I no longer hear the sound of running streams at evening, the silent waterfall has suspended its waters, and often the shepherd at the break of dawn looks at it and listens, and thinks he still hears it. The ice, closing over the huge ponds, imprisons their sad denizens under its wall. The river is fettered in its rapid flow; it would rush out from its solid vault, but rolls imprisoned beneath the victorious crystal.

That wood is crowned with rime and icicles. They glitter as they hang from the withered branch and cover the meadows with a silver veil. But new hoar-frost, gathering in the atmosphere, weighs unmoving on the deserted hillsides, and the vault of heaven, which seems to have sunk lower, slowly deposits the condensed vapour.

Si le fermier parcourt les guérets confondus,
Au milieu de ses champs il ne les connaît plus,
Et la vaste blancheur sur le monde étendue
Déconcerte ses pas et fatigue sa vue;
Ce voile universel dérobe à tous les yeux
Les ouvrages de l'homme et les bienfaits des dieux. . . .

ANTOINE-LÉONARD THOMAS

Ode sur le Temps

LE compas d'Uranie a mesuré l'espace.
O Temps, être inconnu que l'âme seule embrasse,
Invisible torrent des siècles et des jours,
Tandis que ton pouvoir m'entraîne dans la tombe,
J'ose, avant que j'y tombe,
M'arrêter un moment pour contempler ton cours.

Qui me dévoilera l'instant qui t'a vu naître?
Quel œil peut remonter aux sources de ton être?
Sans doute ton berceau touche à l'éternité.

If the farmer walks over the indistinct fields, in the middle of his land he does not recognize it, and a vast whiteness, spread over the world, confuses his steps and tires his sight. This universal veil conceals from all eyes the works of man and the gifts of the gods.

Ode on Time

THE compasses of Urania * have measured out space. O Time, unknown being which the soul alone embraces, invisible torrent of the ages and the days, while your power carries me towards the grave, I dare, before I go down into it, to halt for a moment to contemplate your course.

Who will reveal to me the instant which saw your birth? What eye can look back to the sources of your being? Doubtless your cradle touches eternity. When nothing yet was, buried in the

* The Muse of astronomy.

Quand rien n'était encore, enseveli dans l'ombre
    De cet abîme sombre,
Ton germe y reposait, mais sans activité.

Du chaos tout à coup les portes s'ébranlèrent;
Des soleils allumés les feux étincelèrent;
Tu naquis; l'Éternel te prescrivit ta loi.
Il dit au mouvement: «Du Temps sois la mesure.»
    Il dit à la nature:
«Le Temps sera pour vous, l'Éternité pour moi.»

Dieu, telle est ton essence: oui, l'océan des âges
Roule au-dessous de toi sur tes frêles ouvrages,
Mais il n'approche pas de ton trône immortel.
Des millions de jours qui l'un l'autre s'effacent,
    Des siècles qui s'entassent,
Sont comme le néant aux yeux de l'Éternel.

Mais moi, sur cet amas de fange et de poussière,
En vain contre le Temps je cherche une barrière;
Son vol impétueux me presse et me poursuit.
Je n'occupe qu'un point de la vaste étendue,
    Et mon âme éperdue
Sous mes pas chancelants voit ce point qui s'enfuit.

night of that dark abyss, your germ was there, waiting but inactive.

Suddenly the gates of chaos swung open; the lights of the kindled suns flashed out; you were born; the Everlasting gave you your law. He said to motion: 'Be the measure of Time.' He said to nature: 'Time will be for you, Eternity for me.'

Such, God, is your essence: yes, the ocean of the ages rolls beneath You above your frail works, but it does not approach your immortal throne. Millions of days effacing one another, ages accumulating, are as void and nothing in the sight of the Everlasting.

But I, on this heap of mire and dust, seek in vain some rampart against Time; its rushing wing drives me on and pursues me. I occupy only a point in the vast expanse, and my bewildered soul sees that point slipping away from beneath my tottering feet.

De la destruction tout m'offre des images.
Mon œil épouvanté ne voit que des ravages:
Ici de vieux tombeaux que la mousse a couverts,
Là des murs abattus, des colonnes brisées,
      Des villes embrasées:
Partout les pas du Temps empreints sur l'univers.

Cieux, terres, éléments, tout est sous sa puissance.
Mais tandis que sa main, dans la nuit du silence,
Du fragile univers sape les fondements,
Sur des ailes de feu loin du monde élancée,
      Mon active pensée
Plane sur les débris entassés par le Temps.

Siècles qui n'êtes plus, et vous qui devez naître,
J'ose vous appeler: hâtez-vous de paraître.
Au moment où je suis venez vous réunir.
Je parcours tous les points de l'immense durée
      D'une marche assurée:
J'enchaîne le présent, je vis dans l'avenir.

Everything shows me images of destruction. My eyes, appalled, see only devastation: here, ancient tombs which the moss has covered; there, ruined walls, broken columns, burnt-out cities; everywhere Time's footsteps imprinted on the universe.

Heavens, worlds, elements, all are under its power. But while its hand, in the night of silence, undermines the foundations of the fragile universe, my active mind, borne far from the earth on wings of fire, soars above the ruins heaped up by Time.

Centuries which are no more, and you still to be born, I dare to summon you: make haste to appear. Come and assemble at the moment where I am. I visit every point of the immense duration with confident steps: I enchain the present, I live in the future.

Le soleil épuisé dans sa brûlante course
De ses feux par degrés verra tarir la source,
Et des mondes vieillis les ressorts s'useront.
Ainsi que des rochers qui du haut des montagnes
     Roulent sur les campagnes,
Les astres l'un sur l'autre un jour s'écrouleront.

Là, de l'Éternité commencera l'empire,
Et dans cet océan où tout va se détruire,
Le Temps s'engloutira comme un faible ruisseau.
Mais mon âme immortelle, aux siècles échappée,
     Ne sera point frappée,
Et des mondes brisés foulera le tombeau. ...

JACQUES DELILLE

[*Nice*]

O NICE! heureux séjour, montagnes renommées,
De lavande, de thym, de citron parfumées:
Que de fois sous tes plants d'oliviers toujours verts,

The sun, exhausted in its burning course, will see the source of
its light gradually quenched, and the motive forces of the ageing
worlds will wear out. Like rocks rolling down on the fields from the
tops of the mountains, the stars will one day tumble one upon
another.

Then will begin the reign of Eternity, and in that ocean in which
everything will be destroyed, Time will be engulfed like a tiny
stream. But my immortal soul, having escaped from the ages, will
not be struck down, and will walk over the grave of the shattered
worlds.

Nice

O NICE! happy town, famous mountains scented with lavender,
with thyme, with lemons: how often beneath your always green

Dont la pâleur s'unit au sombre azur des mers,
J'égarai mes regards sur ce théâtre immense!
Combien je jouissais! soit que l'onde en silence,
Mollement balancée, et roulant sans efforts,
D'une frange d'écume allât ceindre ses bords,
Soit que son vaste sein se gonflât de colère,
J'aimais à voir le flot, d'abord ride légère,
De loin blanchir, s'enfler, s'allonger et marcher,
Bondir tout écumant de rocher en rocher,
Tantôt se déployer comme un serpent flexible,
Tantôt, tel qu'un tonnerre, avec un bruit horrible,
Précipiter sa masse, et de ses tourbillons
Dans les rocs caverneux engloutir les bouillons.
Ce mouvement, ce bruit, cette mer turbulente,
Roulant, montant, tombant en montagne écumante,
Enivraient mon esprit, mon oreille, mes yeux,
Et le soir me trouvait immobile en ces lieux. . . .

olive-groves, whose paleness merges into the dull blue of the seas, did I let my eyes wander round that immense scene! What pleasure I took in it! Whether the sea silently, softly swaying and smoothly rolling, girdled its shores with a fringe of foam, or whether its vast breast heaved with rage, I loved to watch the wave, at first a light ripple, whiten in the distance, swell, grow longer, and advance, bound foaming from rock to rock, sometimes writhing out like a supple snake, sometimes, like a thunderclap, fling its mass forward with a horrifying din and engulf its bubbling eddies in the rocky caves. This motion, this noise, this turbulent sea, rolling, rising, falling in foaming mountains, ravished my mind, my ear, my eyes, and evening found me still rooted to that spot.

ÉVARISTE DE PARNY

Le Bouquet de l'amour

Dans ce moment les politesses,
Les souhaits vingt fois répétés
Et les ennuyeuses caresses
Pleuvent sans doute à tes côtés.
Après ces compliments sans nombre
L'Amour fidèle aura son tour;
Car, dès qu'il verra la nuit sombre
Remplacer la clarté du jour,
Il s'en ira, sans autre escorte
Que le Plaisir tendre et discret,
Frappant doucement à ta porte,
T'offrir ses vœux et son bouquet.
    Quand l'âge aura blanchi ma tête,
Réduit tristement à glaner,
J'irai te souhaiter ta fête,
Ne pouvant plus te la donner.

Love's Bouquet

At this moment compliments, good wishes twenty times repeated
and tedious caresses are no doubt being showered upon you. After
these countless congratulations faithful Love will have its turn; for,
as soon as it sees dark night succeeding the light of day, it will
come, escorted only by discreet, tender Pleasure, knocking softly
at your door, to offer you its wishes and its flowers.

When age has whitened my hairs, reduced sadly to gleaning, I
shall come and *wish* you a happy birthday, being no longer able to
give you one.

Le Revenant

J'IGNORE ce qu'on fait là-bas.
Si du sein de la nuit profonde
On peut revenir en ce monde,
Je reviendrai, n'en doutez pas.
Mais je n'aurai jamais l'allure
De ces revenants indiscrets,
Qui, précédés d'un long murmure,
Se plaisent à pâlir leurs traits,
Et dont la funèbre parure,
Inspirant toujours la frayeur,
Ajoute encore à la laideur
Qu'on reçoit dans la sépulture.
De vous plaire je suis jaloux,
Et je veux rester invisible.
Souvent du zéphyr le plus doux
Je prendrai l'haleine insensible,
Tous mes soupirs seront pour vous :
Ils feront vaciller la plume
Sur vos cheveux noués sans art,
Et disperseront au hasard
La faible odeur qui les parfume.
Si la rose que vous aimez

The Ghost

I DON'T know what they do down there. If from the heart of deepest night one can come back to this world, I shall come back, you may be sure. But I shall never appear like those indiscreet ghosts which, heralded by long-drawn moans, see fit to whiten their features, and whose funereal attire, always arousing fear, increases the ugliness one acquires in the tomb.

I am eager to please you and I would choose to remain invisible. Often I will borrow the scarcely perceptible breath of the lightest breeze. All my sighs will be for you. They will sway the feather on your carelessly knotted hair and will disperse at random the subtle scent which perfumes it. If the rose you love revives on

Renaît sur son trône de verre,
Si de vos flambeaux rallumés
Sort une plus vive lumière,
Si l'éclat d'un nouveau carmin
Colore soudain votre joue,
Et si souvent d'un joli sein
Le nœud trop serré se dénoue,
Si le sofa plus mollement
Cède au poids de votre paresse,
Donnez un souris seulement
A tous ces soins de ma tendresse.
Quand je reverrai les attraits
Qu'effleura ma main caressante,
Ma voix amoureuse et touchante
Pourra murmurer des regrets;
Et vous croirez alors entendre
Cette harpe qui, sous mes doigts,
Sut vous redire quelquefois
Ce que mon cœur savait m'apprendre.
Aux douceurs de votre sommeil
Je joindrai celles du mensonge;
Moi-même, sous les traits d'un songe,
Je causerai votre réveil.

its glass throne, if from your lighted candles a brighter flame shines out, if the glow of a fresh carmine suddenly colours your cheek, and if often on a pretty breast the knot, too tight, is loosened, if the sofa yields more softly under your sleepy weight, spare just a smile for all these marks of my love.

When I see again those charms which my hand brushed caressingly, my voice, touching and tender, may well murmur my regrets. And then you will think you hear that harp which sometimes, under my fingers, managed to repeat to you what my heart managed to teach me. To the sweetness of your sleep, I will add the sweetness of illusion. In the guise of a dream, I myself will cause

Charmes nus, fraîcheur du bel âge,
Contours parfaits, grâce, embonpoint,
Je verrai tout: mais, quel dommage,
Les morts ne ressuscitent point.

Que le bonheur arrive lentement!
Que le bonheur s'éloigne avec vitesse!
Durant le cours de ma triste jeunesse,
Si j'ai vécu, ce ne fut qu'un moment.
Je suis puni de ce moment d'ivresse.
L'espoir qui trompe a toujours sa douceur,
Et dans nos maux du moins il nous console,
Mais loin de moi l'illusion s'envole,
Et l'espérance est morte dans mon cœur.
Ce cœur, hélas, que le chagrin dévore,
Ce cœur malade et surchargé d'ennui,
Dans le passé veut ressaisir encore
De son bonheur la fugitive aurore
Et tous les biens qu'il n'a pas aujourd'hui.
Mais du présent l'image trop fidèle
Me suit toujours dans ces rêves trompeurs,
Et sans pitié la vérité cruelle
Vient m'avertir de répandre des pleurs.

your awakening. Naked charms, freshness of youth, perfect lines, grace, agreeable plumpness, I shall see all. But, more's the pity, the dead do not come back again.

How slowly happiness comes! How quickly happiness goes! During my sad youth, if I lived it was for a moment only. I am punished for that moment of ecstasy. Deceiving hope is always sweet and at least consoles us in our suffering, but the illusion flies far from me and hope is dead in my heart. This heart, alas, which grief consumes, this heart, ailing and burdened with misery, would recapture from the past the fleeting dawn of its happiness and all the joys which it does not have today. But the present's too-living image always follows me in these deceitful dreams, and cruel truth comes pitilessly to remind me to weep. I have lost everything –

J'ai tout perdu: délire, jouissance,
Transports brûlants, paisible volupté,
Douces erreurs, consolante espérance,
J'ai tout perdu: l'amour seul est resté.

ANDRÉ CHÉNIER

Bacchus

VIENS, ô divin Bacchus, ô jeune Thyonée,
O Dionyse, Évan, Iacchus et Lénée;
Viens, tel que tu parus aux déserts de Naxos,
Quand tu vins rassurer la fille de Minos.
Le superbe éléphant, en proie à ta victoire,
Avait de ses débris formé ton char d'ivoire.
De pampres, de raisins, mollement enchaînés,
Le tigre aux larges flancs de taches sillonnés,
Et le lynx étoilé, la panthère sauvage,
Promenaient avec toi ta cour sur ce rivage.
L'or reluisait partout aux axes de tes chars.
Les Ménades couraient en longs cheveux épars
Et chantaient Évoé, Bacchus et Thyonée,
Et Dionyse, Évan, Iacchus et Lénée,

rapture, pleasure, burning ecstasy, untroubled joy, sweet follies, comforting hope, I have lost everything: only love is left.

Bacchus

COME, divine Bacchus, O young Thyoneus, O Dionysus, Euan, Iacchus, and Lenaeus. Come, as you appeared on the deserted shores of Naxos, when you came to console the daughter of Minos. The proud elephant, a trophy of your victory, had formed your ivory car with his spoils. Softly enchained with vines, with grapes, the broad-flanked tiger streaked with stripes, and the star-marked lynx and the savage panther drew you and your court along that shore. Gold gleamed everywhere on the axles of your chariots. The Maenads ran with their long hair flowing and sang Evoe, Bacchus, Thyoneus, and Dionysus, Euan, Iacchus, and Lenaeus,

Et tout ce que pour toi la Grèce eut de beaux noms.
Et la voix des rochers répétait leurs chansons,
Et le rauque tambour, les sonores cymbales,
Les hautbois tortueux, et les doubles crotales
Qu'agitaient en dansant sur ton bruyant chemin
Le Faune, le Satyre et le jeune Sylvain,
Au hasard attroupés autour du vieux Silène,
Qui, sa coupe à la main, de la rive indienne
Toujours ivre, toujours débile, chancelant,
Pas à pas cheminait sur son âne indolent.

La Mort d'Hercule

ŒTA, mont ennobli par cette nuit ardente,
Quand l'infidèle époux d'une épouse imprudente
Reçut de son amour un présent trop jaloux,
Victime du Centaure immolé par ses coups.

and all the fair names that Greece had for you. And the voice of the rocks repeated their songs, with the harsh drum, the ringing cymbals, the curving oboes and the twin castanets which were shaken as they danced on your noisy way by the Faun, the Satyr, and the young Sylvan, flocking in disorder round old Silenus, who, cup in hand, and always drunk since the Indian shore, always feeble, reeling, rode slowly along on his sleepy ass.

The Death of Hercules *

ŒTA, mount ennobled by that burning night, when the unfaithful husband of an imprudent spouse received too jealous a token of her love, (and became the) victim of the Centaur slain by his own hand.

* Hercules (Alcides) received from his wife a shirt rubbed with the blood of the Centaur Nessus, whom he had killed. She believed that the blood would act as a charm to make Hercules faithful to her, but instead the shirt burned into his skin, causing unbearable pain. Uprooting trees in his agony, Hercules built his own funeral pyre and perished upon it with his attributes – the club and the skin of the Nemean Lion.

Il brise tes forêts. Ta cime épaisse et sombre
En un bûcher immense amoncelle sans nombre
Les sapins résineux que son bras a ployés.
Il y porte la flamme; il monte; sous ses pieds
Étend du vieux lion la dépouille héroïque,
Et l'œil au ciel, la main sur sa massue antique,
Attend sa récompense et l'heure d'être un dieu.
Le vent souffle et mugit. Le bûcher tout en feu
Brille autour du héros, et la flamme rapide
Porte aux palais divins l'âme du grand Alcide.

Néære

Mais telle qu'à sa mort, pour la dernière fois,
Un beau cygne soupire, et de sa douce voix,
De sa voix qui bientôt lui doit être ravie,
Chante, avant de partir, ses adieux à la vie:
Ainsi, les yeux remplis de langueur et de mort,
Pâle, elle ouvrit sa bouche en un dernier effort:

He breaks your forests. Your dark and wooded height piles up beyond counting in an immense pyre the resinous pines snapped off by his arm. He sets fire to it, mounts it, spreads under his feet the heroic spoils of the old lion and, with his eyes fixed on heaven, his hand on his ancient club, awaits his reward and the hour to be a god. The wind blows and roars. The blazing pyre shines round the hero, and the swift flame bears up to the divine palaces the soul of great Alcides.

Neæra

But as at its death, for the last time, a beautiful swan laments, and with its sweet voice, its voice which is soon to be taken from it, sings before it goes its farewell to life: so, her eyes filled with languor and death, pale, she opened her mouth in a last song:

«O vous, du Sébéthus Naïades vagabondes,
Coupez sur mon tombeau vos chevelures blondes.
Adieu, mon Clinias! moi, celle qui te plus,
Moi, celle qui t'aimai, que tu ne verras plus.
O cieux, ô terre, ô mer, prés, montagnes, rivages,
Fleurs, bois mélodieux, vallons, grottes sauvages,
Rappelez-lui souvent, rappelez-lui toujours
Néære tout son bien, Néære ses amours;
Cette Néære, hélas! qu'il nommait sa Néære,
Qui pour lui criminelle, abandonna sa mère;
Qui pour lui fugitive, errant de lieux en lieux,
Aux regards des humains n'osa lever les yeux.
Oh, soit que l'astre pur des deux frères d'Hélène
Calme sous ton vaisseau la vague ionienne,
Soit qu'aux bords de Pæstum, sous ta soigneuse main,
Les roses deux fois l'an couronnent ton jardin,
Au coucher du soleil, si ton âme attendrie
Tombe en une muette et molle rêverie,
Alors, mon Clinias, appelle, appelle-moi,
Je viendrai, Clinias, je volerai vers toi.

'O you, wandering Naiads of the Sebethus, cut your fair tresses
upon my tomb. Farewell, my Clinias! I, she who pleased you, I,
she who loved you, whom you will see no more. O skies, earth,
sea, meadows, mountains, shores, flowers, melodious woods, valleys, wild caves, remind him often, remind him always, of Neæra
his whole joy, Neæra his love; that Neæra, alas, whom he called his
Neæra, who, sinning for his sake, deserted her mother; who an out-
cast for his sake, roaming from place to place, dared not raise her
eyes to meet the eyes of men.
    'Whether the pure star of the two brothers of Helen (Castor and
Pollux) calms the Ionian wave beneath your ship, or on the shores of
Paestum, under your diligent hand, the roses crown your garden
twice every year, at sunset if your soul, moved, falls into soft and
silent musings, then, my Clinias, call me, call me. I will come,

Mon âme vagabonde à travers le feuillage
Frémira; sur les vents ou sur quelque nuage
Tu la verras descendre, ou du sein de la mer
S'élevant comme un songe, étinceler dans l'air,
Et ma voix, toujours tendre et doucement plaintive,
Caresser, en fuyant, ton oreille attentive.»

Épigramme

(*Inspirée de Properce*)

«LAISSE, ô blanche Lydé, toi pour qui je soupire,
Sur ce pâle berger tomber un doux sourire,
Et, de ton grand œil noir daignant chercher ses pas,
Dis-lui: ‹Pâle berger, viens; je ne te hais pas.› »

– «Pâle berger aux yeux mourants, à la voix tendre,
Cesse, à mes doux baisers cesse enfin de prétendre.
Non, berger, je ne puis. Je n'en ai point pour toi.
Ils sont tous à Mœris, ils ne sont plus à moi.»

Clinias, I will hasten to you. My wandering soul will tremble in
the foliage; on the winds or on some cloud you will see it descend,
or, rising from the heart of the sea like a dream, glitter in the air,
and my voice, still tender and softly plaintive, will caress as it passes
your listening ear.'

Epigram

(*After Propertius*)

‘LET, O white Lydè, you for whom I sigh, a sweet smile fall upon
this pale shepherd and, with your big dark eye deigning to mark his
coming, say to him: "Pale shepherd, come; I do not hate you."
‘Pale shepherd with languid eyes, with tender voice, cease, cease
now to lay claim to my soft kisses. No, shepherd, I cannot. I have
none for you. They are all Moeris's, they are mine no longer.'

Épigramme

O CRÉDULES amants, écoutez donc au moins
De vos baisers secrets ces mobiles témoins,
Ces flots d'azur errants sous vos belles dryades,
Byblis, Œnone, Alphée, et tant d'autres naïades,
Qui murmurent encor de doux gémissements.
Tous furent autrefois de crédules amants
Qui, se fondant en pleurs, et changés en fontaines
Par la pitié des dieux, serpentent dans vos plaines.

L'Amérique

Invocation

SALUT, ô belle nuit, étincelante et sombre ...
Qui n'entend que la voix de mes vers et les cris
De la rive aréneuse où se brise Thétis.
Muse, Muse nocturne, apporte-moi ma lyre.
Comme un fier météore, en ton brûlant délire,
Lance-toi dans l'espace et, pour franchir les airs,
Prends les ailes des vents, les ailes des éclairs,
Les bonds de la comète aux longs cheveux de flamme.

Epigram

O CREDULOUS lovers, at least listen to these moving witnesses of your secret kisses, these azure waters wandering beneath your lovely dryads, Biblis, Oenone, Alpheus, and so many other naiads, who still murmur their soft plaints. All were once credulous lovers who, dissolving in tears and changed into streams through the pity of the gods, wind through your plains.

Invocation

HAIL, lovely night, glittering and dark, you who hear only the voice of my verse and the cries of the sandy shore on which Tethys (Ocean) breaks. Muse, Muse of night, bring me my lyre. Like a proud meteor in your burning ecstasy, launch yourself into space and, to pass through the skies, take the wings of the winds, the wings of the lightning, the bounds of the comet with long hair of flame.

Mes vers impatients élancés de mon âme
Veulent parler aux dieux, et volent où reluit
L'enthousiasme errant, fils de la belle nuit.
Accours, grande Nature, ô mère du génie.
Accours, reine du monde, éternelle Uranie,
Soit que tes pas divins sur l'astre du Lion
Ou sur les triples feux du superbe Orion
Marchent, ou soit qu'au loin, fugitive emportée,
Tu suives les détours de la voie argentée,
Soleils amoncelés dans le céleste azur
Où le peuple a cru voir les traces d'un lait pur;
Descends, non, porte-moi sur ta route brûlante,
Que je m'élève au ciel comme une flamme ardente.
Déjà ce corps pesant se détache de moi,
Adieu, tombeau de chair, je ne suis plus à toi.
Terre, fuis sous mes pas. L'éther où le ciel nage
M'aspire. Je parcours l'océan sans rivage.
Plus de nuit. Je n'ai plus d'un globe opaque et dur
Entre le jour et moi l'impénétrable mur.

My eager verses, springing from my soul, would speak with the gods, and they fly where roving Enthusiasm, the son of the fair night, shines out. Come to me, great Nature, mother of genius. Come, queen of the universe, eternal Urania: whether your feet walk on the star of the Lion, or on the triple lights of proud Orion, or whether afar, an impetuous fugitive, you follow the windings of the silvery way, those suns heaped together in the azure of heaven, in which the common people thought they saw the traces of a pure milk.*

Come down — no, rather bear me up on your fiery path, let me rise to heaven like a burning flame. Already this solid body falls away from me, farewell, fleshly tomb, I am no longer yours. Earth, flee from under my feet. The ether in which the sky swims draws me up. I move through the shoreless ocean. There is no more night. I no longer have the impenetrable wall of a hard, opaque globe between the day and me.

---

* The Milky Way: according to legend, the milk of Juno.

Plus de nuit, et mon œil et se perd et se mêle
Dans les torrents profonds de lumière éternelle.
Me voici sur les feux que le langage humain
Nomme Cassiopée et l'Ourse et le Dauphin,
Maintenant la Couronne autour de moi s'embrase,
Ici l'Aigle et le Cygne et la Lyre et Pégase,
Et voici que plus loin le Serpent tortueux
Noue autour de mes pas ses anneaux lumineux.
Féconde immensité, les esprits magnanimes
Aiment à se plonger dans tes vivants abîmes,
Abîmes de clartés où, libre de ses fers,
L'homme siège au conseil qui créa l'univers,
Où l'âme remontant à sa grande origine
Sent qu'elle est une part de l'essence divine.

Ode a Marie-Anne-Charlotte Corday

QUOI! tandis que partout, ou sincères ou feintes,
Des lâches, des pervers, les larmes et les plaintes
Consacrent leur Marat parmi les immortels,

No more night, and my sight is lost and mingles in the deep torrents of eternal light. Now I am upon those lights which in human speech are called Cassiopeia and the Bear and the Dolphin, now the Crown bursts into fire around me, here the Eagle and the Swan and the Lyre and Pegasus, and further now the twisting serpent winds its luminous coils around my feet. Fertile vastness, noble spirits love to plunge into your living gulfs, gulfs of light where, free from his chains, man sits in the council which created the universe, where the soul, reascending to its great origin, feels that it is a part of the divine essence.

Ode to Marie-Anne Charlotte Corday *

AH, while on all sides the tears and moans, sincere or feigned, of cowardly, perverted minds consecrate their Marat among the

---

* Executed on 18 July 1793 for having assassinated the extremist revolutionary leader Marat in his bath.

Et que, prêtre orgueilleux de cette idole vile,
Des fanges du Parnasse un impudent reptile
Vomit un hymne infâme au pied de ses autels,

La Vérité se tait! Dans sa bouche glacée,
Des liens de la peur sa langue embarrassée
Dérobe un juste hommage aux exploits glorieux!
Vivre est-il donc si doux? De quel prix est la vie,
Quand, sous un joug honteux la pensée asservie,
Tremblante, au fond du cœur se cache à tous les yeux?

Non, non, je ne veux point t'honorer en silence,
Toi qui crus par ta mort ressusciter la France
Et dévouas tes jours à punir des forfaits.
Le glaive arma ton bras, fille grande et sublime,
Pour faire honte aux dieux, pour réparer leur crime,
Quand d'un homme à ce monstre ils donnèrent les traits.

---

immortals, while – arrogantly officiating before that vile idol – an
impudent reptile from the slime of Parnassus † vomits a foul hymn
at the foot of his altars,

Truth is silent! In her numbed mouth, her tongue, impeded by the
trammels of fear, denies the homage justly due to (such) glorious
deeds! Is it so sweet to live, then? Of what value is life when
thought, enslaved beneath a shameful yoke, hides itself timorously
from every eye in the depths of the heart?

No, no, I will not honour you in silence, you who thought to
resurrect France by your death and gave up your life to punish
evil deeds. You took the sword in your hand, great and noble girl,
to shame the gods, to make good their crime, when they gave the
features of a man to that monster.

---

† Probably a certain Michel de Cubières-Palmézeaux, who had
written a poem in Marat's honour.

Le noir serpent, sorti de sa caverne impure,
A donc vu rompre enfin sous ta main ferme et sûre
Le venimeux tissu de ses jours abhorrés!
Aux entrailles du tigre, à ses dents homicides,
Tu vins redemander et les membres livides
Et le sang des humains qu'il avait dévorés!

Son œil mourant t'a vue, en ta superbe joie,
Féliciter ton bras et contempler ta proie.
Ton regard lui disait: «Va, tyran furieux,
Va, cours frayer la route aux tyrans tes complices.
Te baigner dans le sang fut tes seules délices,
Baigne-toi dans le tien et reconnais des dieux.»

La Grèce, ô fille illustre, admirant ton courage,
Épuiserait Paros pour placer ton image
Auprès d'Harmodius, auprès de son ami;
Et des chœurs sur ta tombe, en une sainte ivresse,
Chanteraient Némésis la tardive déesse,
Qui frappe le méchant sur son trône endormi.

So that black serpent, coming out from his foul cave, had the
poisonous web of his hateful days broken at last by your true, un-
faltering hand. From the tiger's bowels, from his murderous teeth,
you came to claim back the livid members and the blood of the
human beings whom he had devoured!

His dying eye saw you, in your sublime exultation, applauding
your own hand and contemplating your prey. Your look said to
him: 'Go, raving tyrant, go and prepare the way for your accom-
plices in tyranny. To bathe in blood was your only delight, now
bathe in your own and find that there are gods.

Greece, O noble maid, admiring your courage, would exhaust all
Paros to place your statue next to Harmodius, next to his friend.*
And choirs round your tomb, with sacred fervour, would hymn
Nemesis, the tardy goddess, who strikes the evil man asleep on his
throne.

---

* Harmodius and Aristogeiton, slayers of Greek tyrants. Paros
was famous for its marble-quarries.

Mais la France à la hache abandonne ta tête.
C'est au monstre égorgé qu'on prépare une fête
Parmi ses compagnons, tous dignes de son sort.
Oh! quel noble dédain fit sourire ta bouche,
Quand un brigand, vengeur de ce brigand farouche,
Crut te faire pâlir aux menaces de mort!

C'est lui qui dut pâlir, et tes juges sinistres,
Et notre affreux sénat et ses affreux ministres,
Quand, à leur tribunal, sans crainte et sans appui,
Ta douceur, ton langage et simple et magnanime
Leur apprit qu'en effet, tout puissant qu'est le crime,
Qui renonce à la vie est plus puissant que lui.

Longtemps, sous les dehors d'une allégresse aimable,
Dans ses détours profonds ton âme impénétrable
Avait tenu cachés les destins du pervers.
Ainsi, dans le secret amassant la tempête,
Rit un beau ciel d'azur, qui cependant s'apprête
A foudroyer les monts, à soulever les mers.

But France gives up your head to the axe. The celebration they prepare is for the slaughtered monster, among his companions – all worthy of his fate. Oh, what noble scorn moved you to smile, when a brigand, seeking to avenge that savage brigand, thought he could make you grow pale at the threat of death.*

It was he who must have paled, and your sinister judges, and our loathsome senate and its loathsome ministers, when at their bar, fearless and friendly, your gentleness, your simple and noble words, taught them that in truth, however powerful crime may be, he who gives up his life is more powerful than it.

For long, under a cheerful and pleasing surface, your inscrutable heart had kept the fate of the monster hidden in its subtle depths. So, while it gathers the storm in secret, the clear blue sky smiles, yet prepares to strike the mountains with thunder, to lash the seas.

---

* No doubt a reference to the public prosecutor, Fouquier-Tinville.

Belle, jeune, brillante, aux bourreaux amenée,
Tu semblais t'avancer sur le char d'hyménée;
Ton front resta paisible et ton regard serein.
Calme, sur l'échafaud, tu méprisas la rage
D'un peuple abject, servile et fécond en outrage,
Et qui se croit alors et libre et souverain.

La Vertu seule est libre. Honneur de notre histoire,
Notre immortel opprobre y vit avec ta gloire.
Seule tu fus un homme, et vengeas les humains.
Et nous, eunuques vils, troupeau lâche et sans âme,
Nous savons répéter quelque plainte de femme,
Mais le fer pèserait à nos débiles mains.

Non, tu ne pensais pas qu'aux mânes de la France
Un seul traître immolé suffît à sa vengeance,
Ou tirât du chaos ses débris dispersés.
Tu voulais, enflammant les courages timides,
Réveiller les poignards sur tous ces parricides,
De rapine, de sang, d'infamie engraissés.

Fair, young, resplendent, led to the executioners, you seemed to
be riding in your bridal car; your brow was still untroubled and
your look serene. Calm on the scaffold, you despised the rage of an
abject populace, servile and rich in insults, and which yet believes
that it is free and sovereign.

Only Virtue is free. Glory of our history, our eternal shame lives
on there (in history) with your fame. You alone were a man and
vindicated the human race. And we, vile eunuchs, a cowardly and
soulless herd, we know how to repeat some womanly whimper, but
the steel would weigh heavy in our feeble hands.

No, you did not intend that a single traitor sacrificed to the angry
spirit of France should suffice to avenge her, or should recover her
scattered remains from chaos. You meant, by firing timorous hearts,
to awaken daggers over all these parricides – fattened on plunder,
blood, and dishonour.

Un scélérat de moins rampe dans cette fange.
La Vertu t'applaudit. De sa mâle louange
Entends, belle héroïne, entends l'auguste voix.
O Vertu, le poignard, seul espoir de la terre,
Est ton arme sacrée, alors que le tonnerre
Laisse régner le crime et te vend à ses lois.

Iambes VIII

ON vit; on vit infâme. Eh bien? il fallut l'être;
　　L'infâme après tout mange et dort.
Ici même, en ses parcs, où la mort nous fait paître,
　　Où la hache nous tire au sort,
Beaux poulets sont écrits; maris, amants sont dupes;
　　Caquetage, intrigues de sots.
On y chante; on y joue; on y lève des jupes;
　　On y fait chansons et bons mots;
L'un pousse et fait bondir sur les toits, sur les vitres,

One scoundrel less crawls in this slime. Virtue applauds you. Hear the majestic sound of its virile praise, heroic maid. O Virtue, the dagger, the only hope of the world, is your holy weapon, as long as the thunder (God's vengeance) allows crime to prevail and sells you into its power.

Iambes VIII

WE live, we live degraded. What of it? It had to be. Degraded, you still eat and sleep. Even here, in its pens, where death puts us to graze, where the axe draws lots for us, fine love-letters are written; husbands, lovers are duped; tittle-tattle, intrigues of fools. There is singing, gambling, skirts are lifted; songs and jokes are made up; someone sends up and bounces on the roofs, on the panes, a

Un ballon tout gonflé de vent,
Comme sont les discours des sept cents plats bélîtres,
Dont Barère est le plus savant.
L'autre court; l'autre saute; et braillent, boivent, rient
Politiques et raisonneurs;
Et sur les gonds de fer soudain les portes crient.
Des juges tigres nos seigneurs
Le pourvoyeur paraît. Quelle sera la proie
Que la hache appelle aujourd'hui?
Chacun frissonne, écoute; et chacun avec joie
Voit que ce n'est pas encor lui …

balloon swollen with wind, like the speeches of the seven hundred
dreary imbeciles, of which the wisest is Barère.*

Another runs, another jumps; 'politicians' and discussers bray,
drink, laugh; and on their iron hinges the doors suddenly grate.
The purveyor of our masters the tiger-judges appears. Who will
be the prey which the axe calls for today? Each shudders, listens,
and each with joy sees that it is not yet he.

* One of the seven hundred members of the *Convention Nationale*
during the Terror. Writing this fragment in prison while in constant fear of execution, Chénier ciphered Barère's name and disguised his meaning in the previous line by writing:

Comme sont les discours des heptsad (700) *plats bélit.*

ANONYMOUS BALLADS AND SONGS

La Blanche Biche

CELLES qui vont au bois,
C'est la mère et la fille.
La mère va chantant,
Et la fille soupire.
«Qu'av'ous à soupirer,
Ma fille Marguerite?»

«J'ai bien grande ire en moi,
Et n'ose vous le dire.
Je suis fille sur jour
Et la nuit blanche biche.
La chasse est après moi,
Les barons et les princes,

«Et mon frère Renaud,
Qui est encor le pire.
Allez, ma mère, allez
Bien promptement lui dire
Qu'il arrête ses chiens
Jusqu'à demain ressie.»

The White Doe

THOSE who go to the wood are mother and daughter. The mother goes singing, the daughter sighs. 'Why are you sighing, Margaret my daughter?'

'There is great anger in me and I dare not tell you why. I am a maid by day and a white doe by night. The hunt is after me, the barons and the princes.

'And my brother Renaud, who is the worst of them all. Go, mother, go quickly and tell him to call off his hounds till tomorrow afternoon.'

«Où sont tes chiens, Renaud,
Et ta chasse gentille?»
«Ils sont dedans le bois
A courre blanche biche.»
«Arrête-les, Renaud,
Arrête, je t'en prie!»

Trois fois les a cornés
En son cornet de cuivre;
A la troisième fois
La blanche biche est prise.
«Mandons le dépouilleur,
Qu'il dépouille la biche!»

Celui qui la dépouille
Dit: «Je ne sais que dire.
Elle a les cheveux blonds
Et le sein d'une fille.»
A tiré son couteau,
En quartiers l'a mise.

En ont fait un dîner
Aux barons et aux princes.
«Nous voilà tous illec:
Faut ma sœur Marguerite.»
«Vous n'avez qu'à manger!
Suis la première assise.»

'Where are your hounds, Renaud, and your pretty hunt?' 'They
are out in the wood chasing the white doe.' 'Call them off, Renaud,
call them off, I beg you.'

Three times he blew on his copper horn. The third time he blew
the white doe was taken. 'Send for the skinner, let him skin the doe.'

The man who is skinning her says: 'I know not what to say. She
has flaxen hair and the breast of a maid.' He took out his knife, in
quarters he cut her.

They made a feast of her for the barons and princes. 'We are all
of us here; my sister Margaret is missing.' 'You have only to eat.
I'm the first in my place.

«Ma tête est dans le plat
Et mon cœur aux chevilles,
Mon sang est répandu
Par toute la cuisine,
Et sur les noirs charbons
Mes pauvres os y grillent.»

Renaud le tueur de femmes

RENAUD a de si grands appas
Qu'il a charmé la fille au Roi.
L'a bien emmenée à sept lieu's,
Sans qu'il lui dit un mot ou deux.

Quand sont venus à mi-chemin:
«Mon Dieu! Renaud, que j'ai grand' faim!»
«Mangez, la belle, votre main,
Car plus ne mangerez de pain.»

Quand sont venus au bord du bois:
«Mon Dieu! Renaud, qu j'ai grand soif!»
«Buvez, la belle, votre sang,
Car plus ne boirez de vin blanc.»

'My head is on the dish, my heart hangs on the hooks, my blood is sprinkled all over the kitchen, and on the black coals my poor bones are grilling.'

Renaud the Woman-Killer

RENAUD has such handsome charms that he charmed the King's daughter. He took her a good seven leagues away, without saying one word or two to her.

When they had gone half the way, 'God! Renaud, how hungry I am!' 'Eat your hand, my fair maid, for you will never eat bread again.'

When they came to the edge of the wood, 'God, Renaud, how thirsty I am!' 'Drink your blood, my fair maid, for you will never drink white wine again.'

«Il y a là-bas un vivier
Où treize dames sont noyé's,
Treize dames y sont noyé's,
La quatorzième vous serez.»

Quand sont venus près du vivier,
Lui dit de se déshabiller.
«N'est pas affaire aux chevaliers
De voir dame déshabiller.

«Mets ton épé' dessous tes pieds,
Et ton manteau devant ton nez.»
Mit son épé' dessous ses pieds
Et son manteau devant son nez.

La bell' l'a pris, l'a embrassé,
Dans le vivier ell' l'a jeté:
«Venez, anguill's, venez, poissons,
Manger la chair de ce larron!»

Renaud voulut se rattraper
A une branche de laurier;
La belle tire son epé',
Coupe la branche de laurier.

'Down there there is a fish-pond in which thirteen ladies lie drowned. Thirteen ladies lie drowned there, you will be the fourteenth.'

When they came near the fish-pond, he told her to undress. 'It is not becoming for knights to see a lady undress.

'Put your sword at your feet and your cloak before your face.' He put his sword at his feet and his cloak before his face.

The fair maid took hold of him, kissed him, into the fish-pond she threw him. 'Come, eels, come, fish, and eat the flesh of this robber!'

Renaud tried to pull himself out on the branch of a laurel. The fair maid drew his sword, she cut the laurel-branch.

«Belle, prêtez-moi votre main,
Je vous épouserai demain!»
«Va-t'en, Renaud, va-t'en au fond
Épouser les dames qu'y sont!»

«Belle, qui vous ramènera,
Si me laissez dans ce lieu-là?»
«Ce sera ton cheval grison,
Qui suit fort bien le postillon.»

«Belle, que diront vos parents,
Quand vous verront sans votre amant?»
«Leur dirai que j'ai fait de toi
Ce que voulais faire de moi!»

La Courte Paille

Il était un petit navire,
     dessus la mer s'en est allé.

A bien été sept ans sur mer
     sans jamais la terre aborder.

'Fair maid, give me your hand, I will marry you tomorrow!'
'Go down, Renaud, down to the bottom, and marry the ladies who
lie there!'
     'Fair maid, who will take you back if you leave me in this
place?' 'Your grey horse, who follows the postilion so well.'
     'Fair maid, what will your parents say when they see you with-
out your lover?' 'I shall tell them that I have done with you what
you wanted to do with me!'

The Short Straw

There was a little ship which sailed away over the sea.
It was at sea a good seven years without ever touching land.

Au bout de la septième année
  les vivres vinrent à manquer.

Faut tirer à la courte paille,
  pour savoir qui sera mangé.

Le maître qu'a parti les pailles,
  la plus courte lui a resté.

S'est écrié: «O Vierge Mère!
  sera donc moi sera mangé!»

Le mousse lui a dit: «Mon maître,
  pour vous je me lairrai manger.

«Mais auparavant que je meure,
  au haut du mât je veux monter.»

Quand il fut dedans la grand' hune,
  a regardé de tous côtés.

Quand il fut monté sur la pomme,
  le mousse s'est mis à chanter:

At the end of the seventh year the victuals ran out.
They must draw lots * to see who will be eaten.
The captain who gave out the straws was left with the shortest one.
He cried: 'O Virgin Mother! So it is I who will be eaten!'
The cabin-boy said to him: 'Captain, for your sake I will let myself be eaten.
'But before I die, I want to climb to the top of the mast.'
When he was in the maintop, he looked round on every side.
When he got up to the truck, the cabin-boy began to sing:

* With straws of different lengths. The drawer of the shortest loses.

«Je vois la tour de Babylone,
Barbarie de l'autre côté.

«Je vois les moutons dans la plaine
et la bergère à les garder.

«Je vois la fille à notre maître,
à trois pigeons donne à manger.»

«Ah, chante, chante, vaillant mousse,
chante, t'as bien de quoi chanter!

«T'as gagné la fille à ton maître,
le navire qu'est sous tes pieds!»

En passant par la Lorraine

En passant par la Lorraine, avec mes sabots,
Rencontrai trois capitaines,
Avec mes sabots, dondaine, oh! oh! oh!
Avec mes sabots.

'I see the tower of Babel, and Barbary on the other side.
'I see the sheep on the plain and the shepherdess watching them.
'I see our captain's daughter, she is feeding three pigeons.'
'Ah, sing, sing, brave cabin-boy, sing, you have plenty to sing about!
'You have won your captain's daughter and the ship which is under your feet!'

Passing through Lorraine

Passing through Lorraine, with my sabots, I met three captains, with my sabots, *dondaine, oh, oh, oh!* with my sabots.

Rencontrai trois capitaines, avec mes sabots,
    Ils m'ont appelé vilaine,
Avec mes sabots, dondaine ...

Ils m'ont appelé vilaine, avec mes sabots,
    Je ne suis pas si vilaine,
Avec mes sabots, dondaine ...

Je ne suis pas si vilaine, avec mes sabots,
    Puisque le fils du roi m'aime,
Avec mes sabots, dondaine ...

Puisque le fils du roi m'aime, avec mes sabots,
    Il m'a donné pour étrennes,
Avec mes sabots, dondaine ...

Il m'a donné pour étrennes, avec mes sabots,
    Un bouquet de marjolaine,
Avec mes sabots, dondaine ...

Un bouquet de marjolaine, avec mes sabots,
    S'il fleurit, je serai reine,
Avec mes sabots, dondaine ...

I met three captains, with my sabots. They called me ugly, with
my sabots ...
    I am not so ugly, with my sabots, since the King's son loves me,
with my sabots ...
    Since the King's son loves me, with my sabots. He gave me for
my present, with my sabots ...
    He gave me for my present, with my sabots, a bunch of sweet
marjoram, with my sabots ...
    A bunch of sweet marjoram, with my sabots. If it flowers, I shall
be queen, with my sabots ...

S'il fleurit je serai reine, avec mes sabots,
S'il y meurt, je perds ma peine,
Avec mes sabots, dondaine, oh! oh! oh!
Avec mes sabots.

Le Mariage anglais

C'ÉTAIT la fille au roi françois
Que l'on marie à un Anglois:
«O mes chers frères, empêchez
De m'emmener!
J'aimerais mieux soldat françois
Que roi anglois.»

Et quand ce vint pour l'épouser,
Dedans Paris fallut passer:
Il n'y a dame de Paris
Qui ne pleurît
De voir partir la fille au roi
A un Anglois.

Et quand ce vint pour embarquer,
Les yeux lui a voulu bander:

If it flowers I shall be queen, with my sabots. If it dies, my
trouble's wasted, with my sabots, *dondaine, oh, oh, oh!* with my
sabots.

The English Marriage *

IT was the French king's daughter who was being married to an
Englishman. 'O my dear brothers, don't let them take me away! I
would rather have a French soldier than an English king.'

And when it came to wedding her, she had to pass through Paris.
There was not a lady in Paris who did not weep to see the king's
daughter going away with an Englishman.

And when it came to going on board, he wanted to blindfold her:

---

* Perhaps the marriage of Henrietta of France to Charles I.
The syllable -ois or -oi in the rhymes was pronounced *ouè*.

«Bande les tiens et laisse-moi,
    Maudit Anglois!
Puisque la mer me faut passer,
    Je la verrai.»

Et quand ce vint pour débarquer,
Tambours, violons de tous côtés:
«Retirez-vous, ô tambouriniers
    Et violonniers!
Ce n'est pas le son des hautbois
    Du roi françois.»

Et quand ce vint pour le souper,
Du pain lui a voulu couper:
«Coupe pour toi et non pour moi,
    Maudit Anglois!
Je ne puis boire ni manger
    Quand je te vé.»

Et quand ce vint pour le coucher,
L'Anglois l'a voulu déchausser:
«Déchausse-toi et laisse-moi,
    Maudit Anglois!
J'ai bien des gens de mon pays
    Pour me servir.»

'Blindfold yourself and leave me alone, cursèd Englishman! Since I must go over the sea, I will see it.'

And when it came to going ashore, drums, fiddles, on every side. 'Go away, drummers and fiddlers! That is not the sound of the French king's oboes.'

And when it came to having supper, he wanted to cut bread for her. 'Cut for yourself and not for me, cursèd Englishman! I can neither drink nor eat when I see you.'

And when it came to going to bed, the Englishman wanted to take her shoes off. 'Take off your own and leave me alone, cursèd Englishman! I have plenty of people from my own country to serve me.'

Et quand ce vint sur la minuit,
La belle n'est pas endormie:
«Retourne-toi, embrasse-moi,
  Mon cher Anglois!
Puisque Dieu nous a assemblés,
  Faut nous aimer!»

Ronde

Dans le pré dansaient
Quatre-vingts fillettes.
Que dit? Que donc?
Que dis-tu? Que dit-on?
Que dit-elle donc?
Dans le pré dansaient
Quatre-vingts fillettes.

Quand passe par là
Le roi d'Angleterre,
Que dit? *etc.*

Toutes salua,
Hormis la plus belle.
Que dit? *etc.*

And when it came towards midnight, the fair lady is not asleep yet. 'Turn round, embrace me, my dear Englishman. Since God has brought us together, we must love each other!'

Dance Song

In the meadow were dancing eighty little girls. What says? What then? What say you? What say they? What says she then? In the meadow were dancing eighty little girls.

When there passed by there the King of England. What says? etc.

He greeted them all, except the most beautiful. What says? etc.

Tu n'me salues pas,
P'tit roi d'Angleterre?
Que dit? *etc.*

Mets l'épée au poing,
Et moi ma qu'nouillette.
Que dit? *etc.*

Et nous nous battrons
En duel sur l'herbette.
Que dit? *etc.*

Pouf! du premier coup
Ell' le couche à terre.
Que dit? *etc.*

Un' fille a battu
Le roi d'Angleterre.
Que dit? *etc.*

Tout est regagné
Par une bergère.
Que dit? *etc.*

You don't greet me, little King of England? What says? etc.
Take your sword in your hand, and I my distaff. What says? etc.
And we will fight a duel on the grass. What says? etc.
Bing! At the first thrust she stretched him on the ground. What
says? etc.
A girl has beaten the King of England. What says? etc.
Everything is won back by a shepherdess. What says? etc.

Nous pouvons danser,
Nous n'aurons plus d'guerre.
Que dit? Que donc?
Que dis-tu? Que dit-on?
Que dit-elle donc?
Dans le pré dansaient
Quatre-vingts fillettes.

Le Petit Cordonnier

Sur les marches du palais,
Sur les marches du palais,
Y a une jolie Flamande, lon la,
Y a une jolie Flamande.

Elle a tant d'amoureux,
Qu'elle ne sait lequel prendre, lon la,
Qu'elle ne sait lequel prendre.

L'un est un boulanger,
L'autre un valet de chambre, lon la,
L'autre un valet de chambre.

C'est un petit cordonnier,
Qu'a eu la préférence, lon la,
Qu'a eu la préférence.

We can dance, we shall have no more war. What says? etc.

The Little Shoemaker

On the steps of the palace, on the steps of the palace, there is a pretty Flemish girl, *lon la*, a pretty Flemish girl.

She has so many suitors that she does not know which to take.
One is a baker and another is a footman.
It was a little shoemaker on whom her choice fell.

Lui fera des souliers,
De maroquin d'Hollande, lon la,
De maroquin d'Hollande.

C'est en les lui chaussant,
Qu'il a fait sa demande, lon la,
Qu'il a fait sa demande.

La belle, si vous vouliez,
Nous dormirions ensemble, lon la,
Nous dormirions ensemble.

Dans un grand lit carré,
Recouvert de taies blanches, lon la,
Recouvert de taies blanches.

Aux quatre coins du lit,
Un bouquet de pervenches, lon la,
Un bouquet de pervenches.

Dans le mitan du lit,
La rivière est profonde, lon la,
La rivière est profonde.

Tous les chevaux du roi,
Viendraient y boire ensemble, lon la,
Viendraient y boire ensemble.

He will make her shoes of Dutch morocco-leather.
When putting them on her he made his proposal.
'Fair maid, if you wished, we would sleep together.
In a big square bed with white pillow-covers.
At the four corners of the bed a bunch of periwinkles.
In the middle of the bed the river is deep.
All the king's horses could come and drink there together.

Et là nous dormirions,
Et là nous dormirions,
Jusqu'à la fin du monde, lon la,
Jusqu'à la fin du monde.

Le Pommier doux

DERRIÈRE chez mon père   y a un pommier doux,
D'argent sont les branches,   et les feuilles itou.
Trois jeunes princesses   sont endormies dessous:
«Tiens,» dit la plus vieille,   «voici que vient le jour.»
«Tiens,» dit la seconde,   «entendez le tambour.»
«Non,» dit la plus jeune,   «ce n'est pas ci le jour,
«C'est son épée claire   de mon ami doux.»
«Il part en campagne   combattre pour nous,»
                              (dit la plus vieille),
«S'il gagne bataille,   il aura mes amours,»
                              (dit la seconde),

And there we would sleep till the end of the world.'

The Sweet Apple-Tree *

BEHIND my father's house there is a sweet apple-tree,
The branches are of silver and the leaves also,
Three young princesses are sleeping beneath it.
'Why,' says the eldest, 'look, the day is coming.'
'Why,' says the second, 'listen to the drum.'
'No,' says the youngest, 'that is not the day,
'It is the bright sword of my sweet love.'
'He's going to the war to fight for us,' (says the eldest),
'If he wins the battle, he shall have my love,' (says the second),

* An alternate title is *Le Pommier d'Août*. In that case the tree
bears August (early) apples, not sweet apples.

313

«Qu'il perde ou qu'il gagne,   il les aura toujours,»
                              (dit la plus jeune).
Derrière chez mon père   y a un pommier doux.

Les Douze Mois de l'année

Le premier mois de l'année
Que donnerai-je à ma mie?
   Un partriole
Qui va, qui vient, qui vole,
   Un partriole
Qui vole dans ce bois.

Le second mois de l'année
Que donnerai-je à ma mie?
   Deux tourterelles,
   Un partriole, *etc. ...*

Le troisièm' mois de l'année
Que donnerai-je à ma mie?
   Trois rats des bois,
   Deux tourterelles, *etc. ...*

'Whether he wins or loses, he shall have mine always,' (says the youngest).
Behind my father's house there is a sweet apple-tree.

The Twelve Months of the Year

The first month of the year what shall I give my love? A partridge flying to and fro, a partridge flying through this wood.

The second month of the year what shall I give my love? Two turtle-doves, a partridge, etc. ...

The third month of the year what shall I give my love? Three woodmice,* two turtle-doves, etc. ...

And so on, until:

* In another version: Three wood-pigeons (*Trois ramiers des bois*).

Le quatrièm' mois de l'année
Que donnerai-je à ma mie?
　　Quatre canards volant en l'air,
　　Trois rats des bois, *etc.* ...

Le cinquièm' mois de l'année
Que donnerai-je à ma mie?
　　Cinq lapins grattant la terre,
　　Quatre canards volant en l'air, *etc.* ...

Le sixièm' mois de l'année
Que donnerai-je à ma mie?
　　Six lièvr' aux champs,
　　Cinq lapins grattant la terre, *etc.* ...

Le septièm' mois de l'année
Que donnerai-je à ma mie?
　　Sept chiens courant,
　　Six lièvr' aux champs, *etc.* ...

Le huitièm' mois de l'année
Que donnerai-je à ma mie?
　　Huit moutons blancs,
　　Sept chiens courant, *etc.* ...

Le neuvièm' mois de l'année
Que donnerai-je à ma mie?
　　Neuf bœufs avec leurs cornes,
　　Huit moutons blancs, *etc.* ...

Le dixièm' mois de l'année
Que donnerai-je à ma mie?
　　Dix poules pondant,
　　Neuf bœufs avec leurs cornes, *etc.* ...

Le onzièm' mois de l'année
Que donnerai-je à ma mie?
　　Onz' coqs chantant,
　　Dix poules pondant, *etc.* ...

Le douzièm' mois de l'année
Que donnerai-je à ma mie?
  Douz' chevaux avec leurs selles,
  Onz' coqs chantant,
  Dix poules pondant,
  Neuf bœufs avec leurs cornes,
  Huit moutons blancs,
  Sept chiens courant,
  Six lievr' aux champs,
  Cinq lapins grattant la terre,
  Quatre canards volant en l'air,
  Trois rats des bois,
  Deux tourterelles,
  Un partriole
Qui va, qui vient, qui vole,
  Un partriole
Qui vole dans ce bois.

Les Menteries

Chanson des bateliers de la Meuse

Ah, j'ai vu, j'ai vu.
– Compère, qu'as-tu vu?
– J'ai vu une vache

The twelfth month of the year what shall I give my love? Twelves horses with their saddles, eleven cocks crowing, ten hens laying, nine oxen with their horns, eight white sheep, seven dogs running, six hares in the fields, five rabbits scratching the soil, four ducks flying through the air, three woodmice, two turtle-doves, a partridge flying to and fro, a partridge flying through this wood.

Tall Tales
Song of the Meuse Boatmen

Ah, I've seen, I've seen. – What have you seen, chum? – I've seen

Qui dansait sur la glace
A la Saint Jean d'été.
– Compère, vous mentez.

Ah, j'ai vu, j'ai vu.
– Compère, qu'as-tu vu?
– J'ai vu une grenouille
Qui faisait la patrouille
Le sabre au côté.
– Compère, vous mentez.

Ah, j'ai vu, j'ai vu.
– Compère, qu'as-tu vu?
– J'ai vu une mouche
Qui se rinçait la bouche
Avec un pavé.
– Compère, vous mentez.

Ah, j'ai vu, j'ai vu.
– Compère, qu'as-tu vu?
– Ah, j'ai vu un loup
Qui vendait des choux
Sur la place Labourée.
– Compère, vous mentez.

a cow dancing on the ice on midsummer day. – Chum, you're
lying.

Ah, I've seen, I've seen. – What have you seen, chum? – I've
seen a frog patrolling the street with a sword at its side. – Chum,
you're lying.

Ah, I've seen, I've seen. – What have you seen, chum? – I've
seen a fly rinsing out its mouth with a paving-stone. – Chum,
you're lying.

Ah, I've seen, I've seen. – What have you seen, chum? – I've
seen a wolf selling cabbages in the Place Labourée. – Chum, you're
lying.

Ah, j'ai vu, j'ai vu.
– Compère, qu'as-tu vu?
– J'ai vu une anguille
Qui coiffait sa fille
Pour s'aller marier.
– Compère, vous mentez.

*Invocation que les filles pourront faire
si elles veulent se marier*

Kyrie, je voudrais,
Christe, être mariée.
Kyrie, je prie tous les saints,
Christe, que ce soit dès demain.
Sainte Marie, tout le monde se marie.
Saint Joseph, que vous ai-je fait?
Saint Nicolas, ne m'oubliez pas.
Saint Médéric, que j'aie un bon mari.
Saint Mathieu, qu'il craigne Dieu.
Saint Jean, qu'il m'aime tendrement.
Saint Thibaud, qu'il soit joli et beau.

Ah, I've seen, I've seen. – What have you seen, chum? – I've seen an eel doing her daughter's hair to go and get married. – Chum, you're lying.

Invocation for Girls Wishing to get Married

Lord, I would like,
Christ, to be married.
Lord, I pray to all the saints,
Christ, that it should be tomorrow.
Holy Mary, everyone is getting married.
Saint Joseph, what have I done to you?
Saint Nicholas, do not forget me.
Saint Merry, let me have a good husband.
Saint Matthew, let him fear God.
Saint John, let him love me tenderly.
Saint Theobald, let him be good-looking and handsome.

318

Saint François, qu'il me soit courtois.
Saint Michel, qu'il me soit fidèle.
Saint André, qu'il soit à mon gré.
Saint Léger, qu'il n'aime pas jouer.
Saint Séverin, qu'il n'aime pas le vin.
Saint Clément, qu'il ait bon cœur.
Saint Nicaise, que je sois à mon aise.
Saint Josse, qu'il me donne un carrosse.
Saint Boniface, que mon mariage se fasse,
Saint Augustin, dès demain matin.

Saint Francis, let him be polite to me.
Saint Michael, let him be faithful to me.
Saint Andrew, let him be to my liking.
Saint Leger, let him not like gambling.
Saint Severinus, let him not like drink.
Saint Clement, let him have a kind heart.
Saint Nicasius, let me be rich enough.
Saint Josse, let him give me a coach.
Saint Boniface, let my marriage take place,
Saint Augustine, tomorrow morning.

INDEX OF FIRST LINES

321

INDEX OF FIRST LINES

INDEX OF POETS